The Great Religions

© 2004 Assouline Publishing for the present edition
601 West 26th Street, 18th floor
New York, NY 10001, USA
Tel: 212 989-6810 Fax: 212 647-0005
www.assouline.com

First published by Editions Assouline, Paris, France.

Printed by R.R. Donnelley

ISBN: 2 84323 611 8

INTRODUCTION BY BRUCE FEILER

The Great Religions

Essential Questions

ASSOULINE

FOREWORD

The origin of this book: a love story and a mixed marriage. He is Jewish. She is Catholic. They celebrate Christmas, Yom Kippur, and Passover together, sitting at the same table...

Pretty soon, questions began to be raised. The answers from the two religions were not the same. Traditions were still alive but the significance was being lost.

A series of books was born: the goal was to explain the meaning of the rituals and cultural symbols of each of the major religions. The first title of the collection, *Symbols of Judaism*, was to be written by Marc-Alain Ouaknin, rabbi and philosopher. Then it was decided that Laziz Hamani would work alongside Marc-Alain Ouaknin: he would take all the pictures of the symbols. They traveled together to Jerusalem, and brought back wonderful pictures. Their friendship still thrives. Next, the *Symbols of Catholicism* were skillfully described by Monsignor Robert le Gall. Then Claude B. Levenson wrote *Symbols of Tibetan Buddhism* and Malek Chebel, *Symbols of Islam*.

For the first time, "religion" was explained not from theoretical texts but from our everyday life. The reality was described in a familiar way in order to help us understand the sense and origins of the four faiths.

The fact that the books were so popular made it clear that people wanted to learn about their religion, but even more about the religions of others, too!

We then felt that we had to unite the symbols of these great religions in order to allow readers to discover the similarities and contradictions among the different practices (though three of them are derived from the same roots).

And we decided to begin the book by asking each of the authors to answer twelve "essential questions."

The underlying idea was to refuse any monopoly over the meaning of life, and overall to open oneself to the different, "the Other." To embrace the difference. Our times are torn between an almost hidden ecumenism and an intolerance visible in too many parts of the world. We are being moved away from a personal dialogue with God and from a real curiosity about "the Other."

May this book be useful to those who are looking for answers to essential questions. May it help us to find the antidote to fanaticism and intolerance.

May it contribute to our being open to others, beyond their religion and traditions.

When one starts to accept "the Other," one paves the way to real and true liberty of the self.

Martine Assouline
Paris, January 2004

INTRODUCTION

In the first week of April 1966, *TIME* magazine published the first issue in its 43-year history that had only words on the cover. The cover was solid black, with three red words stacked ominously on top of one another: "Is God Dead?" The article, written by John T. Elson, took nearly a year to research and was approached with more deliberation than any article in the magazine's history, wrote publisher Bernhard Auer in a note to readers.

Entitled "Toward a Hidden God," the cover story explored the challenge laid down by a radical but influential band of theologians that God was no longer a living force in the world and that churches must learn to get along without him. (Tellingly, the WASP-ish Henry Luce publication made no mention of synagogues or mosques.) A century earlier in *The Gay Science* (1882) Nietzsche raised the possibility that self-serving humans killed off God, but the new thinkers carried the idea even further, declared God absolutely dead, and proposed designing a theology without *theos*. "If nothing else, the Christian atheists are waking the churches to the brutal reality that the basic premise of faith—the existence of a personal God, who created the world and sustains it with his love—is now subject to profound attack."

The magazine went on to favorably quote anti-Nazi Lutheran martyr Dietrich Bonhoeffer in a letter from his Berlin prison cell during World War II: "We are proceeding toward a time of no religion at all." Noting that half the humans on earth lived under totalitarian regimes that condemn religion and that millions more in Africa, Asia, and South America are born without any expectation of being summoned to the knowledge of the one God, *TIME* concluded: "For many, that time has arrived."

Thirty-five years later, in the second week of October 2001, *Newsweek* magazine put on its cover a young Muslim boy, not more than six or eight years old, wearing a white turban. The boy was carrying a black machine gun and the headline, in black and red type, read: WHY THEY HATE US. The immediate sources for this image, of course, were the attacks on September 11th. Noting that Muslim hatred toward the United States extended across the Middle East, from Pakistan to Saudi Arabia to Egypt, author Fareed Zakaria concluded: "The problem is not that Osama bin Laden believes that this is a religious war against America. It's that millions of people across the Islamic world seem to agree."

But the real truth was even larger, and more profound. September 11th was not an isolated example of religious fervor asserting itself into world affairs. Nearly every major international issue at the start of the new century—Afghanistan, Iraq, Iran, Israel, the Palestinian territories, Chechnya, Bosnia, Kashmir—has religion at its center. In the United States, a dizzying array of domestic political issues revolve around religion—abortion, prayer in public schools, gay marriage, the Ten Commandments. Even normally private, intra-mural religious issues have spilled into the public square—the crisis in the Catholic Church over its handling of sex abuse claims, the split in the Episcopal church over the anointing of a gay bishop.

God is not only not dead these days, he practically lives on the front page of every newspaper in the world. So what happened between 1966 and today? And why? And does the return of religion to the crux of international affairs portend a protracted period of violence, or could it also foretell a coming of peace?

The last few centuries have not been good to religion. Beginning with Copernicus (1473-1543) and Galileo (1564-1642), both of whom were religious men, science began to chip away at many of the basic tenets of the divine-centered world view: that the earth was the center of the universe, that the heavens revolved around us (rather than us around them), that we could understand the world by using merely our senses. Francis Bacon (1561-1626), Rene Descartes (1596-1650), and Isaac Newton (1642-1727) took this view even further, develop-

8

ing the scientific method that would become the new bedrock for understanding the way the world works. By the time of the Enlightenment in the 18th century, reason had taken over from faith as the defining model for human progress, and institutional religion became increasingly separated from institutional politics in the structure of Western society.

Particularly in Europe, socialism, communism, and fascism were all examples of secularist philosophies that were openly hostile to religion, famously called by Karl Marx (1818-83) the "opiate of the masses." The ability of Charles Darwin (1809-82) and Sigmund Freud (1856-1939) to galvanize popular as well as academic thinking seemed the final triumph of science over God. As anthropologist and Arabist Malek Chabel notes in this volume, the prestige of science became so great by the late 20th century that its standards seeped into everyday life, making knowledge not known by scientific study seem uninteresting, even unreal. "The power of the men of the church, the imams, and theologians has gradually declined as that of politicians, citizens, and scientists has grown," Chabel writes.

This collapse of faith left what Jean-Paul Sartre called a God-shaped hole in human consciousness, where the divine had once been but then disappeared. Humans, who are uniquely meaning-craving creatures, still longed to fill this hole, and one response was all manner of alternative routes to fulfillment that gained popularity in the West. These quasi-spiritual undertakings included psychoanalysis, yoga, angels, UFOs, ESP, meditation, drugs, sex, alcohol, Alcoholics Anonymous, Body for Life, dieting, pornography, and the Internet. Only religious expression that seemed free of the Judeo-Christian trappings captured appeal, such as Buddhism, Zen, Sufism, and the Ethical Culture movement.

In many ways, the biggest alternative to religion was just plain capitalism, and the promise that the global marketplace could deliver heaven on earth. People were just too busy getting ahead and enjoying the moment to worry about profiting from the past or preparing for the afterlife. And not just in the West. Across the world, including the Middle East, the secular icons of Western capitalism held great appeal. As Fareed Zakaria wrote in *Newsweek*: "I first traveled to the Middle East in the early 1970s, and even then the image of America was of a glistening, approachable modernity: fast cars, Hilton hotels, and Coca-Cola."

Another major response to the collapse of traditional faith was the rise of extreme faith. This is not as paradoxical as it sounds. As Karen Armstrong notes in *The Battle For God*, from the English Revolution to the American Revolution to the Industrial Revolution, "religion has provided the means that get people through the painful rite of passage to modernity." The Technological Revolution would prove no different. Fundamentalism—in Judaism, Christianity, and Islam—would become a major force in international politics during the late 20th century in direct response to globalism. "Fundamentalism rarely arises as a battle with an external enemy," Armstrong writes. "It usually begins as an internal struggle in which traditionalists fight their own co-religionists, who, they believe, are making too many concessions to the secular world." The fundamentalist thus retreats, defensively, into an enclave of pure faith. Unfortunately, this retreat has within it the potential for a future counter-offensive.

If the response to modernity had produced just these two extremes—secularism and fundamentalism—the vast majority of God-bewildered citizens in the middle might have been left with little more to contemplate than the covers of news weeklies. But it did not. In a way the editors of *TIME* could hardly have foreseen, the last decades of the 20th century produced, in the United States and elsewhere, a huge upsurge in popular interest in religion. As Rabbi Marc-Alain Ouaknin writes in this book, in response to the question, "Is religion necessary?": "Religion is undoubtedly necessary, for it enables man to escape the prison of his finiteness, to escape the pettiness of a life closed in on itself and to discover the delights of self-transcendence."

While attendance at churches and synagogues may have declined, Americans in particular took the freedom from institutional religion they had gained in mid-century and set out on their own to re-engage traditional texts. This Back-to-the-Bible movement included surging adult-ed courses, the pop Kabbalah fad, Bill Moyers' popular *Genesis* series on PBS, novels such as *The Red Tent* and *The DaVinci Code*, and dozens of successful non-fiction books by authors such as Karen Armstrong, Thomas Cahill, Elaine Pagels, Jonathan Kirsch, and others, including my own. Even the newsweeklies noticed: *Is God Dead?* produced a flurry of grandchildren proclaiming him alive in the unlikeliest of places, from rock and roll to the Oval Office.

This pronounced return to faith—what George Weigel called the "desecularization of the world"—did not take the West back to its traditional religious roots. Instead, it produced a radically reshaped faith environment, one that held problems, but also great promise for a new kind of religious dialogue. In the 1950s, the American political landscape could be likened to the skyline of a major city, with a series of high-rises that represent the major religions: one for Baptists, say, one for Methodists, one for Lutherans, one for Catholics, one for Jews. Each of these religions was primarily oriented toward its co-religionists.

Fifty years later that skyline has been turned on its side. Each of those religions has undergone, or is undergoing, a seismic internal shift that is splitting it into fundamentalist and progressive factions. This split usually occurs over a variety of issues, specifically the authority of the Bible, the role of women in religious practice, the institution's position on social issues, notably homosexuality, and others. In some cases, like the Baptist Church and possibly soon the Episcopal Church, the schism becomes concrete, with new institutional entities being created. In other cases, the split is reflected in the proclivities of smaller, local bodies: the mainline church on the East Side of town welcomes gays; the evangelical church on the West Side does not.

One consequence of this change is that each of these religions will never again have the institutional coherence or clout that it once enjoyed. Fewer members yield weakened authority in the marketplace of ideas. But the greater impact is that the progressive wings of each religion are finding they are more aligned with the progressive wings of other religions than with their own conservative co-religionists. As one Baptist preacher told me in Georgia, "I have more in common with the Reform rabbi in town than I do with the Southern Baptist preacher up the road." It is this shift that holds the greatest opportunity for changing the way the religions relate to one another, from one of hostility to one of cooperation. It is also the focus of this volume. By outlining the essential questions underlying four of the world's great faiths, Messrs. Ouaknin, Levenson, Le Gall, and Chebel set out to achieve one of the hardest acts of religion: highlighting commonalities among the faiths, while also finding pleasure in difference.

The idea that the monotheistic religions could live alongside one another without compromising their beliefs and without killing one another appears occasionally in history. It was discussed by Cardinal Nicolas of Cusa in the fifteenth century and touched upon in the Council of Trent in the sixteenth century. But true ecumenical understanding did not begin in earnest until the late nineteenth century. The word *ecumene*, from French meaning "the whole inhabited earth," was initially used in the Middle Ages to mean universal and was later adopted by the Catholic Church to signify its claim to represent the entire world. The word was appropriated by Protestants in the late 1800s to signal their desire to once again unify the Christian world. Ecumenical then meant "above and beyond denomination," and ultimately came to mean above and beyond any particular religion.

In 1893, as part of the World's Fair in Chicago to mark the four-hundredth anniversary of Columbus' voyage to America, a lawyer named Charles Bonney proposed inviting members of all the major religions to the event. The World Parliament of Religions is widely regarded as the beginning of the interfaith movement. It was followed by the first World Missionary Conference in Edinburgh (1910), the first World Congress of Faiths (1933), and, following the religious persecution of World War II, the first Council on Churches in Geneva (1948).

For the most part, the force behind these early meetings were Protestants who aimed to bring together disparate factions of Christianity into a unified mission of action and confession. As a bonus, they hoped to unite Christians with believers of other faiths—including Buddhists, Hindus, and others—into what the World Congress of 1933 called a "spiritual Oneness of the Good Life Universal."

The Catholic Church at first dismissed the movement as "pan-Christians" producing a false understanding of God. But the Holocaust, coupled with the growing influence of prosperous and more pluralistic American Catholics, forced change. At the Second Vatican Council in 1962, the Church would issue its own "Decree of Ecumenism" to restore unity among Christians. The new doctrine also praised Jews as "the people most dear" to God because they received his covenant first. It hailed Muslims as those who "profess to hold the faith of Abraham and together with us adore the one, merciful God."

Vatican II accelerated not just a dialogue among religions, but a wholesale reexamination of theology that set out to expunge the angry exclusivism of the past. In relatively rapid fashion, relations between Christians and Jews in particular began to change dramatically, as Jews across the West broke through barriers in business, politics, and social life that had been closed to them for centuries. Universities that, as recently as mid-century, had Jewish quotas now had Jewish presidents. Social clubs that once excluded Jews now held Jewish weddings. And, in 2000, in a remarkable event, which was most remarkable in how few people remarked about it, a Jewish candidate for

Vice President of the United States was part of a ticket that won the popular vote.

September 11, 2001, proved to be a defining moment in the realm of interfaith relations, as it introduced a third major religion into the dialogue that had been taking place, at least in the West, for decades. Islam was an awkward fit at first, as the first introduction that many people had to the faith was through the nose of an airplane crashing into a New York City landmark. In the months after 9-11, some of the most prominent fundamentalist Protestants in the United States, including the Rev. Franklin Graham, son of the Rev. Billy Graham, and the Rev. Jerry Vines, of the Southern Baptist Convention, denounced the faith of over one billion believers. The Rev. Jerry Falwell called Mohammad a terrorist. In an age when we fight wars against terrorists, does this mean the West should declare war on Islam?

The answer, of course, is that the West includes Islam. And millions of Americans expressed that realization by rushing out to buy books, attend lectures, and reach out to their Muslim neighbors in what amounted to a national teach-in on Islam. This is an important first step. The challenge the world faces today is that with religion once more at the forefront of the international conversation, can the religions of the world figure out a way to relate to one another that is not dictated by an effort to extinguish one another? That task—as shown by the variety of answers presented in this book—is surprisingly difficult for it requires embracing the idea that each religion does not contain the exclusive claim on truth. "We need not only a theology of commonality," writes Jonathan Sacks, the chief rabbi of Britain, in his towering manifesto *The Dignity of Difference*. We also need a "theology of difference: why no one civilization has the right to impose itself on others by force: why God asks us to respect the freedom and dignity of those not like us." The charge, in other words, is to see God's image in one who is not in our image. To respect the truth in others even as we uphold it in ourselves.

Is that possible?

The answer, as it's always been in matters of faith, is up to each of us. Reading this book, joining in the process of learning about other's religions, and acknowledging the universality as well as the individuality of the four religions represented here, can be a vital first step. But we must accept that not everyone agrees. The week after *TIME* asked the question "IS GOD DEAD?" on its cover, the magazine ran nearly a page of letters to the editor. Two letters said it best. Richard L. Storatz of Notre Dame, Indiana, wrote in to say, "Sir: Yes." Norine McGuire, of Chicago, Illinois, wrote in to say, "Sir: No."

Perhaps both of them were right.

Bruce Feiler

MARC-ALAIN OUAKNIN
Rabbi and Doctor of Philosophy
Director of the Centre de Recherches et d'Études Juives ALEPH (Paris)
Associate Professor in the Bar-Ilan University (Israel)

DOM ROBERT LE GALL
Theologian
Bishop of Mende

CLAUDE B. LEVENSON
Orientalist and author
Translator of the teachings of the Dalai Lama

MALEK CHEBEL
Anthropologist
Director of the Centre d'Études et de Recherches sur
l'Imaginaire Arabo-Musulman (CERIAMUS, Paris)

BRUCE FEILER
Author
*Walking the Bible: A Journey by Land Through the Five Books of
Moses* and *Abraham: A Journey to the Heart of Three Faiths*

First Part

12 Essential Questions

Second Part
Symbols

12 ESSENTIAL QUESTIONS

Who is God?

MARC-ALAIN OUAKNIN

In Judaism, the question of God is the question of the Revelation of God. To seek to understand God is to seek to understand the specific way—the original manner—in which the infinite enters into contact with the finite, whereby the divine chooses to reveal itself to men.

After the first words addressed to Abraham, God successively revealed Himself to Isaac, Jacob, and Moses, doing so in a different way each time. In the first three instances, the Revelation was made to an individual; in the fourth, when God revealed Himself to Moses on Mount Sinai, God chose to communicate through the intermediary of an individual to the larger group.

For the Jewish people, the Revelation on Mount Sinai is the most important of the four. But why is this instance so important? Does it have an original structure that makes it radically different from the other three? If we re-read the text of Exodus describing this key moment, we see—this is something we know, but it needs to be emphasized—that God as God is only a voice speaking to the people from the mountaintop, through the intermediary of Moses. This God remains withdrawn, invisible, his only incarnation being his voice, the Word that engraves itself on the Tablets of the Law.

It is indeed an astonishing text, for it speaks of a *vision of voices*: "And the whole people saw voices." Commentators explain this verse as the vision of the text that was given, or revealed, on Sinai. The Revelation is above all the Revelation of a text. That is the great revolution brought to us by the biblical account. And the primary, essential relation to God is a relation to this text of the Law.

Jewish mysticism radicalizes this idea in the following formulation: *Qoudcha berikh hou ve torato had hou* ("the Holy One, Blessed be He, and his Torah are but one"). God, then, is The Text! It is through this text that Man comes to know God. God is, above all, the Creator of Heaven and Earth and the whole Universe, which gives Man the status of creature—Man who arrives as God's last creation, on the sixth day, when creation was made complete.

According to this account, God is He who puts order in the world. Each thing has its own place and this must be respected if the equilibrium of the world is to be maintained. This organization is valid for objects and for living beings. It is the Law of the world, both physical and metaphysical, both mathematical and ethical. God the creator is thus a force that organizes worlds and a force that sustains worlds. This God is called Elohim by the biblical text that begins with those famous words: "In the beginning Elohim created the heavens and the Earth."

The question asked is "Who is God?", but Judaism has many ways of saying the divine, and they are not all equivalent. Even if there is only one God, His ways of revealing Himself to men are multiple. There is the God Elohim, the God YVVH, a name in four consonants that cannot be pronounced, an unsayable name that some transcribe as Yahweh or Jehovah, and wrongly so, for the act of transcription is already a questioning of the infinity of the divine. We also find the name Shadai, expressing the self-limitation of God that was necessary for the creation of the world and for Him to remain present in it. In the Jewish mystical tradition, this movement from the infinite to the finite occurs through the text. It is in the light of this that we can understand the great importance of reading and study in Judaism.

For, as I have said, God is the text. This means that the most radical manifestation of the divine occurs through text, through the book and the letters of the alphabet. In other words, through an object of this world, the infinite—God—went into the finite and thus Himself became something finite and therefore limited, as is all text. In the Kabbala there is a name for this movement from the infinite to the finite, this possibility that the finite can exist out of the infinite; it is the *Simsum*, or the contraction of God. This contraction raises an important theological problem: if God puts Himself forward in finite form, can He still be God?

The Kabbalists and Talmudists have been well aware of this problem and of the need to answer it, for, obviously, there is a risk of having a finite God, a God in this world—in other words, an idol. And if God became the Book, then we must in a sense restore the text's status as an Infinity. That is to say, we must use all the means at our disposal to give it an infinite meaning. This is what the Talmudists succeeded in doing. The point of the Talmud is not to better understand the text, or to better understand God, but to interpret the text in such a way that the Word it contains, that one Word, can be understood plurally.

It is precisely because of this plurality of perspectives that we can say that each person has a different perception of God. This plural God is a living God, not a polytheism, but rather a pluralist Judaism, a freedom for each person in the way they perceive their relation to the divine.

DOM ROBERT LE GALL

Between the Father and the Son, and their Spirit, who together are the one God of the Christians, there is a unity that we are called to conjoin, as in Jesus's prayer to his Father before his Passion: "Neither pray I for these alone, but for them also which shall believe on me through their word; that they all may be one; as thou, Father, *art* in me, and I in thee, that they also may be one in us: that the world may believe that thou hast sent me" (John XVII:20-21). The mission of the Son comes from the divine unity and is ordered by it, "in the unity of the Holy Spirit," as is sung in the conclusion to prayers at Mass or other services.

Father, Son, the Holy Spirit, the names of the Three that are One, the Holy Trinity, that are the One God of the Christian faith, are the intimate names that go deep into the heart of what is most precious in our own human lives. Is it not true that in our closest human relations we tend toward unity? Love and friendship accomplish a union, a communion that respects and even helps construct the identity of those whom it bonds.

The Trinity is a mystery in which unity and difference come together, each remaining irreducible to the other. It is not a fusion in which the Father, Son, and Holy Spirit are melded together, but a case of Persons who give themselves up in order to reach their full potential and become One, the One God. We are beings who need relationships in order to develop and define ourselves—in philosophical terms we are relative substances. The divine Persons, who are the only God, are, as persons, subsisting relations, that is to say, a full relation to the other, perfectly coinciding with the divine being.

This is a mystery that accompanies Christians all through their life. Right from their baptism—a word which means "to dip" in Greek—"in the name of the Father, the Son, and the Holy Ghost," they are plunged into the Holy Trinity. Every sign of the Cross is made in the name of those three divine Beings. Every prayer at Mass is addressed to the Father through the Son and in the Holy Ghost. Every psalm ends with "Glory to the Father, the Son, and the Holy Ghost," and so on.

The Trinity is not an insoluble equation in which three is one, but a mystery of life and love, for it takes several beings to love and be loved, in the unity that is the goal of all true dilection.

CLAUDE B. LEVENSON

Unlike monotheistic religions, Buddhism is not founded on the notion of a creator God. It is both a philosophy of life and a spiritual approach anchored in the reality of an exceptional historical figure, Shakyamuni, the "Wise Man of the Shakya," the historical Buddha, whom several years of intense solitary meditation led to enlightenment—hence his name, Buddha: "he who has woken up from the illusions of the world." The *Dharma*, the Law that he enounced for beings in this world, enables each person to follow a path analogous to his own, until they are free of suffering and attain *nirvana*, the supreme state of peace that some call knowledge, wisdom, and the ultimate goal, illumination, or enlightenment. In different centuries and regions, there have been many ways that have led to this ideal. Of these, the Tibetan way, with its numerous ramifications, is no doubt one of the most attractive for the infinite diversity of its divinities and the lively cohort of its smiling or fierce-faced gods. Gods? For the sage in the solitude of the Himalayas, gods and goddesses are above all the projection or the phantasmagoria of the human mind. The gods personify power and embody powerful forces, representing the tendencies that human beings must master or refine in order to reach a state of spiritual or human development. The gods help man to realize his full potential: the gifts and capacities that all men have within them just as they have deep inside the nature of the Buddha. This is the seed of enlightenment that they must tend and bring to ripeness and bloom. The gods, according to Buddhism, are also the inhabitants of a kingdom of happiness that is part of the Wheel of Life. As such, they, like us, are only transient, subject to the ineluctable law of change or transformation—and therefore of impermanence. Human beings can be reborn in this kingdom if their karma, the law of causality, allows it, but they will be no less mortal, even if existence in these fields of bliss lasts much longer than a simple human life. In this view, each person is responsible not only for their own self and their acts but also for others and for the world, which they continue to shape with their presence and their actions.

MALEK CHEBEL

For a sincere Muslim, man cannot apprehend God by his five senses or by any form of intellectual speculation. Such a question might indeed seem blasphemous in the very act of asking it, as well as pointless. The divine self is intangible, there is no entity in the world that has the color, consistency or extent of Allah, no being that He can be compared to. Hence, the inanity of trying to approach

Him by way of any argument whatsoever. Thus, knowledge of God cannot be exhibited: it must be lived as an intimate experience. It is a matter of concrete perception, for to know God is above all to love and serve him. It is a certainty of the heart more than an abstract construction.

However, the Koran does attribute a certain number of qualities to Allah, summing these up in some ninety-nine sacred names, which indicate the many divine prerogatives, including: Allah the Unique, Allah the Omniscient, Allah the All-Powerful, etc.

Muslims believe in another virtue that is aesthetic but equally important: Allah is beautiful. And the prophet Mohammed adds that this Beauteous God is also the God of Beauty, which includes all the virtues that the human character has given itself. To this can be added an infinite number of other attributes, which are one with the Beauteous Names of Allah, such as grandeur, extent, and longevity.

It is by this path that the divine is approached in Islam, as much to measure its truth and power as to establish an authentic veneration. Can one love that majestic entity, which, in its sovereign power, leaves no room for doubt or hesitation? To answer this question, the founding texts of Islam insist on the fact that the veneration of God cannot be imposed from outside or practiced under duress. Now, insofar as this faith cannot be disembodied or artificial, each believer must strive to perceive it for him or herself. This insistence on interiority constitutes the great jewel of the faith (*al-iman*).

As Lord of the Heavens, the Earth, and the Universe (Koran 45:36), God is also He through who, constantly, hour by hour, our world is perfected. We need only look around us and examine nature as it sings His praises in order to observe the accomplishment of Man, to be aware of His presence. The "Living Reign" through which the Creator's act, and thereby his identity, is accomplished—that is the principle on which Muslims can best found their definition of God.

What is the divine?

MARC-ALAIN OUAKNIN

Political space opens wherever several people are together: they are not a community but will construct their community in the very questioning of the meaning of their gathering. A community exists "in-the-process-of-forming" because it does not start with prejudices as to what it is or should be.

However, in spite of this permanent impossibility of knowing the definition of "a good society," we continue to think that democracy is a better choice than totalitarianism. And in a democracy we hold up one value rather than another. What are the reasons for this choice? Why do we choose democracy? It is a conviction, but where does it come from?

If we look to the divine and to the Revelation, there is the risk that we will allow an upsurge of false prophets who, in the name of God, will propose a political orientation based on violence! How can we demonstrate that equality is well-founded? What is the legitimacy of a law instituted by man? By men? This is an authentic question, an "endless question" in spite of the many answers that we may give it.

Political modernity, which excludes the idea of Revelation and transcendence, resides in a paradox that is perhaps the very power of questioning, understood as the eros of thought. Thanks to this, thought *thinks*. The paradox is as follows: there is, on the one hand, the need to provide an ultimate foundation for our ethical and political positions and, on the other, the specifically modern insistence of remaining lucid about the impossibility of founding this position on reason itself. Modernity has lost the faith in an ultimate or original foundation for things, but it has kept the stipulation that all these options should be linked to such a foundation. In practice, it is very much as if we all accepted the existence of a transcendent dimension in relation to any human decision or judgment. Beyond certain limits, humankind's judgments and actions are carried out as if the answer were provided by a God.

Revelation could be seen as precisely that: the subject opening up to something other than itself, to another dimension, without going back to the *ego*-logical. Revelation would be this very possibility of the Same moving toward the Other, a movement that we call transcendence. Revelation as the transcendence of God toward man would thus be the corollary of the transcendence of man "toward...," without going back. Responsibility. Revelation would, in this sense, be primarily ethical.

The structure of Revelation as the recognition of alterity is the limit, the self-limitation, of politics. However, recognition of, and respect for, the existence of transcendence are not enough in themselves. That is no more than a well-directed project. In the final analysis it is men who, even in the perspective of Revelation, make their own history. "In a democracy, the people can do anything—and must know that they cannot do *just anything*. Democracy is the regime of self-limitation; it is therefore the regime of historical risk." Let us face the risk of History.

DOM ROBERT LE GALL

Biblical Revelation defines the divine in relation to the human. For indeed, God had to use a human language to tell us who he was. The last word in this Revelation is the Incarnation, whereby "the Word was made flesh" (John I:14). This Word is the very Word of God. It can therefore speak to us truthfully about God. What does it say about Him? "God is love" (I John IV:8). As we have already seen, God is Three in One; his mysterious unity is a fount of eternal love to which we are invited ourselves. God is being, "He who is" (Exodus III:14). Everything that is comes from him: "All things were made by him, and without him was not anything made" (John I:3). But He is distinct from the beings that He creates. Creation is an act of separation, just as birth separates the child from its mother. And yet the relationship remains and must grow. The same goes for those creatures who, while distinct from God, maintain a constant relationship with Him, one that they must discover and keep vivifying. For Christians, it is not a matter of becoming God, of merging into a great Oneness, like the drop of water in the ocean. God the Creator, the Father, the Son, and the Holy Ghost, who is Love, invites His creatures, whom he has made capable of love, to enter into his divine life. We are invited, not to become God, but to be "divinized" by receiving—but not taking—the gift of His love. At "the foundation of the world," the Father chose us through his son "that we should be holy and without blame before him in love" (Ephesians I:4).

Thus everything that we do in love comes, in one way or another, from God, and brings us closer to Him. But we also know that other forces or tendencies pull us in other directions.

CLAUDE B. LEVENSON

As a higher power, the divine is indefinable and inaccessible to ordinary understanding. If we are to believe certain wise men, it is the reflection or subtle projection of the human spirit. For the Buddhists, divinities and deities represent natural or supernatural forces that creatures of the senses must accommodate in order to maintain their precarious balance.

Gods and goddesses play a protective role, so it is better to be careful to ensure their benevolence rather than bring down their wrath. In fact, Buddhism does not acknowledge "divine revelation" in the sense given to that term by the monotheistic religions, because Siddharta Gautama, who became the Buddha, that is to say, "enlightened," is a human being who lived in a precise historical period, five hundred years before Christ. His persevering, uncompromising spiritual quest led him to formulate a specific vision of the world, which over the years became the basis of Buddhism. This singular approach subsequently shaped generation after generation, mainly in Asia, where it was gradually enriched by legends, commentaries, stories, and individual striving, until it had become the solid trunk, a way of living and experiencing the world that has diverse branches.

MALEK CHEBEL

In the classic formula, the divine is a transfiguring power that manifests itself through the teeming variety of nature and through humankind. But (and how else would we know it?) it also has more abstract, inward qualities: uniqueness, transcendence, and permanence.

Its external forms are multiple, being linked to the number of its attributes (Allah has ninety-nine holy names, each one an attribute or characteristic sign) and other exoteric manifestations (human, animal, vegetal forms, etc.), through which he appears on Earth. But in his essence or in his representations, God is divine only if he is a sublime clock gifted with movement, a kinetic entity, a primordial *pneuma*. Beyond His unsayable or inaccessible aspect, God is divine because He is in perpetual motion, an endless dynamic given concrete form in his act of creation: "I was a hidden treasure. I wanted to be known and I created" (*Hadith Qudsi*). The obvious proof of God's existence—in a word, his definition—is *pneumatic*.

Man, as a sign of the divine, in God and in ourselves, remains the finest medium for the heavenly song.

When a Muslim pronounces the Shahada, *La Ilaha ha Ila Allah* (There is no other God than God...)—this being the basic act of his religion—he is speaking of this supreme being whose essential uniqueness ("He is the One") is the guarantee of His universality ("He is Totality and Multiplicity Reunited").

The other distinguishing aspect of the divine is that it is itself the supra-sensible force that nourishes it. The divine is also that through which the humanization of man is achieved. "We created man; and We know what his soul whispers within him, and We are nearer to him than the jugular vein" (Koran 50:16).

What is faith?

MARC-ALAIN OUAKNIN

In his quest, a Jew doubts. He does not seek truth, but meaning. The question is not "How did God create the world?" but, "Since the text tells me that God created the world, what is the meaning of that for me?"

In the Talmud, man is always in movement, leaving certainty to enter into the disquiet of "not knowing," to use the words of Rabbi Nahman of Bratislava. Man is essentially a "seeker" and his work essentially a "quest." With Rabbi Nahman the word "belief" must be written and placed in quotation marks, so as not to be heard without them or confused with simple faith.

For the Jew, there are always battles to be fought, possible defeats to be envisaged. Choices to be made without rest. This is Jacob's struggle with the angel. And this is how he becomes Israel! Jewish man knows no comfortable, definitive, external certainties. In his "belief," which remains a form of "seeking," there is always a "for" and an "against," and when one chooses the "for," one knows very well that doubt can utter the "against."

"Seeking" or "belief" is the infinite tension between two opposites that cannot be resolved in a third term, a synthesis. The positive term never cancels the negative and, instead of a stable equilibrium of the two, there is a constant back and forth between them, in which sometimes one is dominant, sometimes the other.

A Jewish man as "eternal seeker" has opted—and that option is reversible, otherwise he would have chosen once and for all and have become locked into a system—for a "philosophy of the caress" in which there is never any permanent grip or control. On the contrary, what is produced is "futurity," things to come. What emerges here is a wisdom of uncertainty, of an objective uncertainty. And what can be said of faith applies to other worldly perceptions.

"Do I have faith?" asks Kierkegaard. "That is something of which I can have no immediate certainty, for faith is precisely that dialectical oscillation which, though fearful and trembling, never despairs. It is that infinite concern about oneself, that concern to know if one has faith, and it is this concern that is faith itself."

For a "seeker," for a Jewish man, there is only one certitude, that of the risk of the absolute.

When Rabbi Nahman states that "the world is a narrow bridge thrown over the abyss," an abyss into which man may constantly fall from one side or the other, he is talking about man's objective uncertainty, in relation to the world and in relation to the Other. For it is the movement of uncertainty that is the sign of our relation with the Other. This uncertainty is the very sign of "belief." It is when the individual is not sure of his relation to the Other that the relation to the Other exists. In the domain of faith, "it is when man is not sure of his relation with God that there is a relation with God. Wretched are those who believe they are in a relation with Him, for most certainly they are not."

However, this way of having faith is itself very subjective. In order to have a society based on shared values, the masters of the tradition formulated the "articles of faith," which are the essential principles that Jews must adhere to. The best known articles of faith are the thirteen laid down by Maimonides:

The existence of God.

The unity of God.

The noncorporeality of God.

The eternity of God.

God is the sole object of worship.

Belief in the prophecy.

Moses is greater than all other prophets.

God revealed the Torah to Moses.

The text of the Torah is immutable.

The omniscience of God.

The existence of divine reward and punishment.

The coming of the Messiah.

The dead will live again.

DOM ROBERT LE GALL

Faith lies at the heart of human relations. We cannot live without trusting others. For example, what proof do I have that I am the child of my parents? Spontaneously, we believe what others tell us, when they are bringing us news or relating events. A society in the grip of fear or mistrust—as in those totalitarian states where spying and informing were instituted even within the family—is an unnatural society. To love is to assume that, beyond outward signs, one trusts in the other person's heart: "It is only with the heart that one can see rightly," the Fox says to the Little Prince. "What is essential is invisible to the eye." To give one's faith is to bond with someone, to anchor oneself to their heart.

In the Catholic tradition, we distinguish faith, hope, and love, in accordance with the teaching of Saint Paul in his First Epistle to the Corinthians: "Now abideth faith, hope, charity, these three: but the greatest of these is charity" (I Corinthians XIII:13). Faith will give way to vision, hope to possession, but love has already attained its goal. The limitation of this distinction is that it makes faith an intellectual virtue, when in fact it is the whole person adhering to what God reveals to us: "Faith is the substance of things hoped for, the evidence of things not seen," teaches the Epistle to the Hebrews (XI:1). To believe in the truths of faith presupposes that we have faith in the one who offers them to us.

The whole of Scripture is a call for men to put their faith and trust in God, as stated by this first conclusion to the Gospel of Saint John: "And many other signs did Jesus in the presence of his disciples, which are not written in this book. But these are written that ye might believe, that Jesus is Christ, the Son of God, and that believing ye might have life through his name" (John XX:30-31).

CLAUDE B. LEVENSON

Faith is a way of believing, of trusting in an external force or in one's own powers, and of fighting to the very end, until one attains one's objective; it can be the motor for a way of living and of facing up to the many challenges of simple human life.

One can have faith in a multitude of things: in a divine power (of course) in providence, but also in a guardian angel, in an inner guide, in a master of wisdom, in one's lucky star, in an idea of justice, in a better life (not to be always put off until tomorrow). It would seem that the source of a certain kind of faith is inexhaustible and that it is human beings who endow it with its many different colors and objects, for the duration of their time on Earth. Faith can also be a personal choice, made out of affinity or upon reflection, one that eventually becomes that flickering little light that, so it said, we all carry within us.

MALEK CHEBEL

One day, a man came to the Prophet and asked him: "What is faith?" And he replied, "It is to believe in God, in his angels, in the other life, in the prophets and in the Resurrection."[1] And, the Koran adds, it is to not doubt them afterward (Koran 49:15).

Belief is at the heart of faith. You cannot have one without having the potentialities of the other: faith and belief are the two facets of the same attitude. In the Prophet's answer to the Bedouin who questioned him, we can see the essential stages of the process, for the attitude of belief is supported by an orientation, a project. Faith, that complex and powerful feeling, partakes directly of the Mystery of Creation, resides in an intimate and unshakable conviction concerning our vocation as human beings born to serve a common, universal, and transcendental cause.

In practical terms, faith includes the respect that we owe to the canonical duties (*ibadat*) that constitute Islam, in the exoteric sense of the term. There are five of these: profession of faith, prayer, alms, fasting, and pilgrimage. To these we must add the personal disposition toward God ("serve Allah as if you saw him, for while we may not see him, He sees us") and his Prophet. This is expressed in an attitude of sincere devotion, trust, love, and fear.

The faith in Islam, *al-iman*—the term is derived from *amana*, "to keep safely"—is a natural disposition that religious practice reinforces, though it does not create it, "that they might add faith to their faith" (48:4).

The companions of the Prophet have left us many apothegms and adages on the subject of faith. Most of them show faith to be a disposition founded on a "God-fearing" attitude. But since it is not confirmed by any immediate verification, faith cannot be overly straightforward or lacking in sincerity. It is up to the believer to follow or not follow the divine word, to honor it or to exclude it. This is the meaning of the observation made by Ibn Masud (seventh century) that faith is a certainty and that this certainty is the whole of faith.

The difficulties experienced by the penitent and his long progress toward complete faith are summed up in the prophetic dictum that faith has sixty branches.

Faith is a personal feeling that refuses all artifice: "It is not piety, that you turn your faces to the East and to the West," states the Koran. True piety means believing in the instructions of the sacred texts, fearing God (*khushu*) and respecting His Prophet, without trying to gain advantage from this situation.

1. El Bokhari, *Les Traditions islamiques*, Paris, Adrien Maisonneuve, 1984, vol. 1, p. 28.

What is a prophet?

MARC-ALAIN OUAKNIN

In Hebrew, the word for prophet is *navi*. He is the man who lifts himself up to such a high level of consciousness that he can hear the word of God and is able to translate it so as to make it audible for men.

Contrary to popular belief, a prophet does not foretell the future. He simply awakens men to their duties and informs them of the positive or negative consequences of their acts. He states the logical unfolding of events. A messenger of God, he must translate the fruit of his revelation into popular language. In this sense, the divine word lives within him, but his personality or identity is not subsumed into his status as prophet. The source of the prophecy is in the "word," and not the divine "Spirit," and what makes the individual a prophet is not the Spirit that surrounds him, but the words that he possesses. However, he can enter into a dialogue with the divine and the obligations of his charge do not destroy his free will and are not destroyed by the obligations of his charge.

The prophetic experience is a confrontation. The prophet partakes of the action or the word that he allows into himself; armed solely with the divine word, he becomes an iconoclast by examining the world in accordance with its logic. He does not gain a special knowledge of the divine, but only of its momentary design in history; he is neither a philosopher nor a theologian, but a mediator. He does not embody the finality of a message but is an ordinary man who, having experienced the divine word, must accomplish his difficult task of conveying it to an indifferent or even hostile world. This explains why the styles of the prophets differ. Each is a master in his own way, be it of literary expression, sermons, prayers, parables, or legal judgments. Thus the divine judgment is transmitted through the prism of man: the divine revelation is delivered by a fundamentally human and always unique agent.

The first prophets played an important role in everyday affairs and were often consulted by those seeking knowledge of God's oracles. There are references to them being paid for this purpose (I Samuel IX:8; I Kings XIV:3; II Kings VIII:9). They had a considerable influence on Israel's political destiny, and were so important to the monarchy that some kings had their own court prophets: Men such as Nathan (II Samuel VII:1; I Kings I:8) and Gad (I Samuel XXII:5; II Samuel XXIV:11; I Chronicles XXI:9, XXIX:29). These early prophets combined highly lucid reflections on the present with the power to predict the future, although they did this more in symbolic actions than in literal, verbal pronouncements. They could also work miracles, as did Elias and Elisha. But while all these actions were performed "in the name of God," and *by* God through their intermediary, this position did not guarantee their impunity or safety, or prevent them from being persecuted as Elisa was (I Kings XIX), or put in prison, like Micah (I Kings XXII:27).

In the Hebrew Bible, the second canonic section that follows the Torah or Pentateuch is called Neviim, or "Prophets." This section is divided into two parts and begins with the "First Prophets": the books of Joshua, Judges, Samuel, and Kings, which are in fact "historical books" but which contain the stories of the pre-classical prophets, including Nathan, Elias, and Elisha. The second group, called the "Last Prophets," contains works of classic prophetic literature, those of the three "great prophets" (Isaiah, Jeremiah, and Ezekiel) and the twelve "Minor Prophets" (Hosea, Joel, Amos, Obadiah, Jonah, Micah, Nahum, Habakkuk, Zephaniah, Haggai, Zechariah, and Malachi). The distinction between "Major" and "Minor" prophets reflects the length of their works, and not their relative importance or quality.

The first books contain mainly biographical stories about the prophets, whereas the last cover the contents of their prophecies. Both types share the title "prophet" and the divine inspiration that impels men to deliver their message to the people of Israel in order to preserve its Covenant with God.

The first prophets are sometimes called "seers." A number of them, including Elias and Elisha, worked miracles.

DOM ROBERT LE GALL

Contrary to what is commonly thought, a prophet is not just someone who foretells the future. The word means "to speak in advance" and, above all, "to speak in the place of another" (*phemi* means "to speak," *pro* can mean "for" or "before"). The prophet is thus a man who speaks in the name of God. Moses was the great prophet of the Old Testament, to whom the Lord declared, when he received his vocation: "Go and I will be with thy mouth, and teach thee what thou shalt say" (Exodus IV:12). When he was called, Isaiah's mouth was purified by a coal brought from the altar On High (Isaiah VI:6-7). It was the same for Jeremiah: "Then the Lord put forth his hand, and touched my mouth: and the Lord said unto me, Behold, I have put my words in thy mouth" (Jeremiah I:9).

The prophet is sometimes called a "seer," as the First Book of Samuel tells us: "For he that is now called a Prophet, was before time called a Seer" (I Samuel IX:9). This is how Balaam, who in the book of Numbers becomes a prophet in spite of himself, introduces what he must pass on: "Balaam, the son of Beor hath said, and the man whose eyes are open hath said; he hath said, which heard the words of God, and knew the knowledge of the most High, which saw the vision of the Almighty, falling into a trance, but having his eyes open" (Numbers XXIV:15-16).

The prophet is thus someone who, in one way or another, sees what God sees, listens to what God says, and passes it on to those to whom God wishes to convey a message for the sake of their salvation. Jesus is the pre-eminent prophet, for he is God, and his human words really can say who God is. Who is better able to reveal God than the Man-God? When he makes the confession of Caesarea (where Jesus is acknowledged to be the son of God) Peter, so Jesus tells him, is acting as a prophet: "Blessed art thou Simon Bar-jona: for flesh and blood hath not revealed it unto thee, but my Father which is in heaven" (Matthew XVI:17).

Like the Prince of the Apostles, any man who receives the apostolic witness is also a prophet. Moses desired that all the

50

"Lord's people were prophets" (Numbers XI:29), his wish was accomplished by Pentecost, as announced by the prophet Joel (cf. Joel III:1-2; Acts II:16). Prophecy was commonly practiced in the days of the early Church, as Saint Paul relates (cf. I Corinthians XIV). Insofar as the Spirit of God dwells within us, it is possible for us to speak under its influence. Immersed in the mystery of Christ and marked by the Spirit, the Christian partakes of the triple sacerdotal, prophetic, and royal function of Lord Jesus, as we are taught by the Second Vatican Council.[1]

CLAUDE B. LEVENSON

In Buddhism, there are no prophets, if one defines a prophet by its meaning for monotheistic religions. However, exceptional figures may sometimes appear in the community of men: the bodhisattva, the master, and the oracle. Each plays a precise role among his fellows, but above all they are human beings who, by their perseverance in their quest, have in some sense transcended the common level and raised themselves to a superior degree of humanity.

In a sense, the bodhisattva represents the Tibetan Buddhist ideal in this world: aspiring to enlightenment not for oneself, but to help others by taking upon oneself the suffering of all sentient beings; and, having attained full enlightenment, renouncing nirvana so as to remain among living beings from one life to the next, putting one's accomplished knowledge and limitless compassion at the service of all others. A parallel can be drawn here with the ideal of sainthood in other religious traditions, but we should not overlook the fact that the compassion and wisdom of the bodhisattva are always active and manifest from one life to the next.

The master, or lama or "guru"—the primary meaning of which is he who teaches, trains, and grants the blessing that authorizes the individual to enter into the way—is himself a human being formed according to the traditions. In the Tibetan world, choosing a master or disciple is a very meticulous process both for the disciple and for the lama. It is above all a matter of trust, which is the foundation of a balanced relationship that owes as much to reason as it does to devotion. There can be no blind faith. Any master worthy of the name will take care to remind the candidate for wisdom that Buddha himself warned against credulousness, facility, or haste in making a choice that will shape a whole life. The master never shows off his knowledge or powers; he preaches by example, for only his conduct and his qualities can guarantee the truth that he carries within him.

The oracle, monk, or layman (male or female) does not necessarily become what they are by personal choice. They are "chosen" by a higher power that seeks to express itself through them by making them play the role of medium. The task is tough. It demands from whoever accepts it austere discipline and strength of character. Those who are chosen must be capable of enduring and surmounting the physical and spiritual ordeal to which they are subjected at the onset, as well as in the course of the divinatory trance that brings men to some of the answers to the essential questions.

MALEK CHEBEL

Prophet, messenger of God, or preacher—it is difficult to distinguish the exact attributes of each of these three aspects of prophecy and saintliness in Islam. The words themselves are interchangeable and have multiple uses. One need only read the two main Suras of the Koran about prophets, The Prophets and The Poets, to see how shifting are the respective semiologies of the words prophet, warner, messenger, and lawmaker. Still, the preaching of Islam is very much of the strong, monotheistic kind, for it is articulated around a vertical trilogy: Allah, the Koran, and Mohammed. Mohammed is presented as a witness, he who announces the good news, a warner, and a "brilliant luminary." He is God's Prophet.

To this semantic approach an evaluation of the content can be added, for the different "Envoys of God" do not all have the same prerogatives. Some are messengers (*rasul*) and others prophets (*anbiya* or *nabi*).

According to the Islamic tradition, there have been nine messengers since the creation of the world: Adam, Seth, Noah, Abraham, Ishmail, Moses, Lot, Jesus, and Mohammed, who is considered to have brought the cycle of prophecies to an end. Of these, only five prophets have brought new laws: Noah, Abraham, Moses, Jesus, and Mohammed.

The second category comprises the prophets (prophets/messengers or prophets/announcers) whose number, both mythically and symbolically, is 124,000.

Every prophet is also a messenger, announcer, warner, and legislator, but not all messengers have the capacity to create a new law or introduce a Holy Book.

The prophet is an intermediary between two worlds: the world of heavenly creatures and the world of humans. His virtue is to convey without distorting it a holy message to the spiritually and morally impoverished Earth.

Should the "holy" texts be seen as an act of transcendental will or as the word of superior beings?

MARC-ALAIN OUAKNIN

Text implies reading and readers. The Jewish reading of the Scriptures, and therefore the Jewish understanding of God, is not fideistic, the passive repetition of a text that is locked forever into a single meaning. Reading automatically means exegesis, interpretation, and hermeneutics! Reading is automatically study, commentary on commentary, renewing the immutable letters and the life-giving breath of the Living God.

"God is certainly not incarnate, but in some way inscribed, living His life—or part of His life—in letters: in the lines and between the lines, and in the exchange of ideas between readers commenting on them."[1]

The Talmud is the set of interpretations that commentators have made of the text of the Revelation, from Moses to the present day. Thus the text of the Revelation literally explodes under the effect of interpretation.

The Talmudic masters underline one fundamental idea: the Jewish people are not "the People of the Book" but the "People of the interpretation of the Book," to use a formulation dear to Armand Abecassis.

I said at the beginning of my first answer that "God is the text." This means that the most radical manifestation of the divine comes to us through the text, through the book and the letters of the alphabet; in other words, through an object of this world, as if the infinite—God—passed into the finite and thus Himself became something finite; limited, as is all text.

In the Kabbala, this passage from the infinite to the finite, this possibility that the finite has of existing through the infinite, is called the *Simsum*. This means "the contraction of God." This contraction poses an important theological problem. If God offers Himself to the finite, can He still be God?

The Kabbalists and Talmudists have been well aware of this problem, and of the need to answer it, for obviously, there is a risk of having a finite God, a God in this world—in other words, an idol. And if God became the Book, then we must in a sense restore the text's status as Infinity. That is to say, we must use all the means at our disposal to give it an infinite meaning. This is what the Talmudists succeeded in doing. The point of the Talmud is not to understand the text better, or to understand God better: that would be a way of appropriating God, of hemming in the infinite. No, the point is to interpret the text in such a way that the Word it contains, a Word that is unique, can be understood plurally. The definition of the Talmud consists precisely of that pluralistic word—the plurality of human interpretations. And so you may be able to say one thing about the text, but you can also say another, and yet another. The interpretation never stops. The Talmud does not enunciate the meaning of the Torah; on the contrary, it is constantly opening it to new meanings.

In today's Judaism, we should speak not of one but of two Torahs: the written law, and in an immediate and necessary relation to it, the oral law; that is to say, the law of interpretation.

This is the liberty of men and the liberty of God!

Talmudic discussions and infinite interpretation are a bulwark against the death of God!

To enclose God within a single understanding is to kill him or let him die. The vocation of the Talmud—the Jews' oral law—is to shatter the single word of the biblical Revelation and to restore to God his infinity. This is what is meant when we say that the Jewish people, or Judaism, have a relation not to God but to the Book, to the one Book that is the Bible, interpreted in multiple ways by the Talmud. The Talmud is not the interpretation of the Bible, but the place of Jewish interpretation, of the multiple interpretations of the Bible.

When a Talmudic master proposes an interpretation of a given verse or word in the Bible, there will at once be another master to voice an opposing vision, and a third to put forward yet another meaning. There is no definitive truth here, only meaning, or meanings that oppose, correct, and complement each other. Meaning is the gap or the tension between several meanings, but there is never anything definitive in this. In my language I call that "*lire aux éclats*," a pun that means that we must make the truth "break out."[2] The point is to kill the idol of God, to bring alive the living, infinite God.

DOM ROBERT LE GALL

For Catholics, the Holy Scripture, the Bible, is a library unto itself, for it contains seventy-three books divided into two groups: the Old Testament, which comprises forty-six books (the Jews recognize twenty-four books and exclude the books written in Greek), and the New Testament, which has twenty-seven.

The word "testament" is almost synonymous with the word "covenant": it designates the provisions made by God so that his People should inherit his promise. The two Testaments contain the Revelation made by the God of Abraham, Isaac, and Jacob, who is the Father of Jesus Christ, the Son of God, so that we should enter fully into the Covenant that will be consummated in the heavenly Jerusalem.

The books of the Bible range over several literary genres: history, from Genesis to Chronicles, or in the Gospels and Acts of the Apostles; ritual, as in Leviticus; liturgical prayer, in the book of Psalms; words of wisdom in Job, Proverbs, and Ecclesiastes; prophecy, in the poetry of the Psalms and in all the books of the Prophets; and finally, letters, the letters of the Apostles that form the main part of the New Testament.

The holy authors of the Bible spoke with the charisma of inspiration. Each kept his own personality, his training and his style, and the Holy Spirit used these to achieve, via a complex process, the written books we know today. This is a privileged example of that "synergy," which, according to the Catholic conception of religion, founded on Incarnation, unites but does not mix the divine and the human: God and man each act in their own register. Grace does not take the place of freedom; on the contrary, it extends it.

It is the Church that determined the "canon"—that is to say, the "rule"—of the Scriptures, specifying those books it recognizes as inspired (*Council of Rome*, 382). We can say that the Holy Scripture represents the kernel of the ecclesial transmission of the Revelation (or Tradition): this kernel comes from the life of the People of the Covenant, from its liturgy, its prayers, and its meditations. It in turn "regulates" and nourishes that life. In this sense, the "Sacred tradition and Sacred Scripture form one sacred deposit of the word of God, committed to the Church."[3]

The Holy Spirit, which inspired the Scriptures, is also what gives believers their understanding of them, so that they may live by them and thus add to the living Tradition of the Church. The whole of Christian life is summed up in Saint Paul's words to the Romans: "For as many as are led by the spirit of God, they are the sons of God" (Romans VIII:14), sons in the Son, for the glory of the Father.

CLAUDE B. LEVENSON

For Buddhists of every persuasion, there can be no doubt: the texts that they refer to are the works of human beings whose "superiority" was acquired by effort, study, and personal experience. For Tibetan Buddhists, it is through practice that one can assess the effectiveness of the method followed and appreciate its results. The way chosen by one is not necessarily the way that will suit another.

The two great series of texts that are considered particularly precious, and indeed "sacred" by Tibetan Buddhists, are the works of men: the *Kanjur*, or *Word of Buddha*, consists of 108 volumes of *sutras* and *tantras*; the Tanjur represents over 200 volumes of canonic commentaries by the great masters of Indian Buddhism, which inspired the wise men, scholars, and ascetics of the Land of Snow.

When one reaches a certain level of personal development, the texts that seem most forbidding become luminous and provide the key to the pursuit of one's progress. No doubt the most accomplished masters may be endowed with qualities or powers that seem extraordinary to common mortals, but their disciples hold that the potentialities tirelessly exercised and perfected by these masters by means of strict individual discipline and the judicious use of the appropriate means are in fact shared by all human beings.

MALEK CHEBEL

In the case of Islam, this question is settled from the outset. The prophet Mohammed defines himself as a simple mortal, a man among men, and the Koran is held to be the authentic word of God (this is the concept of the uncreated Koran) about which "no doubt is allowed." A sacred, transcendent text and emancipatory legislation, the Koran resists human evaluation insofar as it founds a new relation to God.

Readers of the Koran often meditate on this dialectic of divine nature: Allah is presented and honored as a "prayer for men," a dynamic presence, all movement. Those who cannot read the holy text, the divine word, hear and appreciate it through sound and psalmody, for its spiritual qualities rest essentially on its symbolic efficacy.

The esoteric movements and brotherhoods of Islam consider the *mushaf* that we know in the form of a bound book as the material replica of a hidden, celestial Koran, a *materia prima* kept from the eyes of the profane and resting on a mysterious Preserved Tablet (*al-Lawh al-Mahfuz*), also known as the Mother of the Book

(*Umm al-Kitab*).

This Koran, which is at once word, will, and manifestation of the divine, can be recognized by another particularity: its inimitability (*i'jâz*). "If men and jinn banded together to produce the like of this Koran, they would never produce its like, not though they backed one another" (Koran XVII:88).

The Koran could be the transcription into human language of a transcendental will that human consciousness can apprehend only through faith, "the eyes of the heart," profound consciousness.

But the debate remains open, and is indeed ancient. We know that Muslim philosophy—see, notably, Averroes's discourse on "double truth" or "double meaning," which opposes rational and revealed truth—sought to transcend the duality of the sacred texts, which, while transcendent, were nonetheless formulated in a linguistic medium that is eminently human.

1. Lévinas, *À l'heure des nations*, Paris: Minuit, 71.

2. "*Lire aux éclats*," literally "to read in or into fragments," or "to explode with reading," is a pun on the common expression "*rire aux éclats*," to burst out laughing.—*Trans.*

Is religion necessary?

MARC-ALAIN OUAKNIN

It is clear from everything that is said in this book on the question of evil and human responsibility, with regard to other men and with regard to God and to the world, that religion—as a social and political structure that makes possible both good and the rejection of evil—is an absolute necessity. Religion is first and foremost the Law, before God himself. A Midrash teaches us that God looked into the Torah and created the world. The world is founded on the Law; there can be no world without laws. Every political and social structure in today's world is based on the law handed down on Sinai. It is significant that human rights, when they were first promulgated in a secular context, were written on two tablets echoing the classic representations of the Tablets of the Law from Sinai.

Can a society function without the commandments not to kill one another, not to steal, and so on?

Man is free to choose between good and evil, but it is the text of the Revelation, the Law, that shows him the path of goodness by indicating the actions to commit and not to commit, a set of rituals that enables him to follow in practice the way of good and goodness. It is not enough to mean well, one must put meaning into action. Hence, in Judaism, the fundamental importance of the Act, or *Mitzvah* in Hebrew.

In my previous answers, I have shown that religion is above all interpretation, responsibility for the Infinite. In this sense, religion is undoubtedly necessary, for it enables man to escape the prison of his finiteness, to escape the pettiness of a life closed in on itself, and to discover the delights of self-transcendence, of self-invention. Religion gives man the freedom to invent so that he may invent freedom.

There can be no idea of freedom without the concrete means to make that freedom real and active. Grand ideas are not enough, it must be possible to make them exist in memory and in the body. If we read the Ten Words or the Ten Commandments attentively, we can see that they are inaugurated by a proposition whose tone orients the ensemble. Commentators point out that God does not present himself as the Creator of Heaven and Earth, but as the liberator of the house of slavery. The God of the Law is a God of liberation. Liberation and liberty are the fundamental principles that organize the Law.

Thus, the Torah is presented as an ethical code, allowing personal and individual fulfillment within a harmoniously balanced and organized society.

DOM ROBERT LE GALL

A human being is never alone. For man, to be isolated is to perish. To exclude him is to prevent him from being human, as the extreme case of wolf-children has shown. Born into a family, man can grow only in a loving home and can develop only in the society of his fellows.

It is often said that the success or comfort of a life is dependent on the number and quality of relationships that it forges. We can do nothing without relationships. We must go further and say that we *are* nothing without relationships. Born of the intimate relationship between a man and a woman—a loving relation—the human being can become himself only if there is a true connection between him and his mother and father: this is the condition of his psychological and emotional stability. On this relational basis are built all the other close relations, working outward to brothers and sisters, comrades and friends, all the way to the foundation of a new home.

In everyday parlance, sexual activity is often described as "having relations." That is a euphemism. In fact, these relations are usually only superficial and short-lived. They frustrate that great yearning, that expectation of the unity sought by a man and a women with a view to forming a stable, fruitful couple—or by men and women collectively, in order to constitute a society that ensures the common good. We feel that we are made for the communion of hearts and souls, and wish for the coming of that "civilization of love" that Christ spoke of in the Gospel: "This is my commandment, that ye love one another, as I have loved you" (John XV:12).

The Latin word *religio* comes from the verb *religare*, meaning "to bind." As for the word "relation," it comes from *referre*, which means to "refer": a relation creates a link, and provides references. We can say that religion is what ties, what binds, and what weaves together all our relationships, all our relations. As human beings, we are constantly involved in a relation to the world in which we live—that is to say, with the visible universe, the cosmos, creation, and with others, with our fellow beings, and with God, who is the ultimate reference, the transcendent bond that we need to exist and survive.

We are, then, made for communion with nature, with others, and with God, and this last relation is the foundation of all the others. "No man hath seen God at any time" (John I:18), for He is invisible, but we know, as the Fox told the Little Prince, that "It is only with the heart that one can see rightly. What is essential is invisible to the eye." When we gaze at the sea, or at the mountains, we feel our heart responding to a call that makes us, in some confused way, drawn to what is beyond the world. In the eyes of the one who loves us and whom we love, we see a source of love.

CLAUDE B. LEVENSON

It may be that religion is necessary, although the current Dalai Lama, the fourteenth in the lineage, readily states that the main thing for a human being is to have a kind heart, to show compassion, and to follow the fundamental ethical principles shared by humanity as a whole and by all religious creeds.

As it is practiced in various latitudes, with its differences of local color, Buddhism is as much a philosophy or art of living as a grid for understanding existence or a religion in the wider sense of the term, since it posits the cardinal link between beings, society, and the environment. By this means, the unknown or the unknowable is named so that it can come into existence and take root in consciousness. Religion (or what takes its place) provides a mooring, comfort, or help when our strength is exhausted in the battle with everyday obstacles.

And perhaps being human requires a challenge beyond its personal ambitions to push it to surpass itself. In this sense religion, which often represents an ideal or perfection, helps support the effort toward this goal. At once conditioning, learning process, and passing-on of spiritual knowledge, religion is intimately linked to the society of men.

It reflects their condition, their contradictions, and their hopes. But as a daughter of the human community, it is spared neither its faults nor its intolerance, despite the higher values to which it lays claim.

MALEK CHEBEL

Religion is both a moral edifice for men and a place of mediation with the Creator, a belief system. In the past, religion was also the framework that made it possible to regulate anti-social, excessive, and deviant behavior. But the power of the men of the church, the imams, theologians, and jurisconsults, has gradually declined as that of politicians, citizens, and scientists has grown. Today, religion plays an important role in managing the irrational and in preparing the faithful for the afterlife. Islam itself regularly undergoes renaissances, which on each occasion indicate a questioning of the existing political system.

In this sense, religion is necessary because it offers men everywhere a salutary norm, a moment of intimacy with the Higher Order of the world.

If it is to become the haven of peace and concord described by theologians, religion must be easy to live with and practice: "Religion is easy to practice, in principle, says the Prophet. Let no one try to be too rigorous in their observance of religion, otherwise they will be defeated by the task. Consequently, keep to a happy medium while trying all the while to come closer to perfection."[1] These words of the Prophet's have given rise to a *codex vitae* (code for living) called the *shari'a*, which the majority of Muslims scrupulously abide by. Finally, religion is a further means of mastering collective emotion, for it draws on unknown resources deep in humanity.

Nowadays religion is asked to prove its nonsectarianism and its nonviolence. If that were not the case, as happened with Sodom and Gomorrah, it would lapse into one of the many forms of heresy: Satanic sect, infernal disorder, or moral depravation.

1. El Bokhari, *Les Traditions islamiques*, Paris, Adrien Maisonneuve, 1984, vol. 1, p. 22.

Can one be religious without having faith?

MARC-ALAIN OUAKNIN

It is all a matter of definition. What do we understand by faith? And what does "religious" mean?

I have discussed the fundamental role of the text, of study, and of action. I have said that the most important part of the Revelation is the introduction of ethics, freedom, and justice and equality for all men. If a man is capable of realizing these life projects without having faith in the existence of God, he will be "religious" in the etymological sense of the word "religion" (which comes from the Latin *religere*, meaning to "bind," "to be in relation with") with other men in a world of goodness. I believe that the best way to answer this question is to tell a short Hassidic story.

One day a religious man came to see a great Rabbi who had many powers as well as immense wisdom and all the remedies for both material and spiritual problems. The man, who was a strong believer and had deep faith in God, spoke to the Rabbi thus:

"Master, I have come to see you because I have heard of your reputation and your great power. I would like you to teach me how to serve God and to learn the 'fear of God.'"

"I am sorry to disappoint you," said the Master, "I know no remedy that immediately imparts the fear of God. But I can show you the path that leads to it."

"You have no potion or elixir that could strengthen my faith and my fear of God, so that I may serve Him better?" The pious man was surprised and disappointed.

"No!" repeated the Master, "but I do know the path that leads there."

"And what is this path?" asked the man.

"This path is respect and fear of men."

DOM ROBERT LE GALL

If the starting point for all things is the mystery of relations that imply mutual trust, if the Redemption re-established relations between God and men, thanks to the Man-God who unites them in his person, then we can see why religion and faith are often linked, although they are perfectly distinct.

Religion is the complete network of relations that ties us to the Universe, to others, and to God. It comprises three elements: a belief, or faith; a ritual or liturgy; a morality, or ethics. It indeed presupposes intellectual notions, shared public acts, and conduct in accord with what one believes and celebrates. Faith is expressed communally in the liturgy and lived both personally and socially in the demands of a morality.

The most visible part of a religion is the liturgy and all the cultural acts. It is, indeed, perfectly natural that belief should be expressed at all levels of the relations formed by religion: the liturgy brings into play not only man's body and soul, with his gestures, words and songs, man in his communal dimension, but also man placed in the world where he finds himself, with water, light, fire, colors, space, and architecture.

The danger for religion lies in not going beyond the visible level. Cultural acts can become an excuse that exempt us from faith and morality. The prophets often warned against this very human tendency. God speaks angrily of religious practice that does not come from the heart: "I hate, I despise your feast-days, and I will not smell in your solemn assemblies. Though you offer me burnt offerings, and your meat-offerings, I will not accept them; neither will I regard the peace offerings of your fat beasts. Take thou away from me the noise of thy songs; for I will not hear the melody of thy viols. But let judgment run down as waters and righteous as a mighty stream" (Amos V:21-24; cf. Isaiah I:11-16).

Similarly, in the Gospel, we see Christ cast out the merchants from the Temple with a whip, crying: "Take these things hence, make not my Father's house a house of merchandise" (John II:16). Jesus says to the woman of Samaria: "Woman, believe me, the hour cometh, when ye shall neither in this mountain, nor yet at Jerusalem, worship the Father.... But the hour cometh, and now is, when the true worshippers shall worship the Father in spirit and in truth: for the Father seeketh such to worship him. God is a spirit, and they that worship him, must worship him in spirit and in truth" (John IV:21-24).

Christ does not reject cultural acts linked to our human nature, he who institutes the sacrifice of the new Covenant by offering, not animals, but his own body and his blood, given for us. But all his teaching shows us that even the flesh that he offers us as food is no use if the heart is not in it: "It is the spirit that quickeneth, the flesh profiteth nothing. The words that I speak unto you, are spirit and life." (John VI:63) The fundamental demand of worship is, to repeat Saint Benedict's expression in the Rule, "that our spirit should be in accord with our voice" (XIX:7).

The Gospel begins with a call to conversion (Mark I:15), to a change of direction that orients our living being toward God and not toward ourselves. Indeed, faith resides in precisely this gaze and this movement of the heart toward God. As we say, on the human level to have faith in someone is to place one's trust in them; faith therefore manifests a relation of superior quality. That is why religion, in itself, is not opposed to faith; on the contrary, every true religion is animated by a faith, that is to say, a confidence in divinity that means that we give ourselves to it, and this faith gives meaning to all religious practices. If religion is only external, then we are not in a true relation to God.

The expression "to enter into religion" means the decision taken by certain Christians, who are conscious of answering God's call, to devote themselves to him wholly in the "religious" life. These "religious," as nuns or monks are sometimes called, place their entire existence in a "relation" to the divine mystery. They want to live the full potential of their baptism and their condition reminds all the baptized of the demands of their faith, as the ultimate point to which they all tend: eternal life. Their state of life is said to be eschatological, since it recalls the ultimate goal of baptismal grace: immersion in the life of Trinitarian relations, in the virginal love of the three Divine Persons.

CLAUDE B. LEVENSON

It is no doubt possible to conceive of religiousness without faith. To be religious does not necessarily imply adhesion to a doctrine that is established, strictly codified, and organized in a more or less rigid social framework.

Religious feeling can certainly be experienced outside divine revelation, simply in relation to a particular sensibility toward the world, without any direct metaphysical implications. Also, an ideology can also be lived as a religious faith (which indicates a profound instinctive need driving human beings to seek the community of their fellows in the quest for a founding identity), as can a profound devotion to beauty, to a specific place, or to an idea.

In the final analysis, whether or not we believe in God, in the widest sense of that word, is a strictly personal matter. But being religious without faith no doubt covers a broader space of possibilities for spiritual development, which is also a personal progress. It is, in sum, a choice that is made by each person's free will, insofar as they are aware of being responsible for their own life.

MALEK CHEBEL

Faith is the first article of religion, the spiritual guide that activates human conduct. The Koran often exhorts us to "Believe and do deeds of righteousness." This idea is repeated no less than 700 times in the holy text. The term "Muslim," in comparison, is used only forty-four times.

There is a discreet controversy opposing those theologians who see man as divine in essence and endowed with faith from birth (*fitra*), and those who consider that man improves himself by the practice of his religion, in accord with his free will. Ultimately, the innatists and the "dogmatics" disagree over the very definition of religion, over its essence and scope.

What is piety without religious practice and without observance of rituals? What is the meaning of sustained practice of a religion if followers do not feel a glimmer of faith?

This kind of essentialist duality is expressed through two attitudes: *mu'min* (believer) on one side and *muslim* (practicing) on the other. One can indeed artificially take up the actions imposed by the dogma without being enveloped by the slightest emotion, or feeling the transport that is called "faith," or feel them only half-heartedly.

In contrast, the sincere believer (who is always a practicing Muslim) cannot imagine even a relative failure to observe the rites of Islam (*ibadat*). Without a solidly grounded faith, he cannot rest content with a cult that will sooner or later lead to an impasse. For the Muslim, rituals are only one vehicle among others for reaching one's destination.

Finally, the question can be turned around: is it possible to believe without practicing, to have a deeply felt faith without ever entering into the slightest ritual? This question is constantly being raised in Islam. In one of many illuminations, the great mystic Al-Hallaj (858-922) recommends the pure and simple suppression of the dogma, the abolition of rituals. In their place, he advocates only mystical transport, the conviction of the heart and fusion with the Creator.

This applies to simple rituals (prayer, fasting, etc.), but also to pilgrimage, which means that the believer would be exempted from having to travel to Mecca.

Such a proposition is certainly unthinkable in today's Islam. However, just as we must recognize the idea of practicing a religion that we do not believe in, so we must make the effort to conceive of a faith exercised without its dogmatic support, or the recourse to any religion in its exoteric sense.

Why does God allow evil?

MARC-ALAIN OUAKNIN

It is written that "God saw everything that he had made, and behold, it was very good." If that was so, then how, and for what reason, can there be evil in the world?

Jewish religious philosophy provides several explanations concerning the origin of evil. Here I will present only one of them. I make no claims that it is the only one recognized by Judaism, for there are no supreme decisions in the field of Jewish thought.

We can, however, distinguish three categories of "evil":
– ethical evil
– physical evil
– metaphysical evil

Let's begin with a basic general remark. Often, human understanding goes astray and confuses "good" and "evil" because it cannot perceive the ultimate consequences of an event of which it sees only the beginning. If men were to look back, they would certainly find many incidents in their life that they initially viewed as calamitous but that, in the end, turned out to be salutary. For our understanding is only partial and limited, incapable of seeing and grasping the links between events and their consequences. This should serve as a warning to us, lest we set ourselves up as judges of the Creator.

Why does evil exist? Why was man not created perfectly good, incapable of doing wrong and sinning and behaving badly? How lucky humanity would have been if all men had been good and if order had reigned in the world! Is that not a universal aspiration? Judaism does not believe in an original sin that can be passed on from generation to generation. It is up to each individual, in their lifetime, to take up the daily struggle so that their good inclinations may triumph over their bad; to fight moral evil in all its forms and abstain from it oneself and oppose those who do it to others. Since we are enjoined to be "a nation of priests and a holy people," it is our task to uproot ethical evil. But the goal is one thing, and how to achieve it is another. If men had been created with only a penchant for good, they would not have had free will and would have done automatically everything the Creator made them do.

That is why two instincts were created: the source of moral good and the source of moral evil came into existence at the same time. However, man was given a chance. If he had willingly heeded the voice of the Creator and had always been inclined to obey His injunctions, and only those, he would never have needed to know good and evil. His freely made choice to always follow the divine way would have kept him clear and spared him that constant struggle. But humanity did not take that path; it infringed God's word. A very profound idea is contained within this single commandment: "But from the Tree of Knowledge of good and evil, do not eat." For as long as man was ready to observe this rule, he had no need to know good and evil. When he made the decision to sin, he ate "of the fruit of the tree" and the war of inclinations became a battle to be fought every day and every moment. And even then, humanity might still have triumphed. If it had chosen good, if it had been constantly aware of the responsibility implicit in its resemblance to God and had cooperated with its Creator, the world could have been perfectly felicitous. But we were not so meritorious.

How often men choose evil, and, instead of letting happiness reign in the Universe, provoke catastrophes! God provides food for all living creatures, and we share it in a way that is neither intelligent nor just. In one country we burn the "surplus" or throw it into the sea, while in another men die of hunger. Humanity abases itself in national, racial, religious, and political persecution. It is to humanity, and not God, that we must address the question of the existence of moral evil in the world. It is ourselves, and ourselves alone, who are responsible for theft and banditry, for the slave trade, murder, and war. Life and death, blessings and curses, good and evil—we were given the choice. We should have chosen good; we opted for evil.

Humanity cannot even claim the excuse of ignorance. A

covenant was made with the sons of Noah; messengers were sent to all the nations. With us, with the Jews, further covenants were made. We were sent the Law and the Prophets, and we had our saints, preachers, and decision-makers, as well as many thinkers. In addition, each people has been vouchsafed the great lesson of history. All men have been able to see the disastrous effects of using force without moral justification. Great countries, powerful nations have disappeared, as if they had never existed. But from all this, humanity has learnt almost nothing. Each new dictator seeks to extend his power to the whole world and finds followers ready to persecute and kill in the name of the "great leader." And so, in the end, people wake up and complain about the catastrophes that they have brought down on themselves. They should not attack God but themselves. God did not create us mute, but in His image, and with a free will. We would not have wished to be created and to live in any other way—to rise and go to bed because we are forced to, to work and rest in spite of ourselves, to turn right or left without our will playing a part. What gives life its value is precisely the power to decide and to act, to give and to refuse, to choose and to be mistaken.

This is the meaning of being Chosen. The Chosen People are chosen to be responsible.

How, if God exists and guides history, could He have allowed something as inconceivable as the Holocaust?

How can a Jew with faith understand Auschwitz? What is the place of the Holocaust in the often tragic millennia-old history of Israel, or in the history of the world? But also, how can the secular Jew still want to be part of the Jewish community?

At Auschwitz, the Jewish communities of Europe were almost entirely wiped out. Millions of Jewish children, women, and men. After Auschwitz, what hopes can there be for the Jewish people? Has a prophet risen up to say that those remaining would return? Is it not absurd to celebrate the memory of those who were lost in torment and are now in eternal oblivion? Would not today's and tomorrow's Jews be better off freeing themselves of their belief and forgetting this catastrophic, bygone past?

But for the Jew there can be no forgetting.

To forget Auschwitz, or even to act for a moment as if Auschwitz had not existed, would be to blaspheme. In the heart of the present, the Jew holds on to a "founding experience." Today, as yesterday, he remains the descendent of Abraham. Therein lies his unquenchable hope.

Like Elie Wiesel, I believe that the Jew can live with God or against God, but not without God!

DOM ROBERT LE GALL

If the source of life is Love and to live is to love, then why does Christianity emphasize the Cross, and, with it, suffering and death? To shed light on this question, we must begin with the mystery of the relation.

The mystery of God-the-Trinity is grounded on love. God's design is to bring us into this world ruled by the gift of the self. The first pages of Genesis show how this design was thwarted by a being of darkness, the snake, the image of the Evil One or Devil (etymologically, the "divider"), who insinuated suspicion into the amicable relations between God and the first human couple (cf. Genesis III:1-13). Original sin is the extension to the whole of humankind the transgression committed by a spirit of light. That spirit was originally called Lucifer, in other words, "bringer of light." He became filled with a sense of his own beauty, refusing to acknowledge that it came to him from his creator. He tried to withdraw from God's power—from his relation to him, and found himself becoming Prince of Darkness (cf. John, XII, 31-35). He cunningly inveigled Adam and Eve into cutting themselves off from God: they wanted to possess the divine privileges and to dispense with the relation to God, whereas the divine intent was to make them one with His life.

All the sins that followed—the Tower of Babel, or the Golden Calf, for example—are repeat occurrences of this desire for self-assertion: to take from God rather than to receive. The same is true of our personal lapses, which are refusals to love or, in other words, refusals to be dependent: for when one loves one wishes to be dependent.

Redemption could have been achieved in many different ways, to return humankind to the dependency of love. The Son of God is in such a relation to his Father. He became a man so that man could again be fully his son. Since the first sin was essentially a sin of pride and arrogance, the Word made flesh was born humbly into this world at Christmas, to die even more humbly on the Cross and rise from the dead at Easter. Out of love for his Father and for us, Christ died for our sins and rose again to restore our filial dignity.

Christ appeared in disguise to the disciples at Emmaus, who were disillusioned after the events of Good Friday, and said: "Ought not Christ to have suffered these things, and to enter into his glory?" (Luke XXIV:26). Saint Paul proclaims that the Cross is a scandal for the Jews and madness for the pagans (I Corinthians I:23). Certainly, we do not wish for evil or suffering or death, but human experience confronts us with them. Christianity is not a religion that dreams, that floats far away from the realities of our lives. It takes on board the whole human condition. Faced with suffering and death, how would we react to a blandly suave, smiling savior?

Christ on the cross shows God's earnestness in coming to take us back, down in the depths—not to stay there with us, but to get us out. The Cross is not the final point, but the point of passage, the Passover: what is final is Christ's victory over death in the resurrection, the prelude to our own. Having vanquished our pride with his own humility, extending even to death on the Cross, Jesus brings us back to his Father by that same way of the Cross. Suffering and death remain, and are manifest in the world, but, through him, they have a meaning, a significance, and a direction. We find it as difficult as ever to understand these, but Christ crucified and raised from the dead gives us the key to our difficult lives, in which an increasingly close relation with him and with his Father offers the fruits of the Holy Spirit: love, joy, peace, patience, helpfulness, goodness, trust in others, control of ourselves (cf. Galatians V:22). All of these come from a relation strengthened by ordeals.

Christians in this world strive to balance joy and the Cross.

Jansenism, or the wars of this century and the last, may have made Christianity seem more like a religion of "sacrifices" in which the Resurrection had little practical importance. In contrast, the three decades of prosperity that began the second half of the twentieth century tended to obscure the reality of suffering and the Cross. This is evident even in certain aspects of Vatican II. The fitting note is struck by the joy that comes from the Cross, that honors the Easter mystery, celebrated from Holy Thursday to Easter Sunday, and echoed, for example, in the Feast of the Glorious Cross on September 14.

The last word is not with evil or with death, but with life. As Saint Paul exclaimed: "Death is swallowed up in victory. O death, where is thy sting? O grave, where is thy victory?" (I Corinthians XV:54-55, and Hosea XIII:14). Yes, "loves is as strong as death," sings the beloved in the Song of Songs. "Many waters cannot quench love, neither can the floods drown it" (Song of Solomon VIII:6-7). The Christ who loved us even unto death is the Prince of Life (Acts III:15).

CLAUDE B. LEVENSON

For a follower of Buddha, the question of evil cannot be formulated in these terms. Insofar as human beings live in a world full of contradictions and opposing forces, no doubt it is almost impossible to conceive of good without evil, just as day answers night, light/shadow, cold/hot, and Heaven/Earth.

In keeping with the Buddhist law of impermanence, the very

notions of good and evil are subject to change, that is to say, to transformation. It is for man to make them his own through his experience and thoughts. And then it is for him to choose his way, knowing that the inflexible law of causality, *karma*, will produce its effects in this life or a later one. Good and evil exist on Earth only because of human beings. It is therefore up to man to take responsibility for his acts, whichever of these two fundamental alternatives they are linked to, and to be fully aware of their consequences.

MALEK CHEBEL

Evil and its corollary, good, exist in a strange association. For us to cease to mention them, must God first forbid them? Or must He maintain them so that, as long as we live, we are rightly distressed at undergoing or embodying their consequences?

Evil is an ordeal, the ultimate test of the solidity of a man's faith and, perhaps, one of its components. How can we recognize the true, the useful, the right, and the good, and make them our own, if we do not avoid, eradicate, or discipline the diabolical temptation?

Furthermore, evil is made of deceit, for it is an indirect incitement: "Like Satan, when he said to man, 'Disbelieve'; then, when he disbelieved, he said, 'Surely I am quit of you. Surely I fear God, the Lord of all Being'" (LIX:16). Here, evil is also a test, a temptation held in check and transcended.

In this sense, whether considered major or minor, evil is a delimitation of good. To be aware of this is a way of cultivating one's religion with greater responsibility and serenity. This discrimination between good and evil is an inseparable part of faith, and clearly not another miscreance. Here, Islam seems to have adopted the wisdom of the old adages: "How can we conceive of the cure if we know nothing of the evil that gnaws at us?"

There is also a pedagogical dimension in the dualistic presentation of good and evil, even if the list of sins in Islam is very rich and not amenable to such a rudimentary opposition. To take an example, for the Mu'tazilites (a ninth-century Islamic rationalist movement), a Muslim who committed a serious sin was not yet beyond the pail of Islam, and would become so only after a precise period had elapsed. He was in an intermediate position (*manzila baïna al-manzilataïne*), which is itself also antithetical to the dualistic opposition of good and evil in the Manichaean sense of the term. Moreover, referring to an important verse of the Koran ("You are the best community there is among men. You order good, you proscribe evil and believe in God" (III:110), the Mu'tazilites argue the absolute primacy of good over evil.

But from the point of view of elementary doctrine, the good/evil dualism has one immediate benefit: it impels the believer to commit acts that are likely to be honored here below, before they are in the beyond. "A corrupt word is as a corrupt tree—uprooted from the earth, having no establishment" (XIV:34). It is divine recompense that gives legitimacy to the acts committed on Earth. But in allowing evil, God teaches us how to combat it. Islam grants unbroken absolution to all believers. Attendance at the mosque, procedures of purification linked to daily prayer (*salat*), and the seeking of forgiveness (*du'a, istighfar*) allows them to redeem themselves, without needing to go before an imam. The Muslim's penitence is acted out away from the confessional and in the absence of his fellows, for they too, even the greatest judges among them, are capable of committing that forbidden evil.

Is religion dangerous?

MARC-ALAIN OUAKNIN

For Judaism, the world does not exist *in itself*. It is always the result of a projection of meaning. It is man who vests meaning in the world. Life is fundamentally hermeneutic.

"In any case, these are interpretations, that is to say, projections of abstract explanatory systems on our sense perceptions made in order to give us a unified representation of it in which the unifying relations are the product of reason" (Henri Atlan).

This hypothesis, it seems to me, is the foundation of all Talmudic thought. It will immediately be understood that the question being posed here is that of the law. For Judaism, the law is a "norm" and not a "dogma." The whole Talmudic enterprise of interpretation rests on this essential distinction. Therefore, the law calls a "norm" what is not a constraint but, on the contrary, the very possibility of openness.

"A normative element, of whatever type, when linked with a method of knowledge and, possibly, coming up against the latter's productions, can open it up and enable it to evolve in cognitive disorganizations followed by incessant reorganizations" (Henri Atlan). However, when "dogma" is instated—in other words, when an interpretation or model are considered the "definitive content of knowledge"—a "corpus that is both theoretical and normative" is constituted, one "in which everyone is called on to believe and to submit themselves in the name of truth." A norm is different from an "objective" knowledge of the nature of things. A norm "deploys a collective project that is more or less interiorized by individuals; it is mythical, symbolic, a social activity of exchange, a source both collective and individual which defines the common ground shared by a society and the individuals that constitute it" (Henri Atlan).

The distinction between the norm and dogmatic knowledge implies the permanent possibility of an evolution or renewal in which the norm itself develops, "but at a different rhythm, with different justifications and mediations of the knowledge contents."

91

Madness, said Lacan, is the theory of a single person. The Talmudic law is the refusal of dogma. It is a norm. The Talmud is conceived as a community in order to avoid madness! The Talmud puts in place a dialogic thought structure, *mahloket*, which guarantees the impossibility of dogmatic confinement, the impossibility of dogmatic truth.

DOM ROBERT LE GALL

All religions are totalizing, in that they gather together all the relations whereby we exist and live: the relation to nature, to others, and to God. Religion is a powerful unifying force. If it is put at the service of others than God, it can become a dangerous, totalitarian power.

We know where fanaticism can lead. In the book of Exodus, the Covenant made between God and his People at Sinai is primarily religious, but it is present in every aspect of the People's life, through the Covenant Code (Exodus XX:21-23), which makes provision even for the practical details of life. Israel is a people whose king is God: it is indeed a theocracy. A day came when the people wanted a more visible king. God disapproved of the request, which indicated a certain lack of faith (I Samuel:VIII). When He did eventually grant them a human king, Saul, he was a failure, but God loved his successor, who, in spite of his sins, was a man of great heart: David, whose distant successor would be the Messiah (I Samuel:XVI). Jesus, Son of God and Son of David, would be the true King of Israel (Luke I:32) "the Prince of the kings of the Earth" (Revelations I:5). However, he took care to point out that "my kingdom is not of this world" (John XVIII:36). The history of the period that followed Jesus Christ shows that the kingdoms of the Earth were often in league against God and his Messiah (Psalms II:1-3). The first Christians were accused of atheism, whereas in fact they were rejecting the paganism of their age and the way in which the Roman emperors had made themselves into gods.

All power tends to become "divine right" so as to extend itself and endure. After the first centuries of persecution, Christianity become the state religion under Constantine, with all the ambiguities that this new situation brought, notably the temptation for the Roman emperors to use religion for political ends, which was called "Caesaropapism." Conversely, when eventually the popes had acquired the political independence that would prove conducive to their mission, their authority sometimes became overly temporal, which proved prejudicial to their specific role. If a certain balance was established under the emperor Charlemagne, there was no lack of quarrels in the centuries that followed, from the investitures controversy in the eleventh century to Louis XIV's Gallicanism.

The Inquisition of the thirteenth century, which needs to be understood in its historical context, represents a kind of collusion between the spiritual powers that be and the "secular arm" intended to purify the Christian people of all heresy. In the 15th and 16th centuries, the Spanish Inquisition was wielded against the Moors and the Jews. Pope John Paul II has encouraged the sons of the Church to see this as one of the errors, infidelities, or inconsistencies for which they needed to repent as they approached the third millennium.[1]

The struggle for Italian unification in the mid-nineteenth century led to the suppression of the Papal States, thus putting Pope Pius IX and his successor in the delicate position of having been despoiled, a position in which the papacy remained until the Lateran Pact under Pius XI. Today, we can say that the Pope's sovereignty over the tiny Vatican guarantees him the necessary independence, but without detracting from the importance of his spiritual mission.

The growing influence of the popes beyond the Church is the sign of a real power that became tangible with the fall of the Communist empire, which, though atheistic and a persecutor of religion, also created its own new religion, complete with dogma, liturgy, and moral system. Today, the Church's social doctrine, which was elaborated at the end of the last century, makes no distinction between communists and liberals, the better to serve all men, and the whole man. The separation of Church and State in most countries has removed many of the ambiguities inherent in collusion in both directions, provided there is an assurance of that religious freedom constantly invoked by the Church, both for itself and on behalf of other authentic religions.

CLAUDE B. LEVENSON

Religion should not be dangerous because in essence religions are supposed to advocate harmony in society and to work toward it in the name of an ideal of perfection founded on love of one's neighbor or fellow. Religion is supposed to guide societies in accordance with the values of equity and justice conducive to the fulfillment of each member, and respecting the interests of all. Like all forms of conditioning, it is also a learning process, teaching us how to live together since, fundamentally, it transmits a spiritual knowledge that seeks to control the contradictory forces of a human society.

However, history, as handed down over the years and through different regimes, tends to show that religion has engendered terrible violence and conflicts whenever one of its leaders or guides has claimed to possess *the* truth. It therefore has an undeniable responsibility in countless massacres, for very often it provided the moral cover for war and plunder.

Like most manmade notions, religion is ambivalent and remains potentially dangerous as long as human beings fail to learn the cardinal meaning of respect for the other.

MALEK CHEBEL

Whenever religion is used to ends other than those prescribed by the Holy Books, it becomes an ideology and, as such, oppressive and deviant. Its normative and legislative virtue, in the human sense of those terms, is overstepped and twisted. Now, the sacred cannot be adulterated or become mentally indolent, no more than it can be reduced to a set of limited measures that answer only the questions of life here below. Islam advocates an inseparable whole, comprising faith and everyday life. Any confusion in one of the two spheres leads to disturbances in the other, or an excess of conformism. Thus, in the case of certain believers, the fear of the afterlife can be seen as a form of paralyzing panic.

But to speak of the deleterious character of religion is a short cut used to justify the lack of faith of those who argue it, and their virtual absence of religious ardor.

In this respect, Islam is exposed to historical aberrations that pursue strategic or political interests in its name.

But humanity cannot sever itself from the divine law that obliges it to respect life. If religion pushes its followers to get rid of the other or negate life, it can become dangerous because of the very things it is meant to fight: intolerance; lack of respect for life; disbelief; and presumption. There is no shortage of examples: Islamic terrorism has, ever since the Hashashins (Assassins, the Ishmailian Shiite sect of Hassan al-Sabbah, 1090-1272), existed in the shadow of the divine word.

The ideological use of religion would not be harmful if schools, universities, and the state and its laws played their role properly.

We can therefore say that education is as important to religion as it is to citizenship and knowledge.

1. Apostolic Letter, 10 November 1994, no. 33.

What is the definition of man?

MARC-ALAIN OUAKNIN

"For man, being is not enough.
He needs to be other."
Louis Aragon

What is man? It is tempting to answer, "man is..." and complete the sentence with some definition or other.

But is it possible to define man? Indeed, is not man precisely that thoroughly singular being who eludes all possibilities of definition? Is not man simply the existing, that whose definition is to have no definition?

Is not the essence of man to have no essence? This paradox is perfectly expressed in the Hebrew language, in which the word for essence, mahut, comes from ma, meaning "what." Essence is therefore "whatibility," a neologism that I put forward here to express this questioning essence of man, this questionability that keeps being open to its possibilities and to its future.

The Kabbala teaches us that the word *ma*, which means "what?" and which, in Hebrew, is spelt *mem-heh*, has a numerical value of 45. *Mem* = 40 and *heh* = 5. It has the same numerical value as the word Adam, or "man," which is spelt *mem-daled-heh*: 1+4+40.

Man is a question, a "what?" a "what is?" a *ma*. This is what I call infinitive man.

The Hebrew horizon is totally defined by "whatibility." It is a staging of questioning. The Book is a "book of questions," from the Bible to contemporary thought via the Talmud, the Kabbala, and Hassidism. But let us come back to God's first revelation to Moses:

"An envoy from God appeared to him... and the bush burned with fire, and the bush was not consumed. And Moses said: 'I will now turn aside to see why the bush is not burnt.' And God saw that he turned aside; God called to him...."

The structure of the story could hardly be more eloquent. Moses sees something strange and questions it, then calls out. The call is akin to the capacity for astonishment. The "why?" is one of the fundamental modalities of being human. The capacity for astonishment, for questioning the event, the nonindifference to events encountered, makes man a free being, free from determinism, leaving the beaten track where everything is decided for him, imposed on him, often without him realizing it. The madua is the word of Moses as he turns aside from the path to go and see why the burning bush is not consumed.

The very possibility of this "why" is the sign of a consciousness that can take responsibility for its own history and, even better, metamorphose destiny into history. For the "why" contains the germ of revolt, the refusal to submit passively to one's destiny.

Man is not the shepherd of being but the sentinel of the question, the guardian of "whatibility." A short anecdote is eloquent on this point:

One day, Primo Levi asked one of the guards at Auschwitz, "Why is all this happening?" And the guard replied: "Hier ist kein Warum!"—"There is no Why here." And that is how humanity foundered, by being "without-why."

DOM ROBERT LE GALL

When God reveals Himself to us in the Bible, He expresses the bond that He wishes to have with us in terms of our most intimate relationships: He is the Husband of his People; he is the Father and we are His sons; He loves us more than a mother loves her children. We are brothers and sisters, for we are all his children.

"For thy Maker is thine husband" chants Isaiah (Isaiah LIV:5), as do all the other prophets and the Song of Songs. For the Jews, this statement is the heart of scripture; for Christians it foretells the mystery of the nuptials between Christ and the Church and emphasizes a theme that runs throughout the New Testament.

The Gospel reveals to us that Christ is the Son of God; more exactly, Jesus himself tell us that he has a Father, with whom he is One: "I and my Father are one" (John X:30). There is a close relation between the Father and the Son, which is sealed in their Spirit, that of their mutual love.

Sent by the Father, this Son comes to speak to us of this eternal life that they enjoy, and is offered to us. To do this, he becomes a man and offers to join with all men, to accomplish the nuptial mystery that makes him and ourselves the total Son. "The kingdom of heaven is like unto a certain king, which made a marriage for his son" (Matthew XXII:2). The Father is the King, the Son is the Husband, and we are the Wife and the Church with which he wishes to be united for eternity.

This union is achieved in suffering and consummated in death on the Cross, that supreme and incontestable proof of Jesus's love for his Father and for us. The risen Christ is "the first born from the dead" (Colossians I:18), "the first-born among many brethren" (Romans VIII:29), who all reproduce the image of the only Son: "I ascend unto my Father, and your Father, and to my God, and your God" (John XX:17).

The Father's unconditional love for us includes and surpasses maternal love, as stated by this moving text from the prophet

100

Isaiah: "But Zion said, 'The Lord hath forsaken me, and my Lord hath forgotten me.' Can a woman forget her sucking child, that she should not have any compassion on the son of her womb? Yea, they may forget, yet I will not forget thee."

Father, mother, husband, sons and daughters, brothers and sisters—the Christian revelation is defined by these relations which are the most intimate and the most necessary. It is fully human and reveals humanity to itself. For the experience of these relations, with their joys and limits, leads us to discover and hope for a fullness of love, of paternal, maternal, conjugal, filial, and fraternal love that is found in God; that is God.

Here is what the mother of a young monk has written to me as I work on these pages: "I am sure you know that for a mother, her son, whether a minister, a bishop, or whatever, is always her little one: she carried him for nine months, gave him life, loved him, pampered, protected, guided, and encouraged him in order to try to make him a responsible being and, if I may put it like this, to bring out the best in him. In most cases it is a hard task, and there is no letup, but love, the love between parents, the love given to one's children, the love between children and parents and, surely the most important, God's love for us all, are of great help. Little by little, I am learning to trust totally in God, our Father, our guide, and not disappoint him, which is not always easy." This mother eloquently expresses very well the fact that God is at the heart of our relationships, and that these fundamental relationships lead us to Him.

How could it be otherwise, if God in Himself is relation?

CLAUDE B. LEVENSON

Man is an animal endowed with reason, or unreason, according to the mood of the times and the circumstances of the moment. He is capable of the best and of the worst in this world, which, according to Buddhism, is the only one that offers him the rare and precious opportunity to seek out true freedom.

Man is a sensitive creature endowed with multiple potentialities that he can, if he wishes, lead to accomplishment by choosing open-heartedness, compassionate attention to others, and disinterested helpfulness to as many people as possible. The human being is responsible for his actions, his thoughts, and his speech; he is capable of thought and can transcend egotistical limits to attain what, depending on the place and traditions, we call wisdom, knowledge, beauty, or enlightenment. Man is a social and sociable being who could not survive without its fellows, even if every human being is a World in its own right, responsible for all, for good and evil, for unhappiness and happiness. It is for men to decide on which side they will bring down the balance in a perpetually changing equilibrium.

MALEK CHEBEL

The human does not exist in itself, for it is a simple reflection of the spiritual activity of men, their emotional synthesis, their structure. In doctrinal terms, it is the living being's reaction to the distant horizons that he allows himself, or that are given to him by religion, spirituality, or belief.

This is how it is understood in Islam: the human is the living, sensitive, creative part of whoever believes in God, loves his neighbor, and respects his commitments. In other words, to have faith in a superhuman force, to accept the outstretched hand of others (society) and accept one's own singularity. A companion of the prophet Mohammed named Anas (seventh century), relates the following utterance: "None of you will really have the faith—will be a Muslim—if he does not desire for his neighbor what he desires for himself." Such a conception implies an element of altruism in man, even if absolute altruism is by definition inaccessible. In reality, the human being is first and foremost a being who observes the divine injunctions, and cultivates them as an immediate given of his consciousness and places them above other preoccupations. The human is therefore that which finds fulfillment in praise and celebration.

In a more philosophical approach, as advocated by Shabestari, the great Iranian mystic who died in 1320, "Man was the last being to be created, for he is the determining cause of creation."[1] Reference is made to the late creation of Adam (Friday afternoon) and the fact that nothing was created after him, in order to distinguish him from the rest of Creation. The human is a part of the self that is realized in contact with others.

Finally, the human is man's capacity for alertness, by virtue of which he is a "being-in-the-world" who is sensitive to otherness, and a virtual consciousness that believes in the beatitude of a creating God, the possessor of the Two Worlds, the World Below, and the World Beyond.

That he must profit fully from his time on Earth does not in any sense thwart his future project, for life on earth is only a stage in his assumption and global outspreading.

1. Sa'd od-Din Mahmud Shabestari, *La Roseraie du mystère*, Paris, Sindbad, 1991, "La Bibliothèque persane" collection. p. 132.

Is man bound to the earth?

MARC-ALAIN OUAKNIN

We try to understand, and so we approach that strange creature whose name is man. In Hebrew his name is *adam*, which comes from the word *adama*, meaning "earth." In the same way, Latin derives *homo* from *humus* for "earth" or "alluvium" or the archaic "glebe." Indeed, "the earthy" or "glebish one" would be a good translation if man were only dust, but he is also life-giving breath, and word. He is the *ruah melaléla*—a speaking breath.

To understand man is to go back to this original breath. To the breath that was a cry when it came to us on the day of our birth, in the very time and place of separation and severance, that of bodies torn from one another. Water and the breath of life exist in an extremely important relation at the moment of birth. No sooner are we torn from our mother and the amniotic ocean of her protective belly than a fountain of air wells up within us, and here is the first cry.

The inaugural breath, the cry, becomes silent respiration. It is expressed in the discreet letter heh, which is the only letter in the Hebrew alphabet that is pronounced without the aid of any part of the mouth: it is pure breath!

Each respiration is a *heh*, a breath, a prayer. To breathe is already to pray!

The Talmud teaches us in the name of Rav Yehuda, son of Rabbi Ilay, that the world was created with the letter *heh*. And so it is written "here is the story of the heavens and the Earth on the day they were created"—*behibaream*. This word should not be read as behibaream: "where they were created," but *heh baream* ("with a *heh* they created them").

The *mah*, the "what?" is written with two letters, *mem* and *heh*, which signify the articulation of water (*mem*) and breath (*heh*). These two letters are combined at the moment of birth. The passage from the amniotic fluid to the world.

To ask these questions is to rediscover the inaugural moment of

107

entry into life. To see the world with new eyes, as if one were seeing it for the first time. Each question is a new birth to ourselves and to the world. A rupture with the old self and the creation of a new way of filling the world with significance.

When the child becomes an adult, a mature man, this marks his accession not to definitive perfection, to completeness, but to the discovery of infinite "whatibility," the question ma that impels man to go on searching, building, inventing, to discover "the infinitive man."

The inaugural force of the beginning: the *mem* of the *ma* inaugurates an archaeological movement, heading in the direction of the origin that takes us back to the emergence of the world. *Mem* does indeed signify "provenance." Not that this return offers us the originary moment, the beginning in which the meaning of life might be deposited, a meaning that we could "reappropriate" like some lost object. The beginning is not a content but a force. To go back to the origin in order to draw from its force, the strength to start afresh every time, to recapture the founding articulation of water and breath, to realize the fact that "to live is to be born at each moment."

To be called back to the beginning is to meet that inaugural force, the force that made the beginning possible.

"Man was created so that there would be a beginning." Every man is a new beginning, and every man must accept that difficult and demanding task: to create time from a new beginning. The letter *mem* that opens man to existence is above all an encouragement to bring into play that human faculty to understand, to undertake, and to take an initiative—and thus to enter into action.

"The life of man, rushing toward death, would inevitably lead to the ruin, the destruction of everything that is human, were it not for the faculty to interrupt this movement and start with something new, a faculty inherent in action, as if to constantly remind us that men, although they must die, are born not to die but to innovate" (Hannah Arendt).

The *meh* says that man, *adam*-the-question, also speaks of water and breath, of the moment of birth. Each instant of life draws its strength from that moment of birth. It reminds us that "with each birth, something uniquely new arrives in the world" (Hannah Arendt). Each birth is the emergence of a new questioning, a new desire to be. To respond to the fact of our birth is to be responsible, that is to say, to protect the questioning and the inaugural moment of birth, which are the womb of our freedom.

"Because we are born, we are condemned to be free" (Hannah Arendt).

DOM ROBERT LE GALL

Born on Earth, the human being lives on a "blue planet," which is not a paradise, and which the ecologists have shown to be in danger, but which is, however, a human world where God became flesh within history. Human life is conditioned by the fragile and unstable balance of our Earth; it is tied to its diurnal and annual rhythms, for the Earth spins on its axis every day and around the Sun every year. Our knowledge depends on what is accessible to our senses, and our will is drawn spontaneously to visible things. However, the human soul, which in its activity is tied to terrestrial realities, transcends Earth. In his search for fullness of existence and goodness Man has always looked to the heavens. He feels bound to something beyond Earth, for which he knows himself to have been made, and his prayer is often like that of the psalm: "Unto thee I lift up mine eyes, O thou that dwellest in the heavens" (Psalms CXXIII:1). The high places of this Earth, like mountains, are where we meet God (Sinai), and that is why the altars in churches are also raised. Man senses that he is made for another world. Religions define this world.

For Christians, God came to this Earth through the Incarnation, in order to lead us to Heaven. Still, we are not simply invited to stay in the clouds: the angels of the Ascension remind the Apostles of their mission down below (Acts of the Apostles I:11). In our hopes, we are already citizens of the heavens (Philippians III:20), but that does not mean we do not have to help build the earthly city. Christians live in an equilibrium between the already and not-yet of their present condition. This is the time of the Church, in its pilgrimage of faith. Jesus Christ, who died and rose again, then ascended to the heavens to make a place for us there as Lord of history, seated to the right of the Father. And to continue his mission through the centuries, he founded the Church, which is, strictly speaking, the gathering of men and women who believe in him, were baptized in his name and spread around the world "a sweet savour of Christ" (II Corinthians II:15).

Entrusting the Church to Peter who, in the name of all the Apostles, had confessed his belief in his divinity, Jesus solemnly spoke these founding words: "Thou art Peter, and upon this rock I will build my church; and the gates of hell shall not prevail against it. And I will give unto thee the keys of the kingdom of heaven: and whatsoever thou shalt loose on earth shall be loosed in heaven" (Matthew XVI:18-19). We know that Peter's power is not understood in the same way in the different Christian confessions.

The ecumenical movement is dedicated to promoting unity among Christians, but its history, and the different sensibilities within the Catholic church, both work against this reunification. Nevertheless, as the Church approached the Jubilee of the Redemption in 2000, Pope John Paul II made numerous gestures signaling the Church's openness, and even went as far as to recognize the wrongs committed by the Church throughout history, and to say, furthermore, that we could reassess the way in which the popes exercised their paramountcy in charity for the sake of unity.

At the turn of the new century, the audience and influence of the Pope are remarkable. When it comes to the teachings of the Church, our contemporaries—even those in the Church itself—have grown used to picking and choosing, but it must be admitted that, even if people do not always follow edicts made unpopular by the media, they are still attentive to what is said, especially given the current loss of moral certainties. The Church's reminders on moral and sexual matters (abortion, contraception, homosexuality) certainly annoy many, but they still sense that the Church's championing of the family concerns the very future of our society. In matters of personal and social morality, people realize that the Church is not working for its own interests, but for mankind and its future.

In spite of its opacities, the Church is not a purely human institution. To repeat the definition of Saint Cyprian, the third-century bishop of Carthage and martyr, it is "the People that takes its unity from the unity of the Father and Son and Holy Ghost" (*De oratione dominica*, XXIII), and this brings us to the heart of Christianity, this mystery of the relations between divine Beings in whose name Christians are baptized and whose infinite, permanent joy they are invited to share. In the introduction to his first letter, Saint John writes: "That which we have seen and heard declare we unto you, that ye also may have fellowship with us: and truly our fellowship is with the Father, and with his son Jesus Christ. And these things write we unto you that our joy may be full" (I John I:3-4). Let us also quote Jesus's great prayer before his Passion, which expresses the true identity of the Church: "And the glory which thou gavest me I have given them; that they may be one, even as we are one; I in them, and thou in me, that they may be made perfect in one; and that the world may know that thou hast sent me and hast loved them, as thou hast loved me" (John XVII:22-23). A People united in the unity of the Trinity, the Body and Wife of Christ, the Temple of the Spirit, the Church gives us all the chance to enter into the plenitude of love of the Three who are One, and to do so through our deepest human relationships.

CLAUDE B. LEVENSON

From the most obvious relations to the most subtle network of correspondences, the founding elements of the world are meshed together to form the fabric of life: man is bound to the Earth, the mother that feeds him, in its most immediate reality and in a sublimated form as a female divinity.

The latter represents the energy without which, it would seem, there could be no living creatures. Man is bound to the Earth if only because he lives on it and looks to it to provide his daily sustenance. It offers him the resources for survival, providing that he remembers that these are not inexhaustible.

In providing human beings with their habitat, the Earth also nourishes their minds and their imaginations, opening up broad vistas reaching both beyond their horizons and on into their spiritual quest. Manifest or hidden, the correspondences between man and his environment reveal an indissoluble link, a subtle play of mirrors sending to each images of their own reality.

MALEK CHEBEL

In Islamic cosmology, a special position is assigned to the Earth, of which man, understood in the general sense, is the main representation. This link between the Earth and man is based on the tradition and history of the Muslim faith and can be explained by the importance of territorial power in the growth of religion and on the more fundamental belief that nourishing the Earth is the only occupation man can be sure of throughout his life, although he is not limited to only that task. The Arabian Bedouin's acute awareness of the "inhabited Earth/uninhabited Earth" in times of old, informs most Islamic representations. The notion of the Earth is thus intrinsic to the Islamic cosmogony, and of the humanity that refers to it. But this Earth is a collective inheritance that belongs to no person in particular. It is an Earth where the Creator sent his apostle, charged him to transmit the new revelation, and blessed him before he in turn blessed others.

Man's filiation attaches him to this earth. He was born from the womb of its clay, while his mission points him to the divinity of the holy text. In this sense, the conception of mankind contrasts with that of the jinns, who are a creation of fire: "He created man of a clay, like the potter's, and He created the jinn of a smokeless fire" (LV:15).

These notions articulate the representation of the world in Islam. They make it possible to precisely define the role and position of man in the sacred architecture of Islam, of which the lived experience implies a particular sensitivity to the Earth—body, mass, and extent—but also in its symbolic meaning as the frontier of the world.

The image of the Earth-dwelling-of-man carries a poetic force that is characteristic of epiphanous entities, and this is expressed by the rhythms of the Koran and its associated phonetic mediations with power and amplitude.

In its profane sense, the question of the Earth—the Earth of the ancestors, for example—exists within collective representations. However, there is no uniform juridical treatment. But the Koran does assign it an undeniable augural impact.

The historical complex that links the Earth and Islam have become increasingly manifest over the years. As early Islam extended beyond its first spatio-temporal characteristics (isolation, dryness, morphology), the notion of rootedness in the Earth gave way to that of extent, to unfolding and conquest. The Earth become a territory, with provinces and a geography.

The lunar world of the Rub al Khali, the stony desert that borders Mecca and Medina, added to the crucial sense of lack in early Islam by making the virtual absence of land physical.

Should Islam's hunger for conquest be seen in relation to the exiguousness of its originary land?

A symbol of divine power (XLI:39), the Earth is also the refuge and protector of mankind (XLI:9). This is where he finds the substance that nourishes him: "It is God who made for you the earth a fixed place and heaven for an edifice" (XL:66). To which we must add that God wanted the Earth to be worthy of Him, spacious and beautiful (LXXX:24-32). But the Earth is also riddled with traps, especially for miscreants. "Look over the Earth and consider how the guilty have ended."

What is the beyond? What happens after death?

MARC-ALAIN OUAKNIN

Judaism proclaims the eternity of the soul. This fundamental truth, that man's destiny continues beyond his earthly existence, is what underpins all its doctrine.

In the Torah, indeed, the commandments are intimately linked to the principle of compensation. Now, according to the Tradition, the main part of this reward is for the soul, and is granted only after death. Thus, the crowning conclusion of life here below, and its full justification, are to be found only within the perspective of the beyond. "Rabbi Yaacov says: 'This world is like a vestibule before the future world: prepare yourself while in the vestibule so that you may enter the palace'" (*Avot*, IV, 16).

Such a conception of life is also a conception of death. This affects only the physical part of man and certainly does not signify the end of being, which resides wholly within the soul. On the contrary, it marks the completion of its mission on earth, and its accession to an eternal world, a place of true beatitude. Death has rightly been compared to a kind of parturition, something admittedly painful in itself, but presiding over the inauguration of a new life.

Furthermore, this idea of the soul's eternity is reinforced and borne out in Jewish thought by the belief—which is one of the articles of faith—in the resurrection of the dead: at the end of time, and in a manner whose ill-defined details have sometimes divided theologians, the souls of the dead, or at least a good number of them (Daniel XII:2) will be reincarnated and enjoy a life of earthly bliss.

Thus the faithful Jew feels neither terror nor helplessness when confronted with death; it is an expected phenomenon about which there is nothing truly harmful in itself.

However, Judaism does recognize the right to feel and manifest pain and sorrow when a loved one dies. Indeed, it even sees this as a duty, since Jewish law has instituted and codified numerous mourning rituals. The reason for this is very clearly expressed in the *Tractate Avot* (IV, 1-7, following the *Mishna* quoted above): "One hour of repentance and good deeds in this world is worth more than the whole life of the future world. And one hour of happiness in the future world is worth more than all of life in this world."

But if the future world is the supreme place of reward and true joy, only the present world allows the individual the possibility to progress, to raise himself up and deserve reward. For only the cohabitation of body and soul—the feature, exclusively, of earthly existence—can create the conditions for a human mission and, subsequently, for its reward. The soul in itself is already wholly with God. But the body solicits the person, pushing them to draw away from Him.

Hence the task assigned to man: to resist physical drives, to submit matter to spirit by carrying out God's commandments, to transform and sublimate the body as an instrument serving God. Moreover, this antagonism between the forces of the body and those of the spirit also conditions free will, which is itself a key condition for any notion of merit or reward.

In other terms, for the soul, the body represents a unique opportunity to ascend and enrich itself. It is the irremediable loss of this source of fruitfulness and wealth that we lament. Seen in this light, mourning rituals are not sterile for those who observe them but salutary and edifying. They lead to an awareness of the true meaning of life, and of the need for each person to act and live as best they can during their short time here below; to minimize the importance of the physical and the material; to refuse, finally, to identify their being with their own body, so as not to disappear with it when it returns to the dust.

DOM ROBERT LE GALL

The beyond is the primordial and final mystery of Trinitarian love, which is already present and active in lives that accept it. The Gospel of Jesus Christ is the Good News of that "kingdom of heaven" (Matthew V:19) where our "Father which is in heaven" (Matthew V:16) awaits us. To reach it, we must heed and put into practice the teachings of Jesus, in other words, live out the paradox of the Beatitudes, which prepare us to enter fully into the Pascal mystery of the sacrificed Lamb.

Our sufferings and our death configure us in the image of Christ, who suffered and died so that we may resemble him in a resurrection like his. At the final moment, intimately and personally, God clearly asks each of us one last question: "Do you want my love? Do you accept the happiness for which you are made, you who are enduring a death similar to my own?"

Between death and entry into the life of God, Catholic tradition recognizes the existence of a time of purification where we learn to "see God"—at least for those who do not die in the fullness of love for their Lord. This is Purgatory, which is not a place of physical suffering because the resurrection of the flesh has not yet taken place, but a time intended to enable the soul, still its own prisoner, to open totally to the virginal love of eternity. The human being does not enter the life of the Father and the Son and the Holy Ghost alone. With his brothers and sisters, he constitutes the Bride of Christ, whom the redeeming sacrifice has made "a glorious church, not having spot or wrinkle, or any such thing, but holy and without blemish" (Ephesians V:27).

Eternal life is a marriage prepared by a king for his son, as Jesus himself revealed to us (Matthew XXII:2)—the marriage of the lamb, as celebrated in Revelation: "The marriage of the Lamb is come, and his wife hath made herself ready. And to her was granted that she should be arrayed in fine linen, clean and white: for the fine linen is the righteousness of saints" (Revelation XIX:7-8). This is the consummation of the Covenant: "Behold, the tabernacle of God is with men, and he will dwell with them: and they shall be his people, and God himself shall be with them, and be their God" (Revelation XXI:3). And as they wait to be immersed in this River of Life flowing from the throne of God and the Lamb (Revelation XXII:1), "the Spirit and the bride say, Come...Amen. Even so, come, Lord Jesus" (Revelation XXII:17, 20).

CLAUDE B. LEVENSON

After physical death there opens a space and a time that are unknown and by definition unknowable since, with only a few rare exceptions—saints, ascetics, poets—no one has ever returned from them. For some, this is a place of happiness and love; for others, of endless horror and suffering; for yet others, emptiness and nothingness. For Buddhists, death is a time of transition in the cycle of existences; for Tibetan Buddhists, it is the temporary world of the *bardo* through which man passes before being reborn in one of the six kingdoms of existence.

For Tibetans, integrating death into life is part of everyday experience. One cannot exist without the other. It is therefore particularly important to live one's death consciously, in order to ensure the best possible rebirth. Unless, that is, one takes that most rare and precious of all opportunities, to recognize the meaning of the Clear Light, which manifests itself during the period of transition and which delivers us forever from the cycle of births, or *samsara*.

To help them achieve this difficult transition, the Tibetans have a guide called the Tibetan Book of the Dead, or *Bardo Thodol Chenmo*, the exact meaning of whose title is "great liberation through hearing in the between." When a lama reads it to someone on their death bed, it is said that this book helps them recognize the different stages of their corporeal and mental dissolution, and not to be afraid of it. Thus, a clear consciousness of what is happening at these crucial moments constitutes the path that leads to nirvana—knowledge, wisdom, or enlightenment—without having to come back to one of the kingdoms in which, in one form or another, suffering manifests itself.

According to Tibetan custom, by preparing ourselves meticulously to live our death, we are naturally applying ourselves to the practice of the teachings, since life, in the final analysis, is like a perpetual flux whose main characteristic is change. When the living body has been transformed into a corpse, all that remains is the most subtle consciousness ensuring the connection between one life and another—unless, that is, this consciousness has recognized the "fundamental luminosity," in other words, the pure nature of spirit. The Tibetans say that the *bardo* between death and rebirth lasts seven times seven days. Once this period has elapsed, either the deceased is fully liberated, or a new life begins under other skies, other latitudes, in other kingdoms perhaps, if not under the same Sun.

MALEK CHEBEL

It is the great mystery of creation: not knowing what will become of our bodies and our souls in the time ahead, and even less so after death.

Whatever the answer, all thought about the beyond implies a particular reading of the teachings of religion, which are the only ones that theoretically identify and delimit where the deceased go, how they are questioned and their actions weighed, and how they are punished. Although it is not named as such in the Koran, purgatory appears immediately after the first questioning in the grave, or "punishment of the tomb" (*adhaab al-qabr*). Thousands of years will go by before the Last Judgment is decreed. But that day is one of the divine mysteries. No man can claim to know the Unknowable.

During this period there occurs the reading of the book where all men's deeds are recorded. The weighing in the heavenly scales. In the final phase, the deceased rises and is asked to take the "narrow bridge" (*Sirat*, or *Cinvat*, to the Mazdeans), before the final verdict made in accordance with what we may describe as absolute equity: "The Word is not changed with Me: I wrong not My servants" (L:29).

Then some are sent to hell, others toward paradise. But even the reprobates may be spared hell, for it is the role of the Prophet to intercede on their behalf.

An intermediary place separates these two destinations. It is a place of rest and waiting that allows those whose fate has yet to be decided to purify themselves: "And between them [Paradise and Gehenna] is a veil, and on the Ramparts (*A'raf*) are men knowing each by their mark, who shall call to the inhabitants of Paradise: 'Peace be upon you!' They have not entered it, for all their eagerness" (VII:45)

The Muslim paradise is, in the descriptions, fabulous. It is the supreme place of rest, a shady, irrigated, perfumed land inhabited by creatures of indescribable beauty. Hell is seen as a terrible place where sinful souls lament without end, while their bodies burn in giant infernos.

This all shows the afterlife to be an immense universe onto which the believer tries to project his expectations and anticipate the great promised rewards. This impenetrable world also has an immediate and, dare I say it, earthly virtue, which is that it disciplines the emotions of those whose commitment is faltering.

Finally, we cannot understand the ideas behind the initiatory procedure if we forget that the believer's awareness is fully engaged during this process, and that it is the place where the joys of paradise and the land of perdition are prepared.

The will of Islam is to liberate all believers from their immediate, vain concerns by giving them greater responsibility. From this point of view, the beyond may prove to be one of its most effective lessons.

Second part

SYMBOLS

SYMBOLS
OF JUDAISM

BY MARC-ALAIN OUAKNIN

THE CALENDAR

HEBRAIC TIME IS BASED ON THE
MOVEMENTS OF THE SUN AND THE MOON.
"TO LIVE IS TO BE REBORN EACH MOMENT."

Months are measured by lunar transitions, but years are defined by the rhythm of the sun. What is unique to the Jewish year is that it sometimes has a thirteenth month. When this occurs, the year is referred to as being "pregnant." According to tradition, Year 1 of the Jewish calendar coincides with the creation of the world. This is calculated as having occurred 3,761 years before the beginning of the Christian era. The difference between the Jewish calendar and the Gregorian calendar used in the West is therefore always 3,760 years. To determine the Jewish year from a year in the Christian calendar, subtract 3,760. For example: 5755 - 3760 = 1995; 5708 - 3760 = 1948.

Conversely, to calculate the Gregorian equivalent of the Jewish year, add 3,760. The year 1789 is therefore 1789 + 3760 = 5549, and the year 2000 in the Christian calendar will be the year 5760 in the Jewish calendar.

The Jewish calendar is governed by the 354-to-355 day lunar year, with twelve months of twenty-nine or thirty days. The names of the months of the Jewish year come from the Babylonians: *Tishrei, Cheshvan, Kislev, Tevet, Shevat, Adar, Adar Sheni* (intercalary month), *Nissan, Iyar, Sivan, Tammuz, Av,* and *Elul. Tishrei* corresponds to the Gregorian equivalent of September-October, and *Elul* to August-September.

To keep the calendar year aligned with the solar year and the rhythm of the seasons, the eleven-day gap between the solar year and the lunar year needs to be filled.

During these embolismic or "pregnant" years, a thirteenth month is added, the intercalary month of *Adar Sheni.* This is a way of ensuring that *Pesach* (Passover) always takes place in early

127

spring, *Shavuot* (Pentecost) at the beginning of the summer, *Rosh Hashanah* (New Year) at the end of the summer, and so forth.

Over a period of nineteen years, a difference of seven months develops between the solar and lunar calendars. Thus, in a nineteen-year cycle, seven years will be "pregnant" ones: the third, sixth, eighth, eleventh, fourteenth, seventeenth, and nineteenth years. For example, the year 5755 (1994-1995) is the seventeenth year of the 303rd nineteen-year cycle. It therefore is an embolismic year. Holidays and feasts are held every month except during the month of *Cheshvan*.

– *Tishrei* (September-October): *Rosh Hashanah* (New Year), *Yom Kippur*, and *Sukkoth* (the Festival of Tabernacles).
– *Cheshvan* (October-November): the only month of the year in which no religious event is commemorated.
– *Kislev* (November-December): *Hanukkah*, the Festival of Lights.
– *Tevet* (December-January): a fast marks the beginning of the siege of Jerusalem.
– *Shevat* (January-February): *Tu Bi-Shebat*, the celebration of the New Year of the trees or Jewish Arbor Day.
– *Adar* (February-March) and *Adar Sheni* (Intercalary): *Purim*, a holiday which commemorates the rescue of the Jews of Persia by Esther.
– *Nissan* (March-April): *Pesach* (Passover).
– *Iyar* (April-May): Israel's Independence Day, and *Lag BaOmer*[1].
– *Sivan* (May-June): *Shavuot* (Pentecost).
– *Tamuz* (June-July): a fast marking the destruction of the Temple of Jerusalem.
– *Av* (July-August): a fast marking the destruction of Jerusalem and of the two Temples.
– *Elul* (August-September): preparations for the celebrations during the month of *Tishrei*.

Rosh Hodesh marks the beginning of each month. In the past, the *Sanhedrin*[2] determined the start of each month after hearing two witnesses testify to having seen the new moon or the *molad* (the precise moment when the moon reappears in the sky as a slender crescent, barely visible). A fire would be lit on one of the hills of Jerusalem, then on another, and another, until the signal had been transmitted across the country, and even as far as Babylon. When the Samaritans, a marginal religious group, began lighting fires at incorrect dates to deceive the Jews, the *Sanhedrin* dispatched messengers from city to city. Finally, to clear up any confusion in faraway communities, the *Sanhedrin* named a second day to mark the beginning of the month. In 358 of the Christian era, Rabbi Hillel, the son of Rabbi Yehuda Hanassi, established a perpetual calendar, which eliminated the need to officially witness the new moon, or send messengers across the country. This calendar has been in use ever since.

In the Jewish calendar, day begins at nightfall, and draws to a close the next day at the same time, when three stars in close proximity appear in the sky. The Sabbath thus begins on Friday at sunset, and finishes Saturday evening at nightfall. The length of other religious days is measured in the same way.

The week is composed of seven days, mirroring the seven days of creation. The first day of the week is Sunday, and the seventh is the Sabbath.

1. The thirty-third day between *Pesach* and *Shevuoth*.
2. The Assembly of the Seventy Elders.

THE TALLITH

THE *TALLITH* IS A PRAYER SHAWL
WORN BY JEWS DURING PRAYER AND AT VARIOUS
RELIGIOUS CEREMONIES

The exploration of Jewish symbols in this book begins with the prayer shawl. According to the Talmud, this exemplary rite is the key to understanding other rites. The spirit of God passes through the *tallith* via the written word. When words, particularly those conveying the names of God, are inscribed upon physical objects of the world, these words send vibrations out into the physical world itself[1].

Words are more than tools for naming, tools that merely give access to objects. They also represent the life of these objects, as well as our own lives in relation to these objects. But only if we learn to listen to the vibrations of life that flow through the matter.

In Judaism, and in particular for the masters of the kabbalah, this life vibration is the name of God or the Tetragrammaton—the four Hebrew letters that are used as a proper name for God in the Bible and is inscribed upon physical matter.

The most exemplary trace is found in the *tallith*. The *tallith* is a rectangular shawl which can be made of any type of material, although wool, linen, or silk are generally used. It is white, and has black, blue, or multicolored threads running through it.

The *tallith* must have four corners from which fringes, or *zizith*, hang.

In principle, the *tzizith* should be made of the same material as the *tallith*. A silk *tallith* should have silk *tzitzioth*; a linen *tallith*, linen *zizith* and so forth. But the most common practice is to use wool for the *tzizith*, no matter what the *tallith* is made of.

Before wrapping oneself in the *tallith*, a blessing is said: "Blessed art Thou, O Lord, our God, King of the Universe, who hast sanctified us by Thy commandments and hast commanded us to wrap ourselves in the fringed garments."

On some prayer shawls, the blessing is embroidered in Hebrew across the top of the shawl, permitting the text to be read. The fabric thus takes on the full meaning of the word "texture."

Some commentators[2] compare the black and blue threads to lines of writing skimming across a blank sheet of paper.

1. Rabbi Nathan of Nemirov, *Likkut Halakhot,* the relevant chapter on the *tallith.*

2. *Menahot* 43b, *Nedarim* 25a, *Shavouot* 29a.

THE TZIZITH

TZIZITH, THE RITUAL TASSEL HANGING FROM THE FOUR CORNERS OF THE *TALLITH*

Observing a ritual requires knowing how to recognize the divine name in its many forms manifest in the reality surrounding us. This is very much the case with the ritual wearing of the *tallith* and its *tzitzioth,* which consists of wearing a garment with four corners, each hung with tassels made of knotted threads. The number of knots and the number of times a thread is wrapped around the others in the tassel corresponds numerically to the name of God. There are two different traditions of how to knot the *tzitzith.*

The first is by writing the Tetragrammaton YHVH in its simplest form. In Hebrew, letters have numerical equivalents. The letters of this Tetragrammaton have the following numerical values:

$$Y = 10; H = 5; V = 6; H = 5.$$

To make a *tzitzith* in this way, four threads are used, one of which is much longer than the others. They are fed through a hole in each of the four corners of the *tallith.* The threads are folded in half, creating

131

eight loose ends, with one thread still being the longest.

Originally, the long thread was azure blue based on the color of a species of shellfish which has since become nearly extinct. Over time, this tradition of one blue thread was lost, but it is undergoing a revival today.

The threads are tied in the following sequence: two knots are made, and the long thread is wrapped around the other threads ten times; another two knots are made, wrapped five times by the long thread; two knots, wrapped six times; two knots, wrapped five times, and finally, two knots alone. In this manner, the name YHVH is written, the Tetragrammaton, whose numerical value is 26:

Two knots; ten wraps (the letter *yod*)

Two knots; five wraps (the letter *hay*)

Two knots; six wraps (the letter *vav*)

Two knots; five wraps (the letter *hay*)

Two knots.

This totals 10 knots and 26 times that the long thread is wrapped around the others threads.

The second traditional method involves writing the Tetragrammaton YHVH with a variant, creating the meaning "God (YHVH) is One (EHAD)." The numerical value in this case is now 39, not 26, as YVMH = 26 and EHAD = 13.

The eight threads are tied in the following manner:

Two knots; seven wraps

Two knots; eight wraps

Two knots; eleven wraps

Two knots; thirteen wraps

Two knots.

This totals 10 knots and 39 wraps.

In the kabbalah, the number 39 is extremely important. It corresponds to what is referred to as a "name in motion."

The Tetragrammaton YHVH representing God cannot be enclosed within the limits of finite language. The letters within an alphabet can thus be put into motion, by turning each letter into the one which follows. An example using English can help clarify this point.

The word "time," for example, names a reality. To release it from its linguistic prison, each letter can be put into motion by substituting the next letter in the alphabet:

$$T \quad I \quad M \quad E$$
$$\downarrow \quad \downarrow \quad \downarrow \quad \downarrow$$
$$U \quad J \quad N \quad F$$

The word "ujnf" is the result of setting "time" in motion. By applying this procedure of alphabetic motion to the Hebrew alphabet and to the Tetragrammaton YHVH, we get:

$$Y \quad H \quad V \quad H$$
$$\downarrow \quad \downarrow \quad \downarrow \quad \downarrow$$
$$K \quad V \quad Z \quad V$$

It thus becomes the word KVZV (pronounced Koozoo) which has the numerical value of 39:

$$K = 20; V = 6; Z = 7; V = 6.$$

As the prayer begins, the person wraps himself in the *tallith*, and enters a world of language in motion, so that the words he utters will carry him into a future which is creative and alive. For the being in motion, a language in motion is necessary and is thus written in the knots and wraps of thread in the *tzitzith* on the *tallith*.

During morning and evening prayer, a liturgical passage called the *Shema Yisrael* is read. It consists of three paragraphs taken from the Hebrew bible. Before the passage is read, the face and the eyes are covered by the *tallith* to emphasize the idea of "hearing," which is taught by the first word of the text, *Shema*—"Hear (O Israel)."

The rite of the *tallith* and the *tzitzith* is set forth in the third paragraph: "Speak unto the children of Israel and bid them that they make them throughout their generation fringes in the corners of their garments, and that they put with the fringe of each corner a thread of blue. And it shall be unto you for a fringe, that ye may look upon it, and remember all the commandments of the Lord, and do them; and that ye go not about after your own heart and your own eyes, after which ye use to go astray; that ye may remember and do all My commandments, and be holy unto your God. I am the Lord your God, who brought you out of the land of Egypt to be your God: I am the Lord God."

During the reading of this passage, the four *tzitzioth* are held in the right hand, and are kissed each time the word *tzitzith* is pronounced. From early childhood onwards, men usually wear a small *tallith* or a *tallith katan* under their clothes. Sometimes the ends of the *tzitzith* can be seen sticking out from under the shirt. The *tallith* is kept for life, and even beyond. There is a custom of burying the dead in a *tallith,* after the *tzitzioth* have been removed.

THE TEFILLIN

TEFILLIN ARE TWO LONG, THIN LEATHER STRAPS, TO WHICH A SMALL LEATHER BOX IS ATTACHED. ONE IS WORN ON THE LEFT ARM AND ONE ON THE FOREHEAD

The *tefillin* contain tiny parchments inscribed with texts from the Torah. They are worn by men during prayer, except on the Sabbath and on festival days. One of the two boxes is attached to the left arm by wrapping the strap around it seven or eight times. The other box is worn on the forehead, positioned between the eyes, and the strap is wrapped around the head and knotted. The straps hang down over the shoulders.

Inside these boxes are tiny parchments: one for the arm, and four different ones for the head. The single parchment for the arm contains four texts, while the four parchments for the head each contain one text. These texts are Exodus 13:1-10; 13:11-16; Deuteronomy 6:4-9; 11:13-21.[1]

The theme of "memory" recurs in these texts as a leitmotiv: "You will wear the *tefillin* like a sign upon thy hand and a memorial between thine eyes." The Hebrew word *zikaron*, or memory, comes from the root Z.K.R., which also means "masculine."

The ritual of the *tefillin* carries with it the idea of *zikaron*—memory and memorial. The four texts of the *tefillin* all express the idea of a "memorial" between the eyes. But the second text uses the mysterious word *Totafot* instead of *zikaron*—mysterious because it is not a Hebrew word. Rashi has ascertained that *Totafot* is a word... from Africa! *Tot* means "two" as does *fot*, in an African language. Why is the word "memory" written in a foreign, in this case African, language? One answer is that it could be a fundamental way of teaching that one person's memory exists through the remembrance of another. It demonstrates openness to other languages and other cultures, a willingness to regard the African as a brother.

This is not a reinforcement of identity by seeking the roots which enclose us, but a questioning of our identity. To remember is to be open, to question.

Rabbi Nahman of Bratslav said: "There is only memory in the world that is to come," or, in a more incisive formula, "remember your future." The future of each person is manifest in the memory of another's existence, which opens us to dialogue and creativity. Wrapped in his *tallith*, language in motion, and bearing the *tefillin*, remembering the future, a man begins his day by a prayer that fills him with creative energy and gives him support in his material, spiritual, and intellectual life. In this ritual, the same idea encountered in the *tallith* surfaces—the inscription of language, specifically the names of God, upon the texture of reality; the written word expressed on and by ritual objects.

Two ways of writing the letter *shin* are inscribed on the *tefillin* worn on the head, one having three strokes, the other four:

The knot, made from the thin leather straps tied on the head, form the letter *daleth*, while the knot by the box on the arm forms the letter *yod* at the box.

letter *daleth*　　　　　letter *yod*

These three letters form the word *Shaddai*, which is one of the names of God. The Talmud gives several explanations for this name. The first divides *Shaddai* into *Sha-dai*, the abbreviation of a longer expression, *Mi-sheamar leolamo dai*—"he who says to his world 'that's enough.'"

God regulates the entropy of the world, introducing limits to the reality of things. Through the rite of the tefillin, man inscribes the feeling of his finite nature onto his own body. It is a lesson in humility and modesty that harmonizes with the idea of opening up the self, mentioned at the beginning of this chapter.

The second explanation analyses the etymology of the word *Shaddai*: *Shad* means a woman's breast, which is both an erotic object and a nourishing one. *Shaddai* literally means "my breasts."

It is a word used by a woman when speaking about her body.

According to the Talmud (Yoma 54a), these breasts are not exposed in a pure and direct nudity, but are covered with a veil. This is not to hide them, but to make them both visible and invisible at the same time. This vision of the breasts, an oddly erotic one, is the vision that the High Priest would have on the Day of Atonement in the most sacred place in the Temple.

Transcendence and eroticism? Eroticism is defined here by that which simultaneously reveals and hides itself, a game of "visible, invisible." Thus, one could say that God appears in an erotic way, both visible and invisible. God completely unveiled would be an idol; entirely veiled, he would be absent.

Here, the "visible and the invisible" is coupled with the "graspable and ungraspable." The text cannot be totally grasped, cannot act as an idol. Its meaning remains enigmatic, a vehicle for time and transcendence. The eroticism of the *Shaddai* reverses the "limitative" aspect of the *Shaddai*, which, according to the first explanation, means the "boundary," the "that's enough."

The *tefillin* allows man in prayer to become conscious of his ability to open up to the infinite, despite the finite nature of his material being and his humanness.

1. The order of the texts can vary according to tradition. We are following the tradition of Rashi.

THE MEZUZAH

THE *MEZUZAH* IS A SMALL PIECE OF
PARCHMENT ON WHICH SEVERAL PASSAGES
FROM THE TORAH HAVE BEEN WRITTEN.
IT IS AFFIXED TO THE RIGHT-HAND SIDE
OF THE ENTRANCE TO THE HOUSE

The *mezuzah* plays a symbolic role as a protector and as a reminder to follow a certain ethic of remaining in a state of being "on the way." the *mezuzah* is a piece of parchment on which the first paragraphs of the *Shema* are written (Deuteronomy 6:4-9, and 11:13-21). The parchment is rolled up and inserted into a tube that is usually of made of wood or metal, though it can be of a different material. The *mezuzah* is fixed onto the right hand side of the front doorpost a third of the way down from the lintel. If the door is too tall, the *mezuzah* should be placed at a reachable level.

Before affixing the *mezuzah*, the following blessing is given: "Blessed art Thou, eternal God of the universe, who hast commanded us to fix the *mezuzah*."

In the *Shema*, the word *mezuzah* also means doorpost. Affixing the *mezuzah* to all the doors in the house (except the doors to the restroom and the bathroom) is a positive commandment that is written in Deuteronomy—"And thou shalt write them upon the doorposts of thy house and upon thy gates" (Deuteronomy 6:9). The *mezuzah* is put up only in permanent houses, not in temporary dwellings, such as the *sukkah*.

The *mezuzah* should be put in place by the owner or the person occupying the home thirty days after moving in. In Israel, they must be put up immediately. Women must also take part.

If *mezuzot* are fixed to several doorposts in a house, only one blessing need be given, as long as the intention to do so is stated before the first one is put up. The *mezuzah* is written by a *sofer*, a scribe who copies the *Sefer Torah* and the *tefillin*, as well as the *mezuzot*. A *mezuzah* is not valid when printed by a machine nor is it acceptable if one letter in the text has been erased.

The Talmud recounts the tale of a man named Artaban who sent a very precious stone to Rabbi Yehuda Hanasi. To thank him, Rabbi Yehuda Hanasi sent Artaban a *mezuzah*. Artaban was greatly surprised to receive the present in return and he replied, "I sent you a valuable stone and you thank me with a simple piece of parchment?" Rabbi Yehuda replied that the parchment had more value than all precious stones put together. Artaban did not answer, but deep down he couldn't help but think that the rabbi had sold him short.

Several years later, Artaban's daughter fell ill. One after another, different doctors tried to help, but each failed.

Then Artaban remembered the rabbi's words. He affixed the *mezuzah* to the doorpost of his daughter's bedroom... and she recovered!

A look at the structure of the *mezuzah* allows for a better under-standing of the meaning of this rite. As with the *tefillin*, this is a text that is not meant to be opened and read. The parchment is rolled up and enclosed in a tube. It is therefore "visible-invisible," "readable-unreadable," which is the same erotic form that was explained in the previous chapter.

The proof of this is that the name *Shaddai* is the word written on the visible, readable side of the parchment. On the back, further words are written upside down.

To read it correctly, the head must be turned upside down. In the chapter on the *tallith*, it was explained how God's name is put into motion by moving the letters forward in the alphabet.

Shaddai and words upside down on the *mezuzah*

Grammatically, the Tetragrammaton YVMH means the past (HYH), the present (HVH), and the future (YHH). The four letters of the Tetragrammaton therefore enable the writing of these three modalities in time that is alive, that is of life, held between memory and hope. Affixed to the doorpost of a home, the *mezuzah* is a reminder to man that he has come a long way, but that the voyage does not end here, and that he must continue to reinvent himself.

The *mezuzah* represents this idea of "setting into motion" and it also suggests how to incite it through language in motion, the key example being that of *Koozoo*.

Man is a creature of language who relates to time, that is to say he lives through a living, breathing language, which is subject to study and interpretation. By questioning single interpretations, he opens words up to multiple and diverse meanings, and in doing so, opens himself up, thus freeing himself from any confinement and sense of lassitude, so as to be able to constantly reinvent himself, to live and be reborn at every instant.

The rite of the *mezuzah* is an invitation to perpetual motion. It is interesting to note that a good number of the texts from the Talmud and the Midrash begin with this idea of being "on the way," for example, "The Rabbi and the Rabbi Hiya were on their way..."

In fact, every text in the Talmud begins with the idea of being "on the way," even if that isn't the specific expression used.

The Talmud, the Midrash, and the Kaballah all contain "thought in motion"—men who think while walking and follow the truth of the path. Without a doubt, this is one of the meanings of the verse: "And thou shalt teach them diligently... and when thou walkest by the way." (Deuteronomy 6:7)

The process of traveling, the way, is everything. We are closer to the place we seek when we are on the way there, than when we are convinced we have arrived, and all that remains is to settle there. As Edmond Jabes wrote: "Never forget that you are a traveller in transit."

The word "way" doesn't necessarily have a spatial meaning. It is not a stroll through a forest or field of our wandering thoughts. It doesn't lead us from one place to another. It is the passage, the movement, of thought itself.

Being on the way sets one in motion, triggers questioning, consideration. It invites and disturbs, incites and appeals. Man "on his way" does not just apply to a Jew, but to man in general.

In one of the most beautiful texts written about the Jewish being, inspired by André Neher, Maurice Blanchot expands and develops this central idea of Judaism. The following is a synopsis of his principal ideas:

"What does it mean to be Jewish? Why does this state exist? It exists so that the idea of being 'on the way' as a movement, and a just movement, may exist. It exists so that along the way and by the way, the experience of that which is strange and unknown may coalesce around us and be experienced in an irreducible way. It exists so that we learn how to speak through the authority of this experience.

"To be 'on the way' is to be perpetually ready to move on; it is a requirement to pull oneself up and away, an affirmation of the truth of nomadic existence.

In this way, the Jew differentiates himself from the pagan. To be pagan is to fix oneself somewhere, fix oneself to the ground to a certain extent, establish oneself through a pact with permanency which authorizes the sojourn and certifies the certitude of territory. Being on the way, being nomadic is a response to a way of being that possession does not satisfy. To put oneself on the way, to be on the way, is already the meaning of the words heard by Abraham: 'Leave your birthplace, your kin, your home.'"

It is important to emphasize that the meaning of these words is positive. Blanchot continues: "If we put ourselves on the way and wander aimlessly, is it because we are condemned to exclusion and barred from having a dwelling because we are excluded from the truth? Isn't it rather that this wandering represents a new way of relating to 'the truth'?"

Rather than an eternal deprivation of a dwelling place, isn't this nomadic existence an authentic way of living, of residing, which does not bind us to a determination of place, nor secure us to a reality that is already justified, certain, and permanent?

It is as though the sedentary state is the goal for all behavior! As though truth itself were sedentary!

It is important to leave one's home, to come and to go as a way of affirming that life is, in fact, 'a journey.'

And this is the message of the *mezuzah*[1].

---

1. The *mezuzah* is fixed slanting to the left, representing the movement of a man's shoulders and arms as he walks.

THE SYNAGOGUE

The architectural design of the synagogue is simple and sparse. In fact, it is not the building itself that is important but the act of gathering together.

There are three daily prayers: *shakharith* in the morning; *minkhah* in the afternoon; *maariv* in the evening. Along with the *Beth Hamidrash*, or the House of Study[1], the synagogue is the central location of Jewish communal life. Three times a day, a *minyan* of at least ten men gather to pray in the synagogue.

While the historical origins of the synagogue are imprecise, the idea of several members of the community gathering on a regular basis has always existed. Its primary period of development was during the time of the prophet Ezekiel and of the Babylonian exile, following the destruction of the First Jerusalem Temple, in 586 B.C.E. The role of the synagogue became vital after the Second Temple was destroyed. The ritual sacrifices offered at the Temple were replaced by institutionalized prayers, whose texts were written down in their definitive form.

It is even said that the synagogue inherited the holiness of the Temple. Respect for the synagogue is mandatory, and therefore behavior within its walls must be proper. Drinking, eating, and sleeping are not permitted inside the synagogue. However, when a House of Study also serves as a synagogue, eating and sleeping there is considered proper behavior.

Originally, synagogues were of a very simple architectural design. In countries where anti-Semitism was rife, Jews did their best to construct very discreet synagogues in the Jewish quarters, with facilities for the *mikvah*, or ritual bath, the community hall, and other communal institutions nearby. Despite restrictions imposed on the construction of synagogues, many were veritable gems in countries such as Italy (most notably in Venice and Rome), Spain, Poland, Egypt, Syria (Aleppo), and Tunisia. In the absence of current restrictions on size, the architectural design of the synagogue has become increasingly diverse, and a considerable amount of attention is devoted to aesthetics.

I. THE INTERIOR ARCHITECTURE

The most important object inside a synagogue is the *Sefer Torah*, the book of the Torah. It sits in the *Aron Hakodesh*, the Holy Ark, located at one end of the synagogue, taking up all or part of the east wall. The Ark is oriented toward Jerusalem, and elevated upon a platform (see chapter 20 on the *Sefer Torah*).

Just in front of the Ark is the *bimah*, the dais for the reader of the Torah and the prayers. The *bimah* is more centrally positioned than the *Aron*. The congregation sit on chairs or benches on either side of the *bimah*, in front of the Ark.

A woman's position in the synagogue is influenced by the sociological context, and differs from one community to another, according to the degree of orthodoxy. Traditionally, women are placed behind the men, separated by a *mekhitsa*, an object which acts as a divider, whether a curtain, a gate, a grating, a folding screen, or a sliding door. Women are often positioned one floor above the men, grouped in a semi-circular fashion, overlooking the men and with a view of the Ark and the *bimah*.

Today, given the growing number of protests by women (justified, in our opinion) over their participation in synagogue rituals, certain communities have placed the *mekhitsa* in the center of the ground floor, with men on the left and women on the right. Other more reformed communities allow women to sit where they like, and they are given the same liturgical rights as men.

II. THE *MINYAN*

At least ten men, thirteen years of age or older, are necessary to form a *minyan*. This assembly is required for any communal prayer, whether the *Kaddish* (the prayer for the dead), a reading from the Torah, or the *keddusha* (given during the silent blessing given while one stands).

III. THE STRUCTURE OF PRAYER

Prayer was institutionalized after the destruction of the Second Temple of Jerusalem. The Hebraic Bible itself contains many examples of individual prayers, such as the one uttered by Moses for his sister, or the prayer of Hannah, the mother of Samuel, to bear a child.

Communal prayer has replaced the offering of sacrifices to the Temple. During the week, three prayers are uttered each day: *shakharith* in the morning; *minkha* in the afternoon, and *ma'ariv* in the evening. On the Sabbath and on holidays, another prayer, the *Musaf*, is added after the *shakharith*.

All prayers are found in the book of prayers called the *Siddur*. Special prayers for certain days, *Yom Kippur* for example, are found in a special *Siddur* called the *Makhzor*, which contains prayers and biblical passages to be read on that day. Thus, the prayers of *Yom Kippur* are found in the *Makhzor* of *Yom Kippur*.

The structure of the prayer is essentially the same for all communities, but sometimes the order or the importance of certain passages to be read differs, according to custom.

All Jews pray facing east, in the direction of Jerusalem and the remnants of its Temple.

1. House of Study (cf. chapter 20).

THE SEFER TORAH

THE HANDWRITTEN PARCHMENT
SCROLL CONTAINING THE FIVE BOOKS OF MOSES
IN THE TORAH IS USED FOR PUBLIC
READINGS IN THE SYNAGOGUE

The making of the scrolls, the distinctive style of the handwriting, the page design, and their decorative details are fascinating from both an intellectual and artistic point of view. One of the most important liturgical acts in the synagogue is that of reading from the *Torah*, the Five Books of Moses:

Genesis: *Bereshith*;
Exodus: *Shemoth*;
Leviticus: *Vayikra*;
Numbers: *Bamidbar*;
Deuteronomy: *Devarim*.

The tradition of reading the Torah in public three times a week began under Ezra, in the sixth century B.C.E. It is read on Mondays, Thursdays, and Saturdays, as well as on festivals, *Rosh Khodesh* (the first day of every Hebrew month), and fast days. In order to perform the public reading, at least ten people (a *minyan*) must be gathered.

Three to seven people are called upon to read a passage or say a blessing before the reading, which is usually given by experts in biblical cantillation. The entire Torah is read over a period of a year. It is divided into fifty-four parts, each called *sidra*, which means order, or *parashah*, which means "piece" or "passage." A different portion is read every Sabbath.

The cycle begins on the Sabbath following the festival of *Simkhat Torah*, which brings the High Holidays to a close; the cycle ends on *Simkhat Torah* of the following year.

Therefore, from week to week, every Saturday, biblical history accompanies the Jewish people, from the creation of the world to the death of Moses and the entrance into the "Promised Land." Jews throughout the world read the same text on the same day.

The name of each of the fifty-four portions is taken from the first word (or one of the first words) of each the *parashah*. In this manner, the first *parashah* is called *Bereshith*—the first word of the first verse of the Torah. The Sabbath adopts the name of the *parashah* that is being read. For example, *Bereshith* Sabbath is when the *Bereshith parashah* is read.

During the public service, after the blessings, the Psalms, the *Shema Yisrael* and the *Amidah* (the silent prayer said while standing with both feet together) have all been read, the Scrolls of the Law, or the *Sifrei Torah* (plural of *Sefer Torah*), are taken out of the Ark. These are kept at one end of the synagogue, facing the entrance, and turned toward Jerusalem.

The location of the Ark is determined by its relative position to Jerusalem.

THE HOLY ARK OR THE *ARON HAKODESH*. The Ark is a chest or receptacle that usually contains several scrolls wrapped in mantles. The mantles richly adorned and embroidered with gold or silver threads on which the names of donors are sewn, as well as the name of the occasion for which they have been donated.

THE ADORNMENTS. Silver plates (or plates of other kinds of metal) are attached to the mantles and bear smaller detachable plates engraved with the name of that week's *parashah*. The ends of the wooden holders on which the scrolls are mounted bear one or two tiny pommels called *Rimmonim* (literally, pomegranates).

THE POINTER OR *YAD*. A finger or hand made of silver, wood, or another material assists the handling of the text during the reading, as touching the scrolls with bare hands is forbidden.

THE *HAGBAHAH* OR THE EXHIBITION OF THE TORAH. A member of the congregation is called upon to open the Ark and to carry the scrolls from the Ark to the reading table in the center of the synagogue. The table is called the *tevah* or the *bimah*. Each scroll is then placed on the table and "undressed" as its outer adornments are removed. The scrolls are opened up to the passage to be read, in order to be shown to the assembly. A member of the congregation comes forward to raise the open scroll and show it to all others present in the congregation. To do this, he turns around, raising his arms up high. This public presentation is called the *Hagbahah*, meaning "to rise up." It is a great honor to be chosen to perform the *Hagbahah* and to recite a blessing aloud before the open scrolls. For special occasions, there is open bidding to determine who will perform these different ceremonies. This is an indirect way of having congregation members donate funds for the upkeep of the synagogue. It is also customary to give a donation when going up to the Torah[1].

TOOLS OF THE SCRIBE. The books of the Torah or of the *Sifrei Torah* are on scrolls made from parched or tanned leather. The scrolls are formed by sewing strips of skin together. The sacred texts are copied onto the scrolls using a calamus reed in the East, and a goose quill in the West. The scribe or sofer writes by hand following a model to avoid mistakes. He uses a special ink that is not easily erased.

THE STRUCTURE OF THE TORAH TEXT. The text uses no vowels. Only consonants form words, which makes the reading difficult, and demands considerable preparation to learn how to read and cantillate properly. There is no punctuation, so nothing indicates the rhythm or the transition from one sentence to the next. Nothing breaks up the flow of these words, except blank spaces, or writing voids, which appear to the untrained eye as gaps in the middle of the writing. The text between two blank spaces is called a *parashah*, or "passage." The books of the Torah are separated by a space of four lines.

Certain letters are topped with small flourishes, called crowns. More specifically, the left side of seven of the twenty-two letters in the Hebrew alphabet are decorated with three small strokes or crowns. These seven letters are: *shin, ayin, teth, nun, zayin, gimnel,* and *tsaddi.*

To fully grasp the meaning of the crowns, it should be added that as Rabbi Tsadok Hakohen of Lublin has pointed out, there is an essential difference between writing Hebrew and Latin letters. It concerns the positioning of the letter in relation to the "baseline." In Latin, the letter sits on a line below it. In Hebrew, however, the letter is suspended from, or hangs below, the line. For example:

Shin   Lamed

The top line represents a barrier. It has a symbolic meaning because it delineates the boundary between the writing and that which exists beyond the writing. With one exception, none of the twenty-two letters of the Hebrew alphabet goes beyond this limit.

The name of the letter in question encloses its meaning in its form. *Lamed* is the semantic root of all things related to study and teaching —teaching that literally follows the directive of this letter, *lamed*, which says "to learn it." To learn is to enter into the movement of going beyond the boundary line of the writing, to go "beyond" the text. *Lamed*, which means "to learn." The word Talmud, the seminal book of Jewish thought, is derived from this letter. The Talmud does not represent a collection of inherited knowledge, but an exacting pursuit of research, questioning, and interpretation. Writing a book is one of the 613 commandments. Writing a book or having a book written in one's name is therefore part of a tradition.

Some communities pool their resources to buy a book of the Torah, with each member buying a letter, a chapter, or an entire passage.

If copies of the *Sefer Torah*, prayer books, *mezuzot*, or *tefillin* are worn out or damaged, they are not destroyed. They are buried in a section of the Jewish cemetery, or grouped together in the *genizah*, which is an area that is usually in a room of the synagogue, or near the synagogue.

The *genizah* in Cairo, which was discovered at the end of the nineteenth century, has proved invaluable to historical research. It

148

contained ancient manuscripts of many sacred texts, as well as precious details about daily life, commerce, customs, and voyages of many Jews over an extended period of time.

1. According to the Sephardic tradition, the *Hagbahah* is done before the reading of the Torah, but in the Ashkenazic tradition the *Hagbahah* takes place after the reading.

THE SABBATH

THE SABBATH IS ONE OF THE MOST IMPORTANT
EVENTS IN THE JEWISH RELIGION. IT IS OBSERVED
AS A HOLY DAY AND A PUBLIC HOLIDAY

In the Hebrew bible, the Sabbath is the seventh day of creation, and it is the day of rest. The word "Sabbath" in Hebrew means to rest from all creative activity. It is a day of rest for the entire Jewish household, whether master, slave, animal, or visitor.

The commandment for observing the Sabbath is the fourth commandment of the Decalogue (the Ten Commandments), which states that Jews must observe this holy day in memory of the Exodus from Egypt.

The fourth commandment is also a reminder that God created the world in six days and rested on the seventh, and this is why he blessed the Sabbath day and made it holy. Although work is not permitted on the seventh day, there are certain duties to be accomplished.

The activities forbidden during the Sabbath are listed in the thirty-nine classes of prohibited work. The activities which must be performed revolve around the *eruv*, the *nerot*, the *Kiddush*, the *challah*, the reading of the Torah, the *seudah*, and the *Havdalah*. These terms will be explored in this chapter.

I. THE THIRTY-NINE CLASSES OF PROHIBITED WORK

Those forbidden on the Sabbath. According to the Talmud, the origin of these classes is found in the interpretation of the following verse: "You will build my sanctuary, yet you will respect my Sabbath." It is understood by this that all labors involved in building the Temple are forbidden on the Sabbath. As the philosopher Abraham Heschel argued in his book with the very apt title *The Builders of Time*, it is a question of man leaving the dimension of space and technique to enter the inner dimension of time. These thirty-nine labors cover a panoply of creative acts.

The basic activities are: 1. sowing; 2. plowing; 3. reaping; 4. binding sheaves; 5. threshing; 6. winnowing; 7. cleansing (crops); 8. grinding; 9. sifting; 10. kneading; 11. baking; 12. shearing (wool); 13. washing (wool); 14. beating (wool); 15. dyeing; 16. spinning; 17. weaving; 18. looping; 19. warping; 20. unwarping; 21. tying a knot; 22. loosening (a knot); 23. stitching; 24. tearing; 25. hunting; 26. slaughtering; 27. flaying; 28. salting; 29. tanning; 30. scraping (a skin); 31. cutting up (a skin); 32. writing; 33. erasing; 34. building; 35. breaking; 36. extinguishing a fire; 37. kindling a fire; 38. striking with a hammer; 39. carrying from one place to another [1].

To this rather lengthy list, the ancients added bans on related labors. It is also forbidden to cook any food on the Sabbath, which is an extension of the ban on baking bread. Many objects must be cast aside before the Sabbath, such as pencils and other writing utensils, or matches for lighting fires, as these objects could easily be picked up and used inadvertently. These additional prohibitions are seen as barriers that reinforce the observance of the Sabbath. It must be noted, however, that they are all instantly annulled if they are involved in saving someone's life, or if a person is in serious danger.

Although these restrictions would appear to impinge on personal freedom, they actually permit man to devote effort and energy to activities of a different nature. During the week, man invests space; during the Sabbath, he invests time. During the week, man's energies are spent with objects; during the Sabbath, his energies are spent on time. The Sabbath is dedicated to rest, but also to study, conversation, walks, and visiting friends. In philosophical terms, putting a distance between object and person allows for self-improvement: improvement of the person in relation to himself and to those around him. All the rituals of the Sabbath highlight the social dimension of camaraderie and meeting with others.

II. THE *NEROT*: THE FRIDAY NIGHT CANDLES

The beginning of the Sabbath is marked by the ritual lighting of two candles. Everything must be ready by the time the Sabbath begins. The house should be cleaned, the meals cooked, the table set, baths taken, and everyone in the family dressed for celebration. Sabbath begins an hour before nightfall on Friday and ends at sunset on Saturday. It lasts twenty-five hours in all.

Two or more candles, or *nerot*, are placed in candlesticks. Candelabra feature prominently in traditional Jewish art, and some of the most beautiful examples can be found among those finely crafted out of filigree silver. In every Jewish household, the candelabrum is a basic symbol of attachment to traditional values.

Today, despite assimilation, the candlesticks still holds a respected place in the home, even if celebration of the Sabbath is only a memory associated with parents or grandparents. The lighting of these candles marks the beginning of Sabbath. It is usually the woman of the house who gives the blessing as she lights each *ner*. The Kabbalists say that the light from the Sabbath candles repairs the damage done by the first man on earth. It erases the darkness brought by original sin. After the candles have been lit, everyone goes to the synagogue to take part in the Friday night service, which differs from those of the other evenings of the week.

Once back in the home, several more psalms are sung, and then it is customary for the father and the mother to bless their children by placing two hands on their head and reciting a few verses from the Torah.

III. THE *KIDDUSH*: THE GOBLET OF WINE

The Sabbath and holy days are times for people to meet with God, and with others. This meeting, or *moed*, is considered a sacred time. The sanctification of time in the Jewish tradition is always marked by a blessing over wine.

The *Kiddush*, which literally means "sanctification," is a ceremony where a blessing is given over a goblet of wine. Time, symbolized by the goblet of wine, is sanctified through this blessing, which inaugurates many festive meals including the first meal of the Sabbath. The blessing is a reminder that the Sabbath marks the creation of the world, that God created the world in six days, and ceased all creative activity to rest on the seventh. This is why man must stop working on this day. It is also mentioned that the Sabbath is kept in remembrance of the Exodus from Egypt and of the wandering through the desert. The Kabbalists point out that the Hebrew word for goblet or glass (of wine), *Koss*, has a numerical value of 86, which is the same as that for one of the names for God, Elohim.

Kabbalist texts explain that wine has a numerical value of 70, the same numerical value as the word Sod, meaning "secret." Numerous speculations are based on these games of numbers and letters, allowing the ritual to be structured by writing the language onto objects. According to the same Kabbalistic tradition, the *Kiddush* glass should be raised with two hands.

IV. *CHALLAH*: THE SABBATH BREAD

After the *Kiddush*, the hands are washed (*netilat yadayim*) in a special receptacle, the *keli*, then a blessing is given over the *challah* loaves, which are covered with a napkin or cloth that is often richly decorated. The Sabbath meal begins with the blessing of the *challah* —two braided loaves of bread which symbolize the two portions of *manna*[2] which fell from the sky onto the desert on Friday. This bread is specially made for the Sabbath.

It is interesting to note that *manna* is one of the underlying themes of Judaism. After the cries of hunger and thirst from the children of Israel reached the ears of Moses, God let a small white grain rain down on the desert, a grain that looked like coriander seed, and that no man had ever seen before. As they came out of their tents on the morning after the *manna* had dropped, each person asked of his neighbor, "What is it?" And Moses answered: "It is bread from the sky, sent to you by God!" And God then told them, "Because you have said 'what is it?,' the name of the bread will be 'what is it?'" [3]. And for forty years, the children of Israel ate "What is it?" It is the fundamental experience of questioning that opens man to both searching and adventure. By beginning the Sabbath with the blessing of the *challah*, one enters the time of the Sabbath via a question, via the questioning of oneself, making the necessary renewal of the self possible.

It has been pointed out several times in this chapter that the Sabbath is a day of rest. A state of emptiness is entered into, not so that the void be filled, but to avoid a life that is too full, which could overwhelm us. The question raised by the *manna* provides us with an opportunity to construct time. The expression that is literally translated as "Here is the *Manna*" also means "time." During the meal, the Sabbath songs, or *Zemiroth*, are sung, and the meal ends with the final blessing *Birkat Ha-nazon*.

V. THE READING OF THE TORAH DURING THE MORNING SERVICE OF THE SABBATH

One of the important moments of the Sabbath is the liturgical reading of the Torah during the morning service of the Sabbath. The Saturday morning service at the synagogue begins with the morning prayer, and is followed by the reading of a passage of the Torah. Every Sabbath section, or *parashah*, is subdivided into seven parts, and for each one of them a person is called up to assist in the reading. A passage from the Prophets is then read, chosen according to the section of the week, the *Haftarah*. The reading is followed by an additional Sabbath prayer, the *Mussaf*, which is the additional service closing the morning service.

153

VI. THE *SEUDAH*

The Sabbath is a time for socializing, for meeting up with friends and acquaintances. This is generally spent sharing meals, where songs are sung and passages of the Torah read during the Sabbath are discussed. Usually, a *seudah* or meal is served three times during the Sabbath. A blessing is made over two loaves of bread at the beginning of the first meal, and at the end the *Birkat Ha-nazon*, the grace is recited. The first *seudah* takes place on Friday night. The second *seudah* begins after the morning Sabbath service. The meal begins with the *Kiddush*, followed by the blessing over the two loaves of bread, as on Friday night. The third meal, or *seudah shelishith*, is served after the afternoon service, just before the Sabbath draws to a close. During this meal, melancholic songs are sung, for it is with a certain sadness that one prepares to leave behind the special and holy feeling of the Sabbath.

VII. THE *HAVDALAH*: THE CLOSING CEREMONY OF THE SABBATH

The Sabbath is brought to a close with a separation ritual. Since the ceremony is very poetic, and the objects are highly symbolic, the ritual has become a source of inspiration for artists. In the dancing shadows from the flickering light thrown by the flame of a twisted candle, a blessing is given over the wine, then over the perfume, over the light, and, lastly, over the separation between the holy time of the Sabbath, and the secular time of the other days of the week.

The word *Havdalah* means separation, the separation of the Sabbath from that which follows the Sabbath. At nightfall on Saturday, a final ceremony is performed, with the first blessing given over the wine, then another blessing over a perfumed plant, which represents the sweet smells of the Sabbath, and the last blessing over the flame.

In its shadow, the fingernails are contemplated to pay homage to the transparency of the first man in contrast to our opaque nature. At the end of the ceremony, a few drops of wine or milk are poured over the flame to extinguish it. *Havdalah* wine is not passed out to all who have assisted, as it is in the *Kiddush*. Instead, it is drunk only by the person who read the *Havdalah*. These days, it is customary to make wishes for the coming week.

The *Havdalah* brings an end to all the restrictions imposed by the Sabbath. Beautifully crafted and extremely valuable examples of the objects used in this ceremony have been produced over the years, namely, of the Besamim (spice box) and the *Havdalah*, the twisted candlestick holders. The most original object of the ceremony is the spice box, which, in Germany and Eastern European countries, is known as *Gewürzbüchse* or *Bessomimbüchse*. Boxes shaped like turrets are the most common, but others can be shaped like fruit such as apples or pears. There are also boxes in the form of flowers, eggs, acorns, fish, and sometimes, steam engines. In fact, there is a great variety of shapes, ranging from swans to roosters, and from windmills to horse-drawn coaches. They are generally made out of solid or filigree silver. For the *Havdalah* ceremony, the boxes are filled with cloves or bay leaves.

What does the perfume ritual mean? Why is the perfume from plants inhaled as the Sabbath draws to a close? According to Kabbalistic communities, man receives an additional soul on the evening before the Sabbath. This soul releases its pungency during the Sabbath, and returns into the world of souls at the end of the Sabbath. Man, feeling this loss, falls into nostalgia, and uses the perfume as a slight "pick-me-up."

1. It is forbidden to carry anything from a private to a public place over a distance of more than four lengths of an elbow (about two steps). However, if an area, even an entire city, is surrounded by a rope or line linking posts that are at least 16 inches high, then this may be considered an enclosed single space, and objects may be carried in it during the Sabbath. This line is called the *eruv*.
2. During the long period of living in the desert, the Hebrews ate *manna* and quail, which fell miraculously from the sky. However, biblical text states that two loaves of bread need to be collected on Friday, as no *manna* fell on the Sabbath.
3. In Hebrew: *Mannehoo*.

THE SHOFAR

THE *SHOFAR* IS A RAM'S HORN USED AS A
MUSICAL INSTRUMENT ON THE DAYS OF *ROSH
HASHANAH*, THE JEWISH NEW YEAR, AND AFTER
YOM KIPPUR, THE DAY OF ATONEMENT

When Abraham was offering his son Isaac in sacrifice by divine commandment, an angel intervened, preventing the murder by choosing a ram to be sacrificed instead. What was called the sacrifice of Isaac became known as "the non-sacrifice of Isaac," which changed the course of man's thinking. Human sacrifice would no longer be committed from this moment on. A ram's horn is blown during certain Jewish ceremonies to pay respect to this animal that saved Isaac's life. Symbolically, the gesture means that if a human must die, the same miracle should occur for him. The *shofar* holds a privileged place at the heart of *Rosh Hashanah* and *Yom Kippur* festivities, days of judgment and pardon.

Three different patterns of notes are sounded on the *shofar*. The first is long and sustained, called *tekiah*, which means "to be fixed, driven into the ground." The second pattern is made up of three notes of equal length, each one-third of the length of a *tekiah*. This pattern is called *shevarim*, which means "broken" notes. The third category is made up of nine short series of notes, all equal in length, all one-ninth of a *tekiah* or one-third of a *shevarim*. This pattern is called *teruah* and means "shaking into motion." When each of these patterns of notes has been played, the sequence is closed with a repeat of the *tekiah* (the long unbroken pattern of notes).

Tekiah —————————————————

Shevarim ———— ———— ————

Teruah — — — — — — — — —

Tekiah —————————————————

The rite of the *shofar* is symbolic of a certain definition of ethical man. The broken notes of the *shevarim* are there as a reminder that man can escape from imprisonment within a closed definition of himself. This is what shapes his freedom, which distinguishes him as being separate from manufactured objects and animals. Objects are defined things, while man is undefined. He is not identifiable or representable. He bears the pattern of broken notes, and refuses to qualify his essence, to enclose himself in any historical or natural definition. In Hebrew, the word that means "I" also means "nothingness." According to the *zohar*, this is to teach man the ability and his duty to not give a concrete definition of his essence. The *zohar* goes even further, emphasizing the numeric coincidence between the word *adam* (man) and *mah* (what? what is it?).

Man is fundamentally a *mah*, a questioning of himself, thus eliminating any risk of fixing himself with a definitive identity, whether it be natural or social. The "what-am-I-man" designates himself as a place of questioning, a process known in Hebrew as *Zeman*, "here is the question," and which signifies time. Human time, infinitive time, as opposed to definitive time.

Prohibition of representation or definition is sounded by the notes of the *shofar*. This prohibition does not concern the idol, but rather man himself. There are no idols, only idolaters. The banning of representation warns man against the never-ending risk of merging with specific determinations of himself. It often happens that by accepting an imaginary representation of himself for a short period of time or permanently, the "what-am-I-man" becomes the "here's-the-man-that-I-am," identifying himself with a character or a role. This being done, he ceases to be part of the great "nothingness." In this reification, he loses a large part of his freedom. Having become the image he is resolved to adhere to, he abolishes distance, the nothingness, his internal difference, the engine of his evolution, and in so doing, he becomes an ethical being.

Returning to the musical patterns of the *shofar*, it could be asked, why are the *shevarim* followed by a *teruah*? Why should the interrupted sound be broken up a second time? This is because there is another derivative of definitive identity, that of a breaking up of identity, which also becomes a system. It is possible to come across beings who are happy with their "broken" image. But the breaking up mentioned earlier should be dynamic, dynamizing. The *teruah* points out the need for a breaking up of what has already been broken, and the momentary reunion with the state of recomposing the "I," or the "me."

It is interesting to note that the word *shofar* also means the esthetic aspect of things which are in a process of improving themselves, of embellishment. The Masters of the Talmud have always analyzed the ethical embellishments in the way we define it: the continual transformation and change of human beings. The word *shofar* could also mean commentary, or interpretation—*perush* (through a game of interchanging letters around, the Hebrew language allows for multiple ways of reading the same word).

The dynamic of breaks, of breaking up the breaks, and of reunifying, fosters close bonds with the interpretation of texts and the world. The relationship of the ethical with interpretation is not just an experience of comprehending words and texts, but also a fundamental existentialist attitude that makes the reinventing of oneself possible.

To interpret, and study, is to interpret oneself...

ROSH HASHANAH

THE JEWISH NEW YEAR

Rosh Hashanah, the Jewish New Year, is a two-day holiday which falls on the first and second day of the month of *Tishri*. This celebration, which starts off a ten-day period leading to *Yom Kippur*, is known as the Ten Days of Penitence.

It is an important event, both spiritually and intellectually, because it provides an opportunity to assess one's actions and thoughts over the past year, and to question one's existence, choices, and options in life. The liturgy, prayers, and biblical texts read at this time all express man's inherent capacity to shake up his existence and find new, original paths.

Rosh Hashanah encourages people to pull themselves out of the daily routine, out of daily habits, and to let go of the weight of being. The continuation of this thinking is found ten days later in the celebration of *Yom Kippur*, which is like a confirmation of the decisions made during *Rosh Hashanah.*

The officiant is dressed in white to bring attention to the solemnity of the celebration, but it is by no means a sad event. To foster inner searching, the *shofar* is blown several times each morning during prayer at the synagogue, as the sound of this horn stirs the being and puts it into question. Every man, woman, and child listens to the blowing of the *shofar.* For people who are ill or unable to come to the synagogue (women who are having difficult pregnancies, for example), the community sends someone to sound the shofar at their homes.

The two evenings of *Rosh Hashanah* provide an occasion for unusual celebrations around the dinner table (this is particularly so in Sephardic households). Specially prepared dishes are used in expressing good wishes for the New Year.

Ashkenazic communities (Jews originating from Eastern Europe) customarily dip slices of fresh apple into honey during these two evenings of celebration, saying "May this year be as sweet for us as this apple dipped in honey." After the bread is blessed, it also is dipped in honey, not in salt, as is otherwise customary.

In Sephardic communities (Jews from Spain and Portugal and their descendants) a true *seder* is organized: the table is sumptuously decorated and laid out with sweet dishes. While certain variations are found, depending on the country of origin, the essential idea is the same: to eat over the next two nights food whose Hebrew or Aramaic names evoke biblical passages, either for blessing the Jewish people or for cursing its enemies. It is a play between food and words. The idea during *Rosh Hashanah* is "let's eat the book!"—an evening of "food for thought, thought for food."

Thus, on a Moroccan table, for example, you would find:
– a fruit dish filled with fresh apples, preferably red ones;
– a small jar of honey in which slices of apple are dipped: may the New Year be as sweet as the apple dipped in honey;
– a small bowl of sesame seeds mixed with granulated sugar: may we be as numerous as the grains of sesame;
– a dish of fresh dates: may all enemies vanish;
– a bowl of pomegranates sprinkled with orange-flower water: may our merits be as numerous as the pomegranate seeds;
– a dish filled with beets: may our enemies move far away from us;
– a dish with a lamb's head: may we always be ahead and not behind;
– a dish with one fish: like the fish, may we always have our eyes open, be on the lookout, and flourish in great number;
– a platter holding seven vegetables: carrots (may all poor decisions made about us be dropped), two types of squash (may all poor judgments be abandoned), chick-peas, beets, onions, and raisins;
– a bowl of green olives, for they are one of Israel's favorite fruits;
– the *kiddush* glass;
– festive breads, also frequently dipped in honey;
– leeks, green beans, quinces, jujubes, or grapes, may also be on the table, depending on the custom, as these seasonal fruits and vegetables are new, like the new year.

Happy new year, *Shanah Tova*!

YOM KIPPUR

THE DAY OF ATONEMENT

Yom Kippur, the Day of Atonement, for Jews around the world, is the most important and significant festival, as it is exceptional both psychologically and spiritually.

On this day, the human being is released from his past. No matter what mistakes, errors, or violent acts he may have committed, he may now be pardoned. The man who decides to change, to question himself, to live in harmony with himself becomes free. He is forgiven, and he may now open himself up to the infinite nature of time. There are three essential paths to follow to arrive at this state of atonement:

– prayer, in which mistakes are listed and atonement is sought;

– fasting, in order to devote oneself entirely to this spiritual awakening;

– charity, or *tzedaka*.

Yom Kippur is the culmination of the Ten Days of Penitence which begin during *Rosh Hashanah*. It is a day of strict fasting, and lasts from sunset until nightfall the next day. It falls on the Hebraic date of *Tishri* 10, in September-October. The day before the fast, it is customary to give money or food to the poor. To this end, collection boxes called *tzedaka* boxes are found all over the world, in Jewish stores, on the streets of Israel, dug into stone walls of houses or affixed to tree trunks. The day before *Yom Kippur*, a ceremony called *kapparah* takes place in which a chicken or hen is swung three times over the head. Afterward, the animal is slaughtered and given to the poor, or else the monetary value of the animal is donated. This is a symbolic way of ridding oneself of the weight of one's errors and mistakes. The same ceremony may also be performed using only money, without the animal.

Near mid-afternoon on the day before *Yom Kippur*, a final meal is served before the fast. The woman of the household lights two candles, as she does for the Sabbath.

Five activities are banned during the *Yom Kippur* fast: eating, drinking, washing, anointing oneself with oils, sexual relations, and wearing shoes with leather soles. Generally, shoes with plastic soles are worn, as no comfort should be sought on this day. Everyone who has reached religious maturity is expected to take part in the fast.

Five prayers are recited during the twenty-four-hour fast. *Yom Kippur* ends with the sounding of the *shofar*, heard as an echo of both hope and freedom.

SUKKOTH

During the celebration of *Sukkoth* or the Festival of Tabernacles, the third pilgrimage in the Jewish year, small booths called *sukkoth* (*sukkah* in the singular) are built outdoors. In memory of the forty years the Jews spent in the desert after the Exodus from Egypt, they are lived in for seven days.

The Festival of Tabernacles takes place after the celebration of *Rosh Hashanah* (the Jewish New Year) during which the *shofar* rite is performed (see chapter nine), and *Yom Kippur* (the Day of Atonement). It lasts seven days in Israel, and eight in the Diaspora. This celebration has several different names: the Festival of Booths, the Feast of Tabernacles, the Harvest Festival, and the Time of Joy.

A booth is built that will stay up for the entirety of the holiday. The word *sukkah* is derived from *skhakh*, which is the thatching used for the roof. The booth is intended to look temporary, in order to represent the dwellings the Jews lived in as they wandered through the wilderness. It pays respect to living, and living precariously. The aim behind the construction of the *sukkah* is to experience what it feels like to live in a dwelling that is in the process of being built, as opposed to a place that is already built. Each year, a new shelter must be constructed for the event (in Hebrew: *Ta'aseh, ve lo min ha'assuya*).

The walls of the *sukkah* can be made of a solid immovable material. The roof should be built of cut vegetable matter, such as wood, boards, rattan, reeds, pine, etc. There must be more shade than sunlight inside the *sukkah*. The roof is the most important element of the *sukkah*. It is the *skhakh*, and gives its name to the entire living space inside. The roof does not represent a limit, but rather an invitation to go beyond. One must go beyond oneself. It is no mere coincidence that the entire month of *Tishri*, the month in which *Sukkoth* takes place, is under the sign of the letter *lamed*, which symbolizes moving beyond (as explained in chapter seven).

The way a human being thinks is very much a reflection of the way in which he lives. In other words, the manner of living on earth, just like that of living in space or the body, reveals as much about the spirit of man as it does his ideas or behavior.

THE LULAV

THE LANGUAGE OF FLOWERS

The other rite of *Sukkoth* is the *lulav*. Each day during the celebrations, a bouquet composed of the following items is brought along to the morning prayer:
– the *etrog*: a citron;
– the *lulav*: a palm branch;
– the *hadass*: three myrtle branches;
– the *aravah*: two willow branches;
The bouquet is named after the *lulav*, one of its elements.

To give blessing to this rite during the morning prayer, the *lulav* is held in the right hand, with the three myrtle branches positioned to the right of the palm branch, and the two willow branches to the left. These three branches are fastened together. The *etrog* is held in the left hand. After the rite is blessed, the two hands are brought together and the four plants are shaken up and down in the direction of the four cardinal points. The the *lulav* ceremony is not performed on the day of the Sabbath. The origins of the *lulav* are associated with Sukkoth, which began as a harvest festival. It consists of thanking God for all species of vegetation.

The *lulav*, or the palm tree, is a tree which bears fruit, but which has no natural perfume. The *hadass*, the myrtle, does not bear any fruit, but has a natural heady perfume. The willow, the *aravah*, does not produce either fruit or a natural perfume, while the citron, the *etrog*, has both fruit and perfume. Meaning has been given to these symbols as a way of classifying the practitioner of the Jewish faith. A

person may be defined by his knowledge of the Torah (perfume), by his practice of it (fruit), by reflection (perfume), and by action (fruit). The *lulav* bouquet represents the Jewish people in its diversity:
– people who practice and study the religion are represented by the fruit and perfume of the *etrog*;
– those who practice the religion without study are symbolized by the *lulav*, the palm branch;
– those who study and have the spirit of the Torah within them are represented by the myrtle branch;
– and finally, those who neither practice nor study are symbolized by the willow.

The bouquet functions as a whole in the rite, emphasizing that everyone has as much value as the other if he or she works together with the others to build the community. The rabbi has as much importance as a simple follower; and a scholar should not be glorified for his knowledge. It is the joy of working together on a common project that is important. The *lulav* is a symbol of the unity and solidarity of the Jewish people.

HANUKKAH

A TREE OF LIGHT

In the second century B.C.E., the Jewish people won a large military and spiritual victory over Greek universalism. The victory was cemented with the reclaiming of the Temple of Jerusalem. All sacrileges perpetrated by the occupiers were purged, and the candelabrum was lit once again—the symbol of restored light. During the construction of the portable sanctuary in the desert, God ordered that certain religious objects be made, namely the *menorah*, a candelabrum with seven branches. The description given in the Bible (Exodus 25: 31-40) is like that of a tree of light. This candelabrum remained lit; it was an eternal light.

In Jewish history, this candelabrum took on a particularly important significance after an event occurred that is fundamental to the Jewish consciousness.

Judea had been under Persian domination until 333 B.C.E., when it fell to the Greeks, led by Alexander the Great. After the death of Alexander the Great, his empire was divided up amongst his generals, one ruling in Egypt and the other in Syria. Following a war of spoils, Judea was controlled by the kingdom of Syria, ruled by the Seleucid dynasty.

Antiochus IV Epiphanes, known as Epimanes (the madman) by the Jews, rose to the throne of Syria in 175 B.C.E. (3585, according to the Jewish calendar). A hot-tempered tyrant who despised the Jewish religion, he wanted to unify his kingdom through the imposition of one religion and culture—Hellenism. The Jewish religion was banned and scrolls of the Torah were confiscated and burned. Practicing the Sabbath, circumcision, and *kashrut* were punishable by death.

The Jews were divided amongst themselves. On the one hand stood the devout believers, or *Hassidim* who, refusing to follow the rules laid down by Antiochus, continued to study the Torah and observe the *mitsvoth*, despite threats of execution. On the other, the Hellenistic Jews were not opposed to assimilation with the Greek culture and religion. They abandoned the Torah and their religious practices and devoted themselves to art and the Olympic games, which at the time were religious in nature. And finally, there were the indecisive Jews, those who did not know whether they should join the *Hassidim* or the Hellenists.

In the small village of Modi'in, not far from Jerusalem, lived the old priest Mattathias, the father of five sons. One day, Antiochus's soldiers arrived in Modi'in and erected an altar in the market square. They called upon the Jews to come forth and offer sacrifices to the Greek gods. The High Priest Mattathias spoke and said: "My sons, my brothers, and I will remain faithful to the covenant of our fathers." At this moment, a Hellenistic Jew came forth to the altar to offer a sacrifice. Mattathias took his sword and killed him instantly, thus triggering

165

a rebellion. The sons and the friends of Mattathias leapt on the Greek officers and soldiers, killing many of them, while others fled. The Jews demolished the sacrificial altar and sought refuge in the mountains. Soon, the faithful Jews and the undecided Jews joined Mattathias and his sons in the mountains, and the rebellion expanded to the entire Jewish population of Judea.

Before dying, the High Priest brought his five sons together, Jochanan, Simon, Jonathan, Judah, and Eleazar, and urged them to continue the combat. He appointed head of the army his son Judah, known as Judah Maccabee—*Makabi* signifies hammer, in other words, Judah the Hammer—for his bravery, or perhaps also because of the slogan printed on his standard: *Makabi* are the initials for: "Who is like You amongst the Powerful, O Eternal." The soldiers of Antiochus, who were led by Appolonius, Nicanor, and Gorgias, all generals at the head of a strong army, were struck down and defeated one by one.

Finally, Judah and his men went to Jerusalem, which they liberated in 165 B.C.E. (3595 in the Jewish calendar). Through the presence of idols, the Temple of Jerusalem had been made impure. Judah Maccabee's companions purged the Temple of all idols and impurities, built a new altar, and consecrated it on *Kislev* 25 of the year 3595. This was the Dedication of the Temple, hence the name *Hanukkah*, meaning "dedication" in Hebrew. *Hanukkah* also means "they rest (from their enemies) on the 25th."

Having purified the Temple, or *Hamikdash*, the Maccabees wanted to light the perpetual light with seven branches. But it had been stolen by the Syrian Greeks. A temporary candelabrum was thus fashioned. But only one flask of pure oil was found to fuel it, a flask that carried the stamp of the High Priest. However, it kept the candles lit for eight days, rather than just one, as was usually the case. The origin of the candlelighting during *Hanukkah* is this miracle of the oil flask. But the real miracle was the victory of a handful of Jews over strong and organized armies which had invaded the East. The candelabrum —the symbol of this spiritual and political victory—has left a profound mark on the consciousness of the Jewish people. Along with the Star of David, it has become the symbol par excellence of Judaism and the people of Israel.

This candelabrum, laden with history, in addition to representing resistance and rebirth, is also the official emblem of the State of Israel. In remembrance of the miracle of *Hanukkah*, Jews light a candelabrum during a period of eight days.

This ceremony has evolved since the initial lighting of the candles. It would have been logical to light a candelabrum with seven branches over a period of eight days. However, the rule that prohibits representation includes objects found in the Temple. The eight-day miracle inspired the design of a new candelabrum—this one with eight branches instead of seven. There was a second official change: the lights (oil lamps or candles) are lit one by one, not all eight at the same time. Thus, one candle is lit the first day, a second the next, and so forth, until the eighth candle is lit on the eighth day. This carries with it the idea of improvement, of continuous renewal. According to the principle set out by the school of Hillel: "One rises with holiness, and one does not descend."

The candle used to light the *Hanukkah* lights (thus making nine in the candelabrum) is called the *shammash*, "the servant"; it is placed on the side or in the center, a little higher or slightly displaced from the candelabrum, so as not to be confused with the eight ritualistic candles.

According to the Kabbalah, the number of candles lit corresponds to the Name of God, EHYH, which is written out as *aleph-hay-yod-hay* and which means "I shall be." It is a setting into motion of this name which means the future. The same relationship to language is found here, as in the "language in motion" concept discussed in the chapters concerning the *tallith* and the *mezuzah*.

The rites are, as such, the memory of historic events of the Jewish people and also the writing of the living name upon the physical matter of the world. The name EHYH written as *aleph-hay-yod-hay* equals the numbers 1-5-10-5.

If these figures are added together according to the principal of lighting the Hanukkah candles, the following sum is obtained:

$$
\begin{array}{r}
1 \\
1 + 5 \\
1 + 5 + 10 \\
1 + 5 + 10 + 5 \\
\hline
= 44
\end{array}
$$

The same principle is applied to the candles. Every day during *Hanukkah*, forty-four candles (thirty-six candles and eight shammashim) are lit, the numerical equivalent of the name "I shall be."

The rite is a reminder in light that "the perfection of man lies in his perfectibility." It is interesting to note that all historical sources concerning *Hanukkah* are in Greek. Thus, the Jewish memory is transmitted by a language other than Hebrew, and through another culture. This is perhaps another one of the lessons of *Hanukkah*: Light is only possible through dialogue between cultures, not through rejection, as an unsophisticated reading of history could lead one to believe. The lights of *Hanukkah* are like hands of light extended outward in the name of dialogue and peace.

TU BI-SHEVAT

THE NEW YEAR OF TREES
OR JEWISH ARBOR DAY

Tu Bi-Shevat is the New Year of Trees, celebrated by a feast of fruit and by the planting of new trees. In Hebrew, *Tu* equals the number 15. The entire word *Tu Bi-Shevat* means the fifteenth of the month of *Shevat*, which falls around January-February.

The New Year of Trees is one of four New Year's celebrations during the Jewish year. It is a happy event, helping to mark the end of winter. During the festivities, at least fifteen types of fruit are laid out on the table. The seven most important are those that grow in Israel (*Shevah ha-minim*): wheat, barley, grapes, pomegranates, figs, dates, and olives. A place of honor is also given to the fruit of the carob tree, which was abundant in Israel when the festival was inaugurated, and to almonds. The almond tree is the first tree to grow buds at the end of winter, and is in full bloom in the middle of *Shevat*.

Some communities, following a mystical tradition, sing hymns especially written for each of the seven types of fruit. In the same tradition, four goblets of wine composed of mixtures of red and white wine are drunk in the following order: the first goblet is filled with red wine; the second contains two-thirds red wine and one third white; the third holds one-third red wine and two-thirds white; and the fourth is filled with white wine.

Red represents rigor, *din*, and white stands for generosity, *hessed*. The four goblets of wine represent a range of possible combinations of behavior which run from the strictest rigor, to the most open generosity.

But the ideal is a balance between *din* and *hessed*, between rigor and generosity, a balance which can only be found after all other possibilities have been exhausted. To embellish the occasion, the rarest and most exotic fruits are sought out—the more kinds of fruit on the table, the better.

In Israel, *Tu Bi-Shevat* is a time when schoolchildren plant thousands of young trees in forests. Their efforts have helped turn the desert green! *Tu Bi-Shevat* is an ecological celebration—bringing man closer to nature, teaching him to respect and care for it. Jews compare the human being to a tree that grows and bears fruit. During wars, for example, cutting trees to make a fence or a weapon is forbidden.

Make trees, not war!

THE MEGILLAH

THE SCROLL OF ESTHER
PURIM: COSTUME AND CARNIVAL

Purim, or the Feast of Lots, is the Jewish carnival, celebrating the victory of the Jews of Persia over Haman, the anti-Semite. The Scroll of Esther, or *Megillah,* is read during *Purim,* and a party is held where everyone attends dressed up in costume.

Purim takes place on *Adar* 14, according to the Jewish calendar (around March) and celebrations revolve around the reading of the story of Esther in the *Megillat* Esther, which is found in the Book of Esther in the Bible. The *Megillah* is a text written entirely by hand with a reed or a goose quill on a roll of parchment paper kept in a box. Both the *Megillah* and the box have been an inspiration to many artists re-creating objects of the Jewish faith.

The Scroll of Esther is read twice during *Purim* celebrations, once the evening before *Adar* 14, and a second time the next morning— when children attend and people come dressed in costume. *Purim* is at the origin of Mardi Gras. It is a celebration of freedom and joy marking the rescue of the Jews from being massacred by Haman. At that time, Jews who lived in exile, following the destruction of the Temple in 586 B.C.E., went even as far as Persia, where they lived peacefully among the native people. One day, Haman appeared, a recently appointed vizier who detested Jews and swore he would see to it that every one of them was exterminated.

Haman chose the date for the massacre of the Jews of Persia by drawing or casting "lots," hence the name *Purim,* or Feast of Lots. The date indicated was the 14th of the month of *Adar.* Haman, who was first Minister of King Ahasuerus (possibly Artaxerxes II), received the King's approval. But the King's wife, Esther, who was Jewish, aided by the sagacity of her uncle Mordecai, delivered the Jews. Esther, Mordecai, and all the Jewish people had fasted for three days in a row. Thanks to their combined efforts in influencing

170

the King, the Jews were saved and Haman and his son were hanged.

The Fast of Esther is held on *Adar* 13 to commemorate that historic fast. And the miraculous liberation of the Jewish people is marked by Purim, a happy event celebrated by dressing up in costumes, enjoying feasts, exchanging gifts, and giving donations to the poor.

For *Purim, Hamantashen* (Haman's pockets), delicious pastries filled with either nuts, raisins, poppy seeds, or other ingredients, are baked in communities in the West. Eating, drinking, and reveling are encouraged during *Purim*, with everyone dressed up in costume, trying to be as anonymous as possible. During *Purim*, the Jews were transformed miraculously from being a persecuted people to a protected people, and from being despised to being honored. The idea behind dressing up is to look entirely different from one's habitual appearance. Who is respected, who is despised? Who is Jewish, who is Haman? Mixing up identities allows each person to reinvent himself, and to be freed from the prison they may have been enclosed in.

The Masters of the Talmud say that the miracle of the *Purim* was a miracle where God was hidden, or remained very discreet. In the text of the Megillah, God's name does not appear at all. The story is presented as a tale of men who take destiny into their own hands. In fact, the name Esther means: "that which is hidden." It is this element of hiding that also exists in the practice of dressing up in costume.

PESACH

PASSOVER

REMEMBERING THE EXODUS FROM EGYPT

Passover festivities last seven or eight days, and during this time it is forbidden to eat anything containing yeast. Unleavened bread or *matzah* is eaten instead of regular bread, and the festivities begin with a special meal called the *seder*. *Pesach* is one of the three pilgrimage celebrations, along with *Shavuot* and *Sukkoth*. It falls on *Nisan* 15, which generally falls in the month of April, and lasts eight days (seven in Israel). The first and last two days are holidays, and the days in between are partial holidays, called *hol ha-mo'ed*.

Pesach is a celebration that is both religious and agricultural in origin. It marks the arrival of spring and of the first barley harvest. It also commemorates the Exodus of the Hebrews from Egypt and the end of slavery. It is important to remember and mark this occasion, as it is one of the major events in Jewish history.

The Jews had been slaves for over 400 years until Moses awakened in them a desire for freedom. The Pharoah kept them in bondage until the Ten Plagues were sent down as divine punishment: blood, frogs, lice, flies, pestilence, boils, hail, locusts, darkness, and death of the firstborn.

The word *Pesach* means "to pass over," as God passed over the homes of the Hebrews during the tenth plague of Egypt, sparing the lives of their newborn. If read aloud *Pesach* could be pronounced "*Peh-Sakh*," meaning "the mouth which speaks." It is a mandatory part of *Pesach* celebrations to tell the story of the Exodus from Egypt, as well as other stories that relate to the Exodus.

There are several activities that are forbidden during *Pesach*, just as there are duties (*Mitzvot*), which must be performed. One cannot eat, have in the home, or even look at *hametz* (anything containing leaven), and also by extension of that rule, any food containing flour or any of the cereals—wheat, barley, oatmeal, spelt, and rye—as these are cereals which ferment. Instead, bread without yeast or unleavened bread, *matzah*, is eaten. It is a symbol of freedom, as it was the bread prepared by the Hebrews the day before the Exodus from Egypt, bread which never rose. matzah also represents misery, as it was often consumed by the Hebrews when they were in bondage in Egypt.

The third mandatory element of the celebration is the *seder* of *Pesach*. During the *seder*, the story of the Exodus from Egypt is read from the *Haggadah*, and food symbolizing the main aspects of the story are laid out on a platter and served as the main dish of the meal.

Discussing freedom is a manner of celebrating the fact that one has freedom of discourse. It is a way of talking about oneself, and of reinventing oneself at the same time.

Several very important preparations are made before the *seder*. All *hametz* found in the house, the car, the workplace, or anywhere else, is thrown out. A derivative of these "cleanings" takes place today even among non-Jews, in the form of "spring cleanings."

The evening of *Nisan* 13, at nightfall, *Bedikat Hametz* takes place: a meticulous search for *hametz* throughout the entire house takes place by candlelight. Any *hametz* found is burned the next morning during the *Bi'ur hametz* ceremony. *Hametz* is put on sale before *Bi'ur hametz* as a way of encouraging people to search thoroughly to be certain they haven't any left in the house by accident. On *Nisan* 14, the oldest boys in each household must fast in remembrance of the death of the firstborn in Egypt and of the saving of the Israelite firstborn. If the boy is not yet of age, his father must fast in his place.

On the evening of *Nisan* 14, everyone gathers around the dinner table, where the seder plate is the central focus.

THE *SEDER*: THE EVENING OF PASSOVER.
THE *SEDER* PLATE.

On a large dish, several symbolic elements are displayed, which are tasted and discussed throughout the Passover evening. This is a very family-oriented evening. The word *seder* means "order," as everything takes place in a very specific order throughout the evening, which is detailed in a text read like a program during the meal.

A copy of this text, called the *Haggadah* of *Pesach*, is handed out to everyone at the table. It is one of the best-selling Jewish texts, and has inspired many Jewish artists. The *seder* plate is placed in the middle of the table. All elements to be served throughout the course of the evening are laid out on the platter. The idea of the evening is to dramatize the elements associated with the Exodus from Egypt, in order to experience the event more profoundly, and to experience the feeling of what it was actually like to live during the liberation.

Questioning is a major part of the *seder*, especially by the children. The questions focus on the unusual objects and customs that take place during Passover. For example, why is *matzah* eaten? Why are bitter herbs and vegetables used? Why must one eat and drink leaning to the left?

Several sentences of the *Haggadah* begin with the Hebrew word "*Mah*" to emphasize the importance of questioning, "*Mah*" meaning "what." For example, the word is found at the beginning of the well-known passage of the four questions. Children wait impatiently for this text to be read aloud, as the youngest must ask: "Why is this night different from all others?" This is one of the questions the *Haggadah* tries to answer throughout the evening.

The *seder* plate contains the main symbols of Passover: a shankbone; a roasted egg; a cup of salted water; a sweet paste called *haroseth*; bitter herbs and vegetables known as *maror* (usually horseradish is used, but Romaine lettuce, radishes, or endives may also be served); herbs with leaves known as *karpas* (parsley or celery), and in the middle of the platter are three cakes of unleavened bread (*matzah*). The location of each one of these items on the platter varies according to local custom.

THE MEANING OF THE SYMBOLS:

1. The shankbone signifies the sacrifice of the paschal lamb the evening before the Exodus from Egypt. Blood from the lamb was used to draw marks over the outside doors of Jewish houses so their newborn would be spared from death. (The description of this event is found in the book of Exodus in the Bible, chapters XII onward.) The sacrifice of this lamb was the first sign of freedom for the Hebrews, for the lamb was a god to the Egyptians. To the enslaved people, the sacrifice of a god was an enormous gesture of trust and hope.

2. The roasted egg signifies the sacrifice that was carried to each pilgrimage festivity. It is also a symbol of mourning for the destruction of the Temple of Jerusalem.

3. *Haroset* is a paste usually made from grated apples mixed with

nuts, cinnamon, red wine, and ginger, or dates, nuts, and apples. It represents the mortar the Hebrews used to bind the bricks to build cities and monuments for the Pharoah.

4. *Maror*, bitter herbs and vegetables, may be Romaine lettuce, endives, radishes, black radishes, or horseradish, according to the community's custom. It is a reminder of the bitterness of slavery, as the Egyptians did more than just over-work the Hebrews. They degraded them psychologically and physically, beating them and forcing them to live under conditions that were so precarious, it was as if the Hebrews themselves were delivering their children to a certain death.

5. *Karpas*, a herb with leaves—usually either parsley or celery—represents the leaves used to smear the blood of the *Pesach* lamb over the doors of Hebrew homes.

6. The salt water in goblets represents the sweat and tears of the enslaved Hebrew people in Egypt.

7. The *matzoh*. There are three cakes, symbolizing either the three patriarchs: Abraham, Isaac, and Jacob, or the three groups of Jewish people: the Cohen, Levi, and Israel. During the *seder*, four glasses of wine are drunk, representing the four languages of freedom used in the Bible to recount the Exodus from Egypt. To further emphasize the importance of the liberation and freedom, the four glasses of wine are drunk leaning on the left elbow, because during the time the *seder* was instituted (the Roman Era) only free men could recline on sofas as they ate.

The end of the *seder* is marked by the eating of the *afikoman*, a small piece of the *matzah*, which is hidden and then found. The word afikoman originates from the Greek, and means dessert, but the Hassidic masters have traced the etymology of the word to the Armaic phrase "Bring on the questioning!" (*Afik-nameh*).

The *seder* ends with the singing of songs, the most well-known being the story of the "One kid, that my father bought for two *zuzim*..." After the second evening of *Pesach*, each night is counted for a forty-nine day period. This continues until *Shavout* (Pentecost). This period is called the *omer*.

LAG BA-OMER

The period of forty-nine days between *Pesach* (Passover) and *Shavout* (Jewish Pentecost) is called the omer. The thirty-third day of this period is called the *Lag Ba-Omer* and is commemorated by a series of pilgrimages and outdoor festivities. The word *omer* has a number of meanings. During biblical times, an *omer* designated a sheaf of new barley. The forty-nine days—seven weeks—between *Pesach* and *Shavout* is called *omer* because an *omer* of barley was brought as an offering of the first fruits of the harvest to the Temple starting on the second day of the Passover holidays.

Lag Ba-Omer is the thirty-third day of the *omer* period. *Lag* written in Hebrew is *lamed gimmel*. *Lamed* has a numerical value of thirty and *gimmel* a numerical value of three, therefore *lag* = 30 + 3 = 33 and *Lag Ba-Omer* is the thirty-third day of the *omer*. The *omer* was originally a very joyous observance of the period of waiting leading up to the Feast of the Revelation of the Torah. This is the period between the Exodus from Egypt and the revelation of the Torah forty-nine days later, during which the Hebrews prepared themselves to receive the Law. And the days during which the Temple was being built constituted a period of joy and celebration linked to the harvest. After the destruction of the Temple, the *omer* became a period of mourning and marriages were forbidden during its observance. How did this come about? According to various schools of thought, several different reasons can be given. We will only cite a few here.

In the year 132 C.E., Israel was under Roman occupation. Certain Jews formed resistance movements and a revolt—a last attempt at independence—broke out under the leadership of Bar-Kokhba. Rabbi Akiva, one of the most eminent masters of the Talmud, supported the revolt because he believed Bar-Kokhba to be the Messiah. But the

Romans crushed the insurrection and Bar-Kokhba succumbed at Bethar in 135 C.E. after a heroic defense.

Following this, the Romans massacred ten great masters of the Talmud, including Rabbi Akiva. The failure of this revolt and the loss of these ten great talmudic figures are mourned during the *omer*.

We mourn for another reason, also in connection with Rabbi Akiva. Rabbi Akiva was the leader of thousands of disciples who brought glory to Israel. But they fell prey to a plague epidemic during the period of the *omer*, which miraculously ended on the thirty-third day. This is why *Lag Ba-Omer* is a half-holiday.

This same day is considered to be the anniversary of the death of Rabbi Shimon bar Yokhai, one of the great founders of the Kabbalah. It is therefore customary to make a pilgrimage to his tomb in Meron, a small village next to Safed in Galilee. The pilgrimage is named the *hillula* of Rabbi Shimon bar Yokhai, and is still celebrated throughout the world by excursions into the country and pilgrimages to the tombs of the holy men.

It is customary to place a small stone on the tomb of the person one is visiting. This practice has several origins, one of which can be derived from wordplay. The word "stone" in Hebrew is pronounced even and written *aleph-bet-nun*. These three letters also represent "father": *av* and "son": *ben*, which, when written together, form the word even, meaning stone. By placing a stone on the tomb we situate ourselves as a son of the deceased, as part of his bloodline and memory.

THE KADDISH

The *Kaddish,* one of the most widely known Jewish prayers, is recited during mourning. Its true meaning is the sanctification of God's name, which continues to be honored despite suffering and mourning. Different customs are followed at the passing away of a loved one: the covering of mirrors, taking off of one's shoes, and even sitting on the floor.

The *Kaddish,* a very old prayer written in Aramaic, is a magnificent hymn to the greatness of God. Before being incorporated into the synagogal liturgy it was originally recited at the closing of the study period. Its function is the separation and articulation of the different parts of prayer.

Later on, the *Kaddish* was also recited by those in mourning at the tomb of their parents or loved ones. It must then be recited during the eleven months that follow the death of a close relative or spouse, three times a day, at morning, afternoon, and evening services and in the presence of ten people or the *minyan.* Even though the *Kaddish* does not, in itself, contain any reference to death, a passage evoking the resurrection of the dead is added at the burial ceremony. The *Kaddish* is, above all, a hymn of praise to God, signifying "holiness," from the word *kaddosh,* meaning "holy." Those in mourning speak of God's greatness, inviting God Himself to take care of the deceased and to welcome them into the other world untormented. The *Kaddish* has become a popular prayer, synonymous with consolation. It is customary for boys, especially the eldest son, to recite this prayer. In Yiddish, the eldest son is called *kaddish,* as he has the privilege of being called upon to recite this hymn of praise. When a person dies without leaving a child, it is said that he has not left a *kaddish*. Nowadays, it is customary for women as well as men to recite the *Kaddish*.

At the announcement of someone's death, whether the deceased is a loved one or not, one says the benediction *Barukh Dayan Ha-Emet*: "Blessed are You, the True Judge." When a person dies, their loved ones must tear one of their articles of clothing. After the burial, those in mourning go either to the home of the deceased or to another house where it will be possible to respect a seven-day mourning period and have a meal of bread and hard-boiled eggs. Other members of the community provide this meal as a sign of their compassion and solicitude.

SHAVUOT

THE DONATION OF THE LAW AND THE *YESHIVAH*: THE RABBINICAL ACADEMY

Shavuot is the festival of the Revelation of the Torah, including the Ten Commandments. It is one of the three pilgrimage festivals. The word *Shavuot* signifies "weeks" as the festival falls at the end of the period of *omer*, the seven weeks of religious observance which starts with the festival of *Pesach* (Passover).

According to the Hebrew calendar, this festival falls on the sixth day of *Sivan*, generally in the month of June, and lasts a day in Israel and two days in the Diaspora. *Shavuot* combines the Festival of the Revelation of the Torah with the celebration of First Fruits and the Grain Harvest festival. It is a day on which all the synagogues and houses are decorated with green foliage, flowers, fruits, and plants.

The Revelation of the Torah took place in the desert on Mount Sinai. The Hebrews, who had gathered at the foot of the mountain, received the Ten Commandments which were engraved on the Tablets of the Law carried by Moses. Tradition tells us that on that day the Hebrews received the entire Torah with all the commandments. There are 613 commandments in all, consisting of 365 prohibitions and 248 mandatory commandments. These constitute the fundamental principles of Judaism and regulate the life of the Jew in the context of family, society, and his or her surroundings.

At the morning synagogue prayer during *Shavuot*, the Ten Commandments reading is supplemented with a reading from the Book of Ruth, a pastoral evocation of the grain harvests. It is customary during this festival to consume chiefly dairy. There are several reasons for this, one of which is linked to the white color of milk, a symbol of purity. Another possible explanation links this tradition to the date of the festival at the beginning of summer, when lighter foods are eaten. And there is yet another: on the sixth of *Sivan*, the Hebrews received the Torah as well as all the recommendations concerning the ritual slaughter of animals and the separation of meat and dairy foods. At that time, there was neither meat fit for consumption nor the proper utensils to prepare it. The Hebrews, therefore, ate dairy foods, which did not need long preparation.

It is also said that the sixth of *Sivan* is the date on which the baby Moses was saved from the Nile River by the Pharoah's daughter, and that he would only be nursed with milk from a Jewish woman.

Traditionally, the entire night of *Shavuot*, until the small hours of the morning, are spent reading the texts of the Torah, the Talmud, and even the Kabbalah.

Scriptural study is the foundation of Judaism. Setting aside time to study the Torah is one of the most important commandments in Jewish life.

Let us now make a brief visit inside a theological academy. In Hebrew, the academy is called *Beth Hamidrash* or *yeshivah*. If you are accustomed to the religious silence that normally reigns in libraries, you would be surprised by the disorderliness, noise, and constant comings and goings in a *Beth Hamidrash*. The academy, which also serves as a synagogue, and frequently, a dining-hall or place to hold festivities, is the centre of intellectual and spiritual life. Some academies receive hundreds of students, all crowded in the same room and studying out loud at the same time.

Talmudic scholars are not monks: silence is not a rule. Piles of books of all different sizes, opened and closed, are piled high on randomly positioned tables. Students, some sitting or standing, an occasional one with his knee resting on a bench or chair, pore over the texts of the Talmud. Sometimes they study side by side, but more often than not they sit facing each other. They read out loud while rocking back and forth or from side to side, punctuating difficult articulations of reasoning with wide gestures of the thumb, or by thumping impetuously on books, tables, even the shoulder of a study companion, known as the haver. They leaf feverishly through books of commentary which they take from the shelves of the immense bookcases lining the hall.

The protagonists in this "war of meanings" are trying to understand, interpret, and explain texts. Rarely in agreement with each other about the meaning of the passage being studied, these scholars go off to consult the Master who listens, explains and then calmly—at least for a moment—takes a position on the various theses propounded in this passionate dispute.

At a table a little further on, a student has fallen asleep with his arms crossed over his Talmudic text. Next to him, another student sips coffee and smokes a cigarette with a meditative air. Day and night hum with constant movement, the sound of voices and study in the exuberant atmosphere of the *Beth Hamidrash*.

THE DIETARY LAWS

THE LAWS IN THE TORAH
GOVERNING KOSHER COOKING

One of the fundamental principles of Judaism is called the *kashrut*, a generic term covering all dietary laws, such as which animals can or cannot be consumed, and which dietary combinations are forbidden (*taref*).

Food and the culinary arts are at the root of all cultures. Cooked is to raw what culture is to nature. Nourishment is essential to humankind; it was through the acquisition and preparation of food that man came first to speech and then to thought. Dietary customs construct a body of dietary rituals that commemorate and transmit the history of a group of people. They act as a constant reminder of this history, thereby effectively ensuring the group's cohesion.

Basic Jewish dietary prohibitions concern the consumption of certain animals and the mixing of milk and meat, or milk-based foods with meat-based foods. The latter respects the commandment "Thou shalt not seethe a kid in its mother's milk." While there are numerous interpretations of this, we believe it to be a symbolic ritual that permits the separation of the mother from the child to prevent incest.

As for the first prohibition, all animals designated for consumption must be slaughtered by a person who knows the laws governing ritual slaughter (*shekhitah*). This person is called the *Shokhet*. Using a special knife, he slits the animals' throats. The *Shokhet* then lets the blood drain out, never to be consumed. Each piece of meat is soaked in water, salted to get rid of all the blood, and finally rinsed. It is only now that the meat is fit for consumption. Blood is not consumed, as it is considered to symbolize the life and soul of the living being.

Since the Temple's destruction, the table has come to represent the altar, and the meal is one way in which the sacrifices and rituals practiced by the priests are remembered. Because of this, one should eat not only in a state of cleanliness but also purity. It is therefore customary to wash one's hands with a special implement called a *keli* that purifies the hands before each meal at which bread is eaten; bread is considered to be a reminder of the priests' nourishment in the Temple.

With the food and words of the *kashrut*, we enter into a covenant with God. (See also the introductory chapter on the prohibition of consumption of the sciatic nerve.)

THE MIKVAH

THE RITUAL BATH

The *mikvah* is a small pool built according to precise rules. The quantity and source of the water it contains are also regulated. The mikvah is used to purify people and objects.

The *mikvah* must hold at least 175 gallons of water. The term *mikvah* is found in Genesis 1:10. "And the *mikvah* (gathering together of the waters) He called seas." The water of the *mikvah* possesses a purifying virtue. It must be natural and come either from a spring, rain, ice, or snow water. Seas, rivers, lakes, and reservoirs filled with rainwater are also sources of purifying water.

People and objects become unclean for a variety of reasons and they must be washed in the *mikvah*. Uncleanliness in people may be linked to death; for instance, people who have been under the same roof as a dead person are unclean.

Menstrual blood resulting from non-impregnation and the death of an egg renders the female unclean. Sexual relations are forbidden during the period of uncleanliness—the period of menstruation, as well as the seven days following menstruation—and are not re-authorized until the woman has been immersed in the *mikvah*.

The rule requiring women to abstain from sexual relations during their period of uncleanliness, and to then immerse themselves in the *mikvah* constitutes what is called the laws of familial purity (laws of *Niddah*). The immersion in the *mikvah* is called the *tevilah*.

While numerous in the time of the Temple, the occasions of purification and self-purification are now clearly fewer, but the importance of the act has not diminished.

Nowadays, the *mikvah* is used by women on the eve of their wedding and by married women who come to immerse themselves each time after giving birth or menstruating. People who have converted to Judaism also come to the *mikvah*, an immersion that is the origin of baptism.

It is visited by men on the Friday before the Sabbath as well as on the eve of *Yom Kippur*, but these visits are not obligatory. For the Hassidim, immersion in the *mikvah* is a mystical act of rebirth and a drawing nearer to God. Physical purity is inextricably linked to spiritual purity and so the mikvah is indispensable to them, and carried out with great fervor each morning before prayer.

THE CHUPPAH

THE NUPTIAL CANOPY

Couples are wedded under a nuptial canopy called the *chuppah*. In Jewish society, the family, rather than the individual, constitutes the smallest nucleus. Stated in the Torah is an obligation to marry and bring children into the world. The family therefore begins on the day of the wedding. Depending on the community in which they originate, the symbols and customs of the wedding and the nuptial canopy are numerous and extremely diverse. For example, wedding rings can be perfectly circular or slightly squared on their outer surfaces, in accordance to kabbalistic custom. All marriage customs share a common goal: to bring happiness to the young couple and to wish them a fruitful marriage.

For some people, the wedding day is similar to *Yom Kippur*, and is therefore a day of fasting, a day on which the bride and groom are purified of past mistakes and brought together, under the marriage canopy, as pure as newborn babies. The young bride-to-be immerses herself in the *mikvah* several days before the wedding so that she will be physically pure on that important day. Although the bride often wears white, it is not obligatory. This tradition, now adopted in almost every country, comes from a rabbinical law prohibiting married couples from being too richly dressed. This is so as not to bring shame upon those who cannot afford to buy or have beautiful clothes made for their wedding. The white wedding dress is a sort of uniform that permits one to forget social disparities on that sacred day. In this way, for one day, the bride is made to feel like a true queen. The wedding ceremony is generally conducted under the marriage canopy by a rabbi who recites two benedictions from the *erusin* or *Kiddushin* over a cup of wine. The two fiancés drink from the cup and then the bridegroom (*khaltan*) slips a ring on the index finger of the right hand of the bride (*kallah*) while reciting the appropriate sentence. After this, the *ketubbah* or marriage contract is read. In many weddings, this is also the time for speeches. This is followed by the ceremony of the *Nissu'in* in which the seven marriage benedictions are pronounced over a second cup of wine. The wedding is usually concluded with a gesture commemorating the destruction of the Temple of Jerusalem: the young bridegroom crushes a glass under his foot. Then, to symbolize their new intimacy, the newlyweds are brought to a private room where they are left alone for a few moments.

The week after the wedding is a period of rejoicing, during which a feast ending with the seven marriage blessings is held each day.

THE KETUBBAH

THE MARRIAGE CONTRACT

Under the *chuppah*, the rabbi or person conducting the wedding ceremony puts before the bride and groom (the *hallah* and the *khaltan*) a "marriage deed," the *ketubbah*. Literally, the word *ketubbah* means "that which is written," an abbreviation of the expression "written commitment."

The *ketubbah*, which is inaccurately translated as a marriage contract is, in fact, a divorce insurance. It guarantees that in the event of an official separation the husband will give the wife enough money to live on for several years, for however much time it takes her to find a stable situation. It is a standard legal document which is signed by the future husband in the presence of two witnesses before the wedding and given to the young wife during the ceremony.

Written in Aramaic, this document enumerates the husband's obligations, especially financial, to his wife on a daily basis and in the case of a divorce. The oldest existing *ketubbah*, found in the south of Egypt, goes back to the fifth century B.C.E.

For two essential reasons, it inspired the art of calligraphy, illustration, and manuscript illumination. The *ketubbah* is not subject to any restrictions concerning its binding, nor to its size, shape, or lettering. It is associated with marriage, which is, by definition, a joyous occasion. Therefore, all patterns, colors, techniques, and innovations are permitted.

The problem of the *ketubbah* occupies a privileged place in Talmudic law. An entire treatise entitled *Ketubot* details all the legal formulations in the writing of the *ketubbah*. So many points of law are discussed concerning this matter that the *Ketubot* treatise has been called *Shas Katan*: the *miniature* Talmud.

THE BRIS MILAH

CIRCUMCISION

The word *milah* is derived from both the Hebrew verb "to cut"and the verb "to be face to face." It is may also be connected to the root of the Hebrew verb "to speak."

Circumcision is a way of introducing language into the body and bringing the body of the infant into the sphere of language. Circumcision is a sign of the covenant between God and the Hebrew people. Despite persecution, it is one of the obligations that Jews have observed over their entire anguished history. It involves the removal of the foreskin from the penis of a baby boy on the eighth day by a *mohel*, a specialist in this type of procedure. It is at this time that the infant is given his name or names.

According to the scriptures, Abraham was the first person to be circumcized. He was 99 years old at the time. His son, Ishmael, the father of Islam, was circumcized at the age of thirteen, and this is why Moslems circumcize boys at this age. Isaac was circumcized when he was eight days old, and this came to be the rule for later generations of Jews.

The ceremony can take place on any day of the week including the Sabbath or even *Yom Kippur*. But if the infant is too small or is jaundiced, the *bris* is considered dangerous and is postponed until the baby is out of danger. At the moment of circumcision, the baby is placed on a special high-chair called the "Chair of the prophet Elijah" as, traditionally, the prophet Elijah is invited to each circumcision.

The *mohel* uses ancient instruments: a double-edged knife, a stylet or probe that detaches the foreskin from the glans, and the *magen* (shield) that protects the glans during the incision. The ceremony ends with the giving of the blessing specific to circumcision, followed by a *seudah* or feast.

Gentiles are also circumcized when they convert. If they are already circumcized, it is sufficient to spill a drop of blood.

We believe that the incompleteness rendered by circumcision enables human beings to enter into the dimension of language. Circumcision removes a part of the man so that he will experience a sense of loss or incompleteness. This leads him to reconstruct and reinvent himself. Obviously, one would ask, "What is the form of circumcision for females?" In the dialectical relationship between man and woman, the woman already carries this loss which inscribes her in the dynamic of desire. She does not therefore need to be circumcized.

THE BAR MITZVAH

AND THE *BAT MITZVAH*: THE RELIGIOUS AGE OF MAJORITY

The age of majority in Judaism is thirteen for boys and twelve for girls. This joyous and festive occasion marks a very important step in the life of an adolescent.

From a religious point of view at thirteen, a Jewish boy achieves the status of a responsible adult. Literally, *Bar Mitzvah* means "son of the commandment." From this moment on, the child will come under all the obligations of manhood and is held responsible for his actions, both good and bad.

The closest Monday or Thursday to the thirteenth birthday in the Hebrew calendar is the occasion for religious celebrations. On this day of great ceremony, the young boy performs certain rituals for the first time in his life. First of all, he wears the *tefillin* to the synagogue and prays there for the first time. Now that the boy has reached the age of majority, he can be a member of the *minyan*, the quorum of ten men required to say a prayer together. On the Sabbath following the *Bar Mitzvah*, the boy recites the morning or evening service before the entire community. In the morning, he is called upon to read from the Torah, and it is customary to read all or a portion of the week's *parashah* (see the chapter on the scrolls of the Torah). A *seudah* is held either on the Sabbath or during the week. Throughout this ritual meal, the young Bar Mitzvah delivers a speech to demonstrate his capacity to grasp the subtlety of the commentaries on traditional texts.

For girls, there is a ceremony called *Bat Mitzvah* that takes place when a girl turns 12, instead of 13. This is because girls are considered to mature faster than boys. It is only recently that the *Bat Mitzvah* has also become the occasion of a celebration. Nevertheless, although traditions are slowly changing, this has not yet become a general rule.

THE CLOTHING CUSTOMS

HATS, BEARDS, SIDE LOCKS, WIGS, AND SCARVES

With the exception of the *tallith* and the *tefillin*, which are obligatory and essentially the same for all Jews, clothing customs vary from country to country.

Some Jews of Eastern European origin, such as the Hassidim, observe eighteenth-century clothing customs: long black coats, long socks, and a fur-trimmed, wide-brimmed hat called a *shtreimel*.

Other Jews who are from the same region but are disciples of different masters always wear black jackets and trousers, with white shirts and Borsalino-type hats that look like Spanish and Portuguese traditional peasant dress. Certain clothes are only worn on special occasions, such as the long, white robe which drapes the officiating minister on *Yom Kippur* and recalls the dress of the High Priest during the time of the Temple.

The origin of the wearing of beards and sidelocks (called *pe'ot* in Hebrew and *payess* in Yiddish), lies in a biblical prohibition of the use of any cutting or slicing objects on the face. Symbolically, this signifies that man's face must not be the object of aggression, that violence must not be done to the humanity of man.

For women, the emphasis is on modesty (*Tseniuth*). She should, of course, be dressed in a modest fashion, but above all, she must keep her head covered if she is married.

The head may be covered by a scarf, like North African women, by a wig or *shaytl*, worn by women from Eastern Europe, or even a beret or small hat for more modern young women.

THE KIPPAH

A SMALL, EMBROIDERED
OR PLAIN CLOTH SKULLCAP THAT MEN
WEAR ON THEIR HEADS

The shape and size of the *kippah*, often referred to as the *yarmulka*, differs depending on the community. In the Braslav communities (mystic Jews originating from Russia), the *kippah* is very large and covers the whole head. It is embroidered, white or cream-colored and has a little pompon on the top. In Orthodox Sephardic communities (Jews from Spain and Portugal and their descendants), the *kippah* is worn under a black hat and is clearly smaller than the Braslavian *kippah*. It is also embroidered, but black in color.

In Orthodox Ashkenazic communities of German or Eastern European origins, the *kippah* is also worn under a black hat but is made of black cloth. In those non-Orthodox communities that accept modernity and are, in general, Zionist—those who recognize the legitimacy and centrality of the state of Israel—the *kippah* is embroidered, knitted, or tatted, and can be of any color. In reality, the Torah states no obligation regarding the wearing of the *kippah*; rather, it is a custom which has become obligatory through the passing of time.

Since the eighteenth century, the *kippah*, which has gradually replaced the turban among Sephardic Jews and the large hats among the Ashkenazim, has become a sign of piety and Jewish identity. The exact meaning of the *kippah* is not known; above all it is a sign of man's humility in his relationship to God.

Man may place a symbolic limit above his head as a sign of his finite nature. But the *kippah* can also be seen as the necessity of placing a limit above one self in order to overcome and go beyond it.

THE TEMPLE

AND ITS MEMORY: THE WESTERN
OR WAILING WALL. THE *KOTEL*

Since the beginning of time, man has needed specific places for worship and prayer. The first Hebrews built an Ark, or *Mishkan*, (house of God), which accompanied them during the forty years in the desert. Later, this traveling temple was replaced by a more permanent one built by King Solomon.

Built on Mount Moriah in Jerusalem, the Temple is the House of God, the centre of worship for the Jewish people.

King Solomon had the first Temple built in the tenth century B.C.E. on one of Jerusalem's hills, Mount Moriah, that was acquired by his father, King David, for this very purpose. The construction lasted seven years and resulted in a magnificent building that housed the Holy of Holies and the Holy Ark, the incense altar of perfumes, and the Golden Candelabrum, as well as many other cult objects to which Solomon added.

The Temple was 60 cubits (8 feet) long, 20 cubits (2.5 feet) wide, and 30 cubits (4 feet) high. It had a high portico, sculpted cedar-paneled walls and solidly barred windows. The Ark of the Covenant was reached through a cyprus and olive-wood door covered in gold. In the Holy of Holies, the most sacred place in the House of God, cherubim with outspread wings, colocynths, and flowers in bloom were carved out of cedar and olive-wood, and covered in a layer of pure gold.

The floor, walls, and ceiling were also covered in gold. On the two bronze pillars at the entrance of the Temple, Solomon had the word *Yakhin* engraved on the pillar on the right and *Boaz* on the pillar on the left.

During King Solomon's reign, the Temple was the center of worship. Daily sacrifices were made there, as well as all Sabbath and festival sacrifices. Three times a year, during the pilgrimage festivals, the entire population would go the Temple to offer the sacrifice specific to the festival. After King Solomon died, the kingdom was divided and the central role of the Temple diminished considerably.

The first Temple was destroyed in 586 B.C.E. by Nebuchadnezzar. Ezra and Nehemiah had it rebuilt and it was inaugurated in 516 B.C.E. The second Temple, which Herod had restored and expanded, was destroyed in year 70 C.E. by Titus and his Roman army.

According to tradition, the first Temple was destroyed as a result of idolatry, incest, and the shedding of blood and the second, because of gratuitous hatred among the Jews. The anniversary of the destruction of the two Temples on the 9th of the month of *Av*, is a day of great mourning and fasting for the Jewish people.

The masters of the tradition had the foresight to build another Temple immediately after the destruction of the second — an invisible temple of spirit and study. It is the creation of Rabbi Yochanan ben Zakkai, who asked one thing of Vespasian when he became Roman emperor: "Permit me to build a school in the city of Yavneh." Thus an "invisible building" was constructed that could never be destroyed, a living culture constantly renewed through the reading of texts and the infinite movement of their commentaries.

THE MAGEN DAVID

THE STAR OF DAVID

The *Magen David*, or Star of David, is the most widely known symbol of Judaism. Literally, *Magen David* means "Shield of David." It is a geometric sign formed by two intertwined, equilateral triangles. This symbol, often inscribed in a circle, was common to many peoples several centuries before the common era.

It was not until the fourteenth century that this geometric motif was definitively associated with the expression "*Magen David*" in a kabbalistic work.

Generally, its purpose was to provide protection from demons and evil spirits and it has only very recently become the symbol of the Jewish people. It now appears on all sorts of cult objects, from Europe to the confines of Russia.

In his book, *Star of Redemption*, Franz Rosenzweig attributes an essential idea to each point of the star: Creation, Redemption and Revelation, Humanity, the world, and God.

In 1897, the first Zionist Congress chose the *Magen David* as its emblem, and it later became the central emblem of the Israeli flag; the much more ancient and authentic *Menorah* symbolizes the State. In his book, *Jewish Messianism*, Gershom Scholem argues that the sanctity of an authentic living symbol has been conferred upon the *Magen David* by the segregation and degradation, the annihilation, the humiliation, and the horror that drove millions of people marked with this yellow star to the gas chambers.

Under this sign, the Jews were assassinated and, under this same sign, which has become worthy of illuminating the path to life and reconstruction, the Jews have become reunited in Israel. It is precisely because of the ultimate humiliation, suffering, and terrifying finality with which this symbol has become so charged that it has acquired such noble title and bearing.

SYMBOLS
OF
CATHOLICISM

BY DOM ROBERT LE GALL

THE TRINITY

THE MYSTERY OF A SINGLE GOD IN THREE BEINGS IS THE SOURCE OF ALL UNITY AND ALL COMMUNION

The foremost symbol of Christianity is that of the Holy Trinity, which is altogether as abstract as a mathematical sign. The Trinity designates the unity of three divine beings, the Father, the Son, and the Holy Spirit, as a *triune*. From this word that mysterious and unfathomable equation 3=1 and 1=3 is derived. Although unique, God is indivisibly made up of three persons. The posing of this undemonstrable axiom, the beginning and the end of all things, explains nothing, and this notion of a triunal and absolute unity barely touches us.

The abstract Trinity is visually portrayed through the geometric symbol of an equilateral triangle, which is often a feature at the top of baroque altarpieces. The three angles and the three sides are equal, but they constitute only a single surface. An eye is depicted in the center of the triangle to show that God sees all—but this single eye, in its cyclopean force, does not so much suggest a look of love as that terrible conscience that pursues Victor Hugo's Cain in "La Conscience."

The word "trinity" allows us to express the mystery of a single God in three beings. According to the three monotheistic religions of Judaism, Christianity, and Islam, God can only be unique, for any multiplicity would be a sign of insufficiency or weakness. As is demonstrated in Greek and Roman mythology, several gods inevitably become adversaries. As the inheritor of Israel's monotheism, Christianity considers that a single God is nevertheless not solitary. First and foremost, Love exists within him and he spreads it throughout his creation. The mystery of God is a mystery of mutual love, of procreation. Our daily experience of life makes it easy for us to understand what a father is, or a son, or a sigh of love. As the origin of all things, God is not a being who is locked up inside himself, but is at the same time a Father full of tenderness, a Son who is the apple of his eye, and a Spirit of love, which is a living link between them.

The Old Testament, which Jews and Christians alike venerate as the Word of God, already reveals this divine fatherhood. The prophet Hosea expressed it in these astonishing terms: "I myself taught Ephraim to walk, I myself took them by the arm, but they did not know that I was the one caring for them, that I was leading them with human ties, with leading-strings of love, that, with them, I was like someone lifting an infant to his cheek, and that I bent down to feed him" (Hosea 11:3-4). Isaiah adds that this fatherly love also contains maternal tenderness: "Can a woman forget her baby at the breast, feel no pity for the child she has borne? Even if these were to forget, I shall not forget you" (Isaiah 49:15).

His only Son came to reveal that Father full of tenderness, whose eternal love fills the New Testament.[1] It was first to Mary, the future mother of the Messiah, that the Archangel Gabriel revealed the mystery of a single God in three persons. The Immaculate Conception of the Son of the Almighty was to be the work of the third person of the Trinity, the Spirit of Love. The whole of the Trinity was expressed at the moment of the Annunciation.[2]

The Gospel according to Saint John defines the relationship between Christ and his Father, who are one. According to the divine plan, we should participate with the Spirit in that unity between Father and Son.[3] That is why Saint Paul's epistles are scattered with Trinitarian formulations, such as the following salutation: "The grace of the Lord Jesus Christ, the love of God, and the fellowship of the Holy Spirit be with you all" (2 Corinthians 13:13).

We are baptized in the love that unites the three divine persons: the sacrament—which is dispensed in the name of the Father, and of the Son, and of the Holy Spirit—is recognized by all three Christian confessions (Catholic, Orthodox, and Protestant). Love and friendship are emotions that we experience in our daily lives. They inspire in us a lasting communion with other people, but without causing a total fusion between individuals. As a guide towards divine love, the Trinity presents us with a perfect example of total communion, because its three persons are of one substance, and yet distinct.

There are numerous representations of the Trinity in Christian art. In contrast to Jews and Muslims who, in their infinite respect, refuse any depiction of God—this is the meaning of the commandment that Yahweh gave Moses on Mount Sinai[4]—Catholics and Orthodox Christians justify making images of God by the mystery of the Incarnation. Since one of the persons of the Trinity became man, it is then possible to depict him as a human in paintings or sculptures, and simple examples of this had already appeared in early Christianity. Similarly, the Holy Spirit, which manifested itself in the form of a dove, can be thus depicted. Nobody has ever seen the Father, the divine "source."

The oldest representation of the Trinity depicts the baptism of Christ: "And at once, as he was coming up out of the water, [Jesus] saw the heavens torn apart and the Spirit, like a dove, descending on him. And a voice came from heaven, 'You are my Son, the Beloved; my favor rests on you'" (Mark 1:10-12). The iconographic tradition depicts the hand of the Father emerging from the clouds to point out his Son, who already has the dove of the Spirit fluttering above him.

Much later, depicted as an old man with abundant hair, a bushy beard, and occasionally wearing a crown, a seated Father can be seen bearing up the Cross on which his Son has died, while the dove flutters between their two heads.

An episode in the story of Abraham was, from the days of the early Church, often used to evoke the mystery of the Trinity: the visit to him of three angels who are, in the biblical text, referred to alternately in the singular and plural (Genesis 18:1-15), and in whom Christian tradition sees a prefiguration of the Trinity. As early as the fifth century, this scene can be found among the mosaics of Santa Maria Maggiore in Rome, which were commissioned by Pope Sixtus III. It can also be seen depicted in Ravenna. The monk Andrei Rublev's famous icon of the Trinity has become a familiar image, but it in fact depicts the visit of the three angels to Abraham. Their gazes are drawn in a circle, expressing their mutual love, and this circle is centered on a lamb, in the middle of the altar-table around which they are sitting. We too may enter into this circle of love through the sacrifice of the Eucharist, which gives us access to that supreme love demonstrated by Christ the Savior on the Cross.

The eucharistic prayer in fact finishes with a Trinitarian statement, which reveals all the meaning of the mystery of Christianity: "Through him Christ, with him, in him, in the unity of the Holy Spirit, all glory and honor is yours Almighty Father, for ever and ever." To which the entire congregation replies with a resounding Amen (in Hebrew "truly, assuredly").

1. "No one has ever seen God; it is the only Son, who is close to the Father's heart, who has made him known" (John 1:18).
2. "The Holy Spirit will come upon you, and the power of the Most High will cover you with its shadow. And so the child will be holy and will be called Son of God" (Luke 1:35).
3. John 17:20-21 (loc. cit.)
4. "You shall not make yourself a carved image or any likeness of anything in heaven above..." (Exodus 20:4).

JESUS CHRIST

THE SON OF GOD BECAME MAN
TO SHARE OUR CONDITION AND ENABLE US
TO PARTICIPATE IN HIS DIVINITY

As far as historians are concerned, there is no doubt as to the actual existence of Jesus. It is attested that he lived two thousand years ago, at the beginning of our system of dating. He was crucified by order of Pontius Pilate and, during the following centuries, the faith that he inspired among his disciples was to become a determining factor in the history of the Roman Empire, and the rest of the western world. At the turn of the third millennium, this faith is still flourishing.

The Christian faith professes that Jesus is the Son of God, that he himself is God. As we have already pointed out, the divine plan is to bring about the salvation of mankind by offering us the chance to enter into communion with the three persons of the Trinity, the Father, the Son, and the Holy Spirit. In order to allow us to participate in this mystery, it was necessary to create a living connection with us, and this was done through the Incarnation. One of the three became one of us, he came to share in our human condition so that we might dwell in their love. The mystery of the Trinity is, then, part of the mystery of the Incarnation: the Son of God became "the Son of Man."

This mystery is the inspiration behind some fundamental sections of the New Testament, and in particular the poetic prologue to the Gospel according to Saint John: "In the beginning was the Word: the Word was with God and the Word was God... The Word became flesh, he lived among us, and we saw his glory... No one has ever seen God; it is the only Son, who is close to the Father's heart, who has made him known" (John 1:1; 14:18). The "Word," in its primary sense, here signifies the word conceived in the thought of God. This God born of God (*Credo*) was born in Bethlehem of the Virgin Mary, an event celebrated by the festival of Christmas.

The Son of God was announced under the name of Jesus—in Hebrew Yehoshuah or Yeshuah—which literally means "Yahweh has saved," or, more simply, "salvation." When the Angel of the Lord appears to Joseph in the first pages of the New Testament, he explains to him the essence of this mission of salvation.[1]

Jesus has been given the additional name of "Christ," which, in Greek, means "anointed" (*christos*), which is also the meaning of the Hebrew "Messiah" (*mashiach*). The Christian tradition in fact recognizes his triple anointment as king, prophet, and priest, which makes of him simultaneously the heir to King David and the great prophet whom. Israel was awaiting (and whom the Jews are still awaiting today). The anointment that he received is that of the Holy Spirit, the Love that unites the persons of the Trinity, and that was clearly expressed by the Father during his baptism in the Jordan.[2] When they are baptized, then confirmed, Christians also receive this anointment of the Holy Spirit and so become other christs, for Jesus was to be "the eldest of many brothers" (Romans 8:29).

Jesus can also be called Immanuel, which the Angel of the Lord (who we have already mentioned) translates as "God-is-with-us."[3] Immanuel has, in the unity of his being, both divine and human nature "without confusion, without change, without division, without separation," according to the venerable phrase of the Council of Chalcedon. At once God and man, he becomes the mediator of a New Covenant, he is the "bridge" between heaven and earth. This is the true meaning of "pontiff" (in Latin *pontifex*, a "bridge-builder"). At the head of the priesthood, the Sovereign Pontiff represents the Priest-Christ in his role as a mediator, just as each bishop does in his diocese.

From this mystery of the Incarnation, conceived as an act of mediation, Christianity derives a full range of symbolism: a physical gesture such as the laying-on of hands, or earthly produce such as water, bread, and wine, take on a spiritual dimension in the sacraments. By becoming man, Christ magnifies all of our images, since the depiction of God now becomes possible. The excesses caused by the creation of images even brought about a violent quarrel, which led to the eighth-century movement of iconoclasm. The Second Council of Nicaea settled the question in 787 by the resolution that holy images were orthodox.

Both the West and the East have faithfully observed these commands. They have created a large cultural heritage of masterpieces depicting the Son of God as a man, from the Good Shepherd of the Catacombs to Rouault's Christ. Mosaics, frescoes, statues, paintings, and eastern icons have been produced by image-makers in prayer and fasting. Churches and museums teem with paintings of a highly religious inspiration. Only the Reformation of Calvin, for whom God was a spirit, forbade any decoration with such images on the bare, austere altars on which the sacred rite is celebrated. The Lutherans have adopted a more moderate position.

Jesus's divine humanity is perfectly expressed in the Transfiguration, which revealed his human face illuminated with divine glory before the apostles Peter, James, and John. The Transfiguration was intended to strengthen their faith just at the moment when Christ was about to pass from this world to his Father's side by means of the Cross of Redemption. It lights up the disfigured face of the crucified Christ, who had sacrificed himself completely to the very end of his life on earth .[4]

1. "You must name him Jesus, because he is the one who is to save his people from their sins" (Matthew 1:21). The identity of Jesus is abbreviated in the letters of the Greek word *ichthus* (fish): "Jesus Christ, Son of God, Savior." This is why, in the catacombs, the fish is one of the symbols of Christ.
2. "This is my Son, the Beloved; my favor rests on him" (Matthew 3:17).
3. Matthew 1:23. Cf. also Isaiah 7:14
4. "There in their presence he was transfigured: his face shone like the sun... " (Matthew 17:2).

THE CROSS

THE CROSS ON WHICH JESUS DIED
FOR OUR SALVATION REMAINS A SIGN
OF COMPLETE SELF-SACRIFICE

In its combination of the horizontal and vertical axes, which thus embrace the whole symbolism of the cardinal points, the cross has established itself in every culture and in all religions. The intersection of these two lines is a point of meeting, of convergence and of synthesis. Conversely, the cross also evokes images of torture, suffering, and confrontation.

The Cross of Christ contains this dual symbolism since it is at once the sacrificial altar, which must reconcile mankind to itself and bring it nearer to God, and also the instrument of execution on which Jesus died. The cross is without doubt Christianity's most widespread and immediately recognized symbol and we must now try to grapple with its true significance.

Jesus had come to earth with a mission of redemption and "went about doing good" (Acts 10:38), but he became a target for the jealousy of his nation's religious leaders, whose small-mindedness he protested against. The power of his preaching and the size of the movement that he had created made them plot against him, and they were to triumph at the moment of Easter. Pontius Pilate, the Roman Procurator of Judea, gave way in spite of himself under the Jews' pressure and condemned him to death for the capital offense of claiming to be the Son of God. But, for Christians, Jesus's death was not the end of his destiny. Christ was resurrected and dwells at his Father's right hand. Like Moses and Jeremiah, Jesus had to bear the brunt of his people's refusal "by taking their guilt on himself" (Isaiah 53:11) and, by his death and resurrection, fulfill Isaiah's prophecy: "Ill-treated and afflicted, he never opened his mouth, like a lamb led to the slaughterhouse" (Isaiah 53:7). Christ was not ignorant of this destiny, which was clearly stated from the beginning of the Gospels when John the Baptist presents Jesus as the Lamb of God.[1] He walked on knowingly towards his destiny and announced his imminent suffering and death on three occasions to his apostles.[2]

This "paschal" suffering by execution and death in fact obeys a mysterious necessity in the divine plan of salvation, as Jesus, when resurrected, explained to the disciples of Emmaus: "Was it not necessary that the Christ should suffer before entering into his glory?" (Luke 24:26). The humiliation that Christ suffered and the crucifixion are, for Saint John the Evangelist, nothing less than a royal investiture. Pilate asks him if he is a king, and the soldiers mock him by calling him "king of the Jews."[3] On Pilate's own orders,[4] and in latter-day representations, the cross carries a notice bearing four letters: I.N.R.I. (*Iesus, Nazarenus Rex Iudeorum*), "Jesus the Nazarene, King of the Jews." The only way to understand Jesus's willing sacrifice is by seeing it as the supremely lucid expression of his love for us and for his Father.[5] This love is such that the Son of God unreservedly submitted himself to the plan which the Father had made for our salvation. This is how he spoke before the Passion, in his last conversations with the apostles: "The prince of this world is on his way. He has no power over me, but the world must recognize that I love the Father and that I act just as the Father commanded" (John 14:30-31).

The Cross of Glory is, then, the ultimate revelation of perfect love. Its importance is explained to us by Jesus during the Last Supper, when he inaugurates the sacrament of the eucharist.[6] Some depictions of the crucifixion link it to the symbolism of the Trinity, in the same way that has been described for the baptism of Christ: a dove, symbolizing the Holy Spirit, hovers above the crucified figure. Indeed, the Son of God died as a man on the cross and "gave up his spirit" (John 19:30), that is to say that he communicated the Holy Spirit to us.

The water and the blood that flowed from his pierced side gave birth to the Church. A certain similarity can be seen here with the birth of Eve, whom God had shaped from Adam's rib.[7] The Church Fathers also say that the Cross is the nuptial bed on which the Church, the Bride of God, is impregnated by Christ the Bridegroom.[8]

The Cross is thus at the center of the history of the Christian world. The motto of the Carthusian order is even: *Stat crux dum volvitur orbis*, "the Cross stands firm in the swirling of this world." That is why our universe is full of crosses. Most churches are built in the shape of a cross: the nave and the choir form the vertical axis, the transept (made up of two wings) the horizontal one. The fact that the choir is often off-center can be explained by the way the crucified Christ's head leant to one side when he "gave up his spirit." Inside the church, the twelve crosses of consecration symbolize the "Apostles of the Lamb" (Revelation 21:14). Christians often wear a cross around their necks, and the pectoral cross is the distinguishing mark of prelates. Christian tombs have, since antiquity, been marked by a cross.

The sign of the cross, which is used to give the blessing, joins the mystery of the Holy Trinity to the mystery of Redemption because, while tracing the cross, the names of the three persons are pronounced: "In the name of the Father [on the forehead], and of the Son [down to the waist] and of the Holy Spirit [from the left to the right shoulder, or the other way round for the Orthodox]. Amen." This symbolic progression summarizes life in its entirety, inspired by a love that carries on through to the end and, which, going beyond our sufferings and our death, leads us to eternal life with Christ.

1. "The next day... [John] said, 'Look, there is the lamb of God that takes away the sin of the world'" (John 1:29).
2. Matthew 16:21; 17:22-23; 20:18-19
3. John 18:33-37; 19:3-14
4. John 19:19
5. John 13:1
6. Matthew 26:26-28
7. John 19:34 and Genesis 2:21-24
8. Ephesians 5:25-27

THE VIRGIN MARY

THE CONSECRATED IMAGE OF MATERNAL TENDERNESS, THE MOTHER OF GOD DRAWS US STRAIGHT TO THE HEART OF DIVINE LOVE

The Archangel Gabriel announced to the Virgin Mary that she was going to conceive a son, who would be the descendant of David and whose reign would be everlasting. This designated him as the Messiah Israel had been waiting for. The Annunciation holds an important place in Europe's cultural heritage and has been painted on numerous occasions. The moment when Mary was summoned to become the Mother of the Savior, and our Mother too, is the basis of her dignity.

We have already pointed out that the complete Trinity is presented to Mary in the announcement of Gabriel, who has been sent by the Father, as a messenger of the Incarnation of the Son, which will take place through the agency of the Holy Spirit. This divine plan of salvation mysteriously hangs on the agreement of a humble maiden from Nazareth. She gives it in her *Fiat*: "You see before you the Lord's servant, let it happen [in Latin, *fiat*] to me as you have said" (Luke 1:38).

Mary gives birth to the baby Jesus in Bethlehem. Forty days later he is presented at the Temple of Jerusalem. Wise Men from the East come to worship him, then King Herod's jealousy forces the holy family to hide for a time in Egypt. After the king's death, Joseph, Mary, and Jesus return to Nazareth where, for the next twenty years, Jesus grows up in obscurity.

Mary has a discreet role to play in the New Testament. Leaving aside the stories of Jesus's childhood in Matthew and Luke, what comes out most strongly is the important episode at the marriage feast in Cana where, following his mother's suggestion, he turns water into wine, the miracle that marks the beginning of his public life.[1] Mary is then seen again standing by the Cross. Just before dying, Jesus points out John, the "disciple whom he loved," and says to her: "Woman, this is your son." He then confirms this by saying to the disciple: "This is your mother."[2] The scene shows us that, when dying, Christ gave us his mother. Seven weeks later, while waiting for Pentecost, Mary is praying ardently with the apostles and is among them when the Holy Spirit comes down in the shape of tongues of fire.[3]

Mary is thus present at the essential moments of Jesus's birth, his death and the founding of the Church. The early councils of the undivided Church profess her discreet yet essential place in the plan of salvation. She is at the heart of the *Credo*, the profession of faith: "By the power of the Holy Spirit, he took flesh of the Virgin Mary and became man." Mary is not a female divinity. She is God's humble servant, but becomes his mother according to the nature of humanity. She provides Christ's human side, just as the Father provides his divine nature. It is then easy to understand how profound her relationship is with the Father and the Son, as well as with the Holy Spirit who impregnated her. Mary can be said to be the human revelation of God's maternal tenderness.

As the centuries passed, the devotion of the Catholics and the

Orthodox to Mary continually increased. On the other hand, the Reformation considered that mankind's addresses to the Virgin—which were at times excessive and exclusive—were an offense to Christ's unique role as mediator. The Catholic Church believes that Mary has a maternal mediatory influence with her Son, and tradition dubs her *Omnipotentia supplex* ("the all-powerful suppliant"). The Dogmatic Constitution of the Church in the Second Vatican Council teaches that: "Mary's function as mother of men in no way obscures or diminishes this unique mediation of Christ, but rather shows its power" (N°60). Mary is the Mother of God and the Mother of the Church, but she is neither above God nor above the Church. "She is hailed as pre-eminent and as a wholly unique member of the Church" (N°53). In the image of the Mystical Body of Christ, she is not the Head, but the Neck, through which all her influence flows. The Church, the bride of God, is also a virgin and a mother.

The liturgical calendar shows the importance of Mary's place in Christian life. Following the chronological order of her life, her first festival is that of the Immaculate Conception, on December 8. This dogma, which was fixed by Pope Pius IX in 1854, professes that the Virgin was preserved from original sin in anticipation of the Redemption. Nine months later, on September 8, comes the Nativity of the Virgin; her presentation at the Temple is celebrated on November 21. March 25 (nine months before Christmas) is the Annunciation of the Lord to Mary. On May 31, the Visitation commemorates her welcome by her cousin Elizabeth. Each year, January 1 is the festival of Mary's divine Motherhood. The Presentation of the Lord at the Temple, or Candlemas, is on February 2. Our Lady of Dolours is celebrated on September 15 and her Assumption on August 15 (this dogma was established by Pope Pius XII in 1950). October 7 is the Feast of the Holy Rosary. Hardly a month goes by without there being a celebration of the Virgin Mary, leaving aside local festivals and countless pilgrimages of the Virgin.

The Rosary that has just been alluded to is a recitation of "Hail Marys" in fifteen decades, made up of five joyful, five sorrowful, and five glorious mysteries. It is known as the "poor man's Psalter": the number of prayers thus pronounced—150—being the same as the number of psalms. By means of a humble repetitive prayer, which can be found in all religions (such as the Orthodox "Prayer of Jesus"), the Rosary enables us to enter alongside Mary into the mystery of salvation.

1. John 2:1-12
2. John 1:26-27
3. Acts 1:14; 2:1-4

THE CHURCH

THE CHURCH IS THE ASSEMBLY OF THE PEOPLE OF GOD SERVED BY THE BISHOPS, PRIESTS, AND DEACONS

The Church is often considered to be an institution that is at once solid and fragile, firm and overbearing, whose religious and moral demands are excessive or outdated. Throughout history, the Church and Churches have experienced tensions, schisms, and scandals. The mystery of the Church lies elsewhere. As the Latin and Greek word *ecclesia* suggests, it is an "assembly" which has been called together (from the Greek verb *ek-kaleein*). The first of these "assemblies," which marked the birth of the People of God, took place on Mount Sinai after the escape from Egypt.[1] It consists in a liturgy of Covenant, from the Greek *leitourgia*, which originally meant any service given to the community by one or several of its members. In this case it is first God who "serves" his people, even before they "serve" him. The liturgy is the work of God and of his people, which is renewed in the New Testament with the mystery of Pentecost.

The first symbolic reality of Christianity is the Trinity; we shall be returning to this fundamental element throughout this book. The Church's true identity is in the union of the faithful tied up with the mystery of the Trinity as defined by Saint Irenaeus, bishop of Lyons and second-century martyr: "Hence the universal Church is to be a people brought into unity from the unity of the Father, the Son, and the Holy Spirit." [2] Churches are places where the Church comes together. In architectural splendor, hewn stones must receive living ones.

The People of God take the primary place in the Church. They are the Bride of God summoned to join herself with her God, depicted throughout the Bible and The *Song of Songs*. According to the New Testament, the Groom of this Bride is the incarnated Son, whose wedding day has been prepared for him by the Father. [3] In the Book of Revelation, this image is linked to that of the Holy City. [4] Quite the opposite of the Tower of Babel, the builders of which wished to unite themselves against God and violate his kingdom, the Church is a gift of God which comes down from heaven, and thus is "a sign and instrument, that is, of community with God and of unity among all men" (*Lumen gentium*, N°1).

To this nuptial image, Saint Paul adds the image of the Mystical Body of Christ: he is the head and we are the members. [5] This is where it becomes necessary to organize the People of God, so that each person should play his part, like the members of a body, and the hierarchy of the bishops grouped around the Pope is at its service. "For you, I am a bishop; with you, I am a Christian," said Augustine to the faithful of Hippo. These two complementary symbols affirm how profound the unity is that exists between Christ and the Church. This nuptial mystery makes the assembly of Christians into "the Full Son," the temple of the Holy Spirit, begotten of the Father, whom they invoke as *Abba* ("papa" in Armenian).

Christ entrusted his Church to Saint Peter. Despite the persecutions of the early Christians in the Roman Empire, Saint Peter carried out his mission by going to Rome and living there until he too was martyred. This is why Saint Peter is considered to be the first Bishop of Rome, and his successors bore the same title. When the Emperor Constantine was himself converted to Christianity (312-

313) and the Bishop of Rome started to exercise his ministry in S. Giovanni in Laterano, Saint Peter's tomb in the Vatican's necropolis began to be venerated, and a magnificent basilica soon rose there, which has been enriched throughout the centuries. The Council of Chalcedon (450-451) consecrated the primacy of the Bishop of Rome and entrusted him with the mission of attending to the unity of the Church, thus making the capital of the Western Empire, badly shaken by barbarian invasions, into the capital of the Christian world.

Christians, however, have not been able to avoid some painful separations. Since 1054, the Orthodox Churches have been independent of Rome, even though their faith and spiritual practices are virtually identical. The Churches created by the Reformations of Luther and Calvin have moved even further away from the Catholic Church. As the third millennium approaches, Pope John Paul II launched an appeal for church unity through a commitment to ecumenism in his encyclical of May 25, 1995. Leading by example, he asks us to confess what separates us from unity, to intensify our dialogues and prayers, and even now to live out the unity of all who believe in, Jesus Christ.

The adjective "catholic" expresses the Church's universal vocation, for "universal" is precisely what it means in Greek (*katholikos*, from *kath-holou*: "according to all"). The article of the Credo that deals with the Church clearly states this demand for unity: "We believe in one, holy, catholic, and apostolic Church." Ecumenism aims to recover this universal mystery of the Church, since the Greek word oikoumene means "the inhabited world" (from *oikos*, "house") and, by extension, the entirety of the known universe.

The churches in our towns and villages symbolize the unity of the human community. Their steeples, which point up towards heaven, display our common upward desire for God. The East prefers cupolas, which symbolize the protective heavenly vault and, even more, God's tenderness that envelops us.

1. "Yahweh gave me the two stone tablets inscribed by the finger of God, exactly corresponding to what Yahweh had said to you on the mountain, from the heart of the fire, on the day of the Assembly" (Deuteronomy 9:10).
2. Quoted at the beginning of the Dogmatic Constitution of the Church in the Second Vatican Council (N°4).
3. "The kingdom of Heaven may be compared to a king who gave a feast for his son's wedding" (Matthew 22:2).
4. "I saw the holy city, the new Jerusalem, coming down out of heaven from God, prepared as a bride dressed for her husband" (Revelation 21:2).
5. 1 Corinthians 12:12-26

THE ANGELS

ANGELS WERE PRESENT AT EACH SIGNIFICANT
MOMENT IN THE LIFE OF CHRIST. THEY ARE
OUR COMPANIONS AND OUR GUARDIANS

On the ceilings of the Baroque churches there is an abundance of plump cherubim with golden wings. In two, or often three, dimensions they escort Christ, the Virgin, or the saints, or else are positioned around the edges of the clouds. But are these angels anything more than just pious decoration? For many of our contemporaries, they are a pleasantly picturesque expression of inaccessible perfection, or simply of an escape into unreality. They are the inhabitants of some imaginary "seventh heaven."

But the liturgy, as well as Holy Scripture, talks constantly of angels and makes them into discreet, yet efficient, participants in the story of salvation, messengers of God and mankind's companions. In Greek, the word angel literally means "ambassador" or "messenger." Angels are the witnesses of God's tender attentions to us. As such, they are our guardian angels.

In the Gospels, angels are always present at the key moments of the mystery of Jesus Christ. The best-known scene in which an angel plays a part is probably the Annunciation.[1] At Christ's birth, "a great throng of the hosts of heaven" greets him by singing God's praises.[2] After the temptation in the wilderness, angels "looked after him"[3] and, at the moment of the agony in Gethsemane, "an angel... coming from heaven" comforted him.[4] On Easter morning, two angels announce the news that Jesus has risen to the holy women,[5] and when Jesus ascends to heaven, they are once more there to reassure the apostles that he will return.[6]

Following the example of Christ's life, the entirety of the liturgy is accompanied by angels, who are the perfect singers of God's glory. The "Glory to God" of festive days is sung in unison with the angelic choir at Bethlehem. During the mass, we are asked to join our voices to their song of praise by chanting "Holy, Holy, Holy."[7] The angels are part of that "invisible world" which is mentioned in the first article of the *Credo*.

Thus we approach "Mount Zion and the city of the living God, the heavenly Jerusalem where the millions of angels have gathered for the festival" (Hebrews 12:22). We must love the angels, sing praises with them and pray to them. They are faithful, efficient friends who allow us to understand, like Saint-Exupery's fox, that "the essential is invisible to our eyes."

1. Luke 1:26-38
2. Luke 2:13
3. Mark 1:13
4. Luke 22:43
5. Matthew 28:2-7
6. Acts 1:10-11
7. Isaiah 6:3; Revelation 4:8
8. Psalms 138:1

THE SAINTS

AFTER A LIFE ON EARTH DEVOTED TO THE
SERVICE OF GOD, SAINTS ARE AN EXAMPLE
TO US AND ALSO PROTECT US

Both the time and the space we live in are full of Saints. From St. Petersburg to Santiago de Compostela, from St. Ives in Cornwall to St. Paul in Minnesota, our world is littered with towns and villages named after saints. If, in the early days of Christianity, Saint Paul called all the believers in Christ "saints" or "holy people,"[1] this title has, since the eleventh century, been reserved for those whom the Holy See has canonized, and who are venerated by the Church. At the time, it was absolutely necessary to regulate the occasionally excessive worship, which, since the Roman persecutions, had been accorded to martyrs, as well as all Christians who had displayed outstanding virtue. The custom was to celebrate the day on which they died, or on which their relics were transported, and the tradition still continues today with the calendar of Saints' days.

The procedure of beatification, then canonization, was defined by Pope Alexander III in the twelfth century, and it has been revised on numerous occasions since. It calls on the authority of the Church to declare that a given person has entered into the Glory of God and should be venerated as a saint. An investigation is carried out, followed by a "trial" that includes several adversarial exchanges between the promoter of the cause (for) and the Devil's advocate (against).

After the Virgin Mary, whose vital place in the Church we have already discussed, the saints include apostles and martyrs, a few Popes and prelates, clerics of all ranks, and some lay people. A saint is someone who, guided by the Holy Spirit, has consecrated his or her life to God and to others. They lend their names to parishes and monasteries, and each of us receives a name at baptism which puts us under the protection of a given "patron" saint. Saints are generally depicted with their heads surrounded by a halo, which symbolizes God's Holiness radiating from them. Since the days of the Old Testament, men like Moses and Elijah have been transfigured by the light of God; that is why they stood alongside Christ on Mount Tabor at the moment of the Transfiguration.[2]

But the worship that we give to the Saints in no way reduces the worship we first owe to God and to Christ. As the Preface of Saints' Feasts puts it: "You are glorified in your saints, for their glory is the crowning of your gifts." Worship of relics has also been part of the Catholic tradition since earliest times. This is perfectly consistent with the mystery of Incarnation that respects the body, the members of Christ, of the Holy Spirit.[3]

1. 2 Corinthians 1:1
2. Exodus 34:29; 2 Kings 2:11; Matthew 17:3
3. 1 Corinthians 6:15-19

BAPTISM

AS AN INITIATION INTO CHRISTIAN LIFE, BAPTISM IS A SECOND BIRTH INTO THE CHURCH

Baptism is the first of the Sacraments, or "Sacred Acts," which are both visible and instruments of invisible grace. They are symbols in the true sense of the word: by means of concrete gestures they bring about spiritual effects, uniting mankind with God through the interaction of body and soul.

The sacraments are an essential part of Catholicism and are derived from the mystery of the redeeming Incarnation. This close link between words (the "form") and material elements (the "matter") allows the Church to carry on its mission of salvation, through the Son of God who became man. It is necessary to make a distinction between his humanity, which provides an "espousing" instrument of our salvation, and sacraments that are "discrete" from him. But the governing symbolism of both is of the same nature. Sacraments perpetuate and personalize Christ's redemptive mission and are accessible to all those who wish to enter into their mystery.

The Church itself can be considered to be the "Original Sacrament." The seven sacraments take their source from here as the main channels of divine grace, having been instituted more or less clearly by Christ and attested in the New Testament. They are baptism, confirmation, the mass, holy orders, matrimony, penance, and the anointing of the sick. These sacred acts are present throughout a believer's life, and are the outward signs of his religious commitment until the last moments of his earthly life.

Baptism (from the Greek verb *bapto* or *baptizo*, "to plunge") effectively "plunges" the believer into the mystery of the Trinity, into the mystery of the death and resurrection of Christ, and into the community of the Church. The most significant form of baptism is by triple immersion, associated with the words: "I baptize you in the name of the Father and of the Son and of the Holy Spirit." But it is most frequently administered by ablution: water is poured onto the head of the person being baptized. In accordance with ancient traditions, Catholics generally baptize young children, in preparation for a religious upbringing, but an increasingly large number of adult believers are also baptized.

Born again of water and of the Spirit,[1] the baptized believer enters into the Mystical Body of Christ, thus becoming, according to Saint Paul, one of its living members,[2] one of the "heirs of God" (Romans 8:17). He is called upon to grow up in the Christian faith, and the other sacraments will mark the various stages of this growth.

1. John 3:5
2. "For as with the human body which is a unity although it has many parts—all the parts of the body, though many, still making up one single body—so it is with Christ." (1 Corinthians 12:12).

CONFIRMATION

THE GIFT OF THE SPIRIT,
THROUGH THE APPLICATION OF HOLY OIL,
TURNS A BAPTIZED BELIEVER INTO AN
ADULT IN THE FAITH

Confirmation completes and perfects what Baptism began. In simple terms, it is the sacrament of growing into a mature Christian. A young believer could well remain a "child" and never become a "grown Christian," just as we talk of a "grown man," if he didn't receive the gift of the Spirit during this ceremony, which more strongly "confirms" his existence in Christ.

In order to receive the sacrament of confirmation, an adolescent has already publicly and willingly professed the faith that he has received from his family (and which, from the age of reason onwards, can be celebrated in a private Eucharist). That is why the expression "profession of faith" is extremely fitting. Customs differ widely between countries: in France, for example, there is the "solemn communion" and believers can be confirmed before making their profession of faith. Whatever the practice, confirmation plays the same indispensable part in our lives as the Pentecost, which brought an end to the mystery of Easter and allowed the apostles to go forth and bear witness to their faith.

The most important part of the confirmation ceremony is a light anointment with chrism, a holy oil that is consecrated by the bishop and the priests on Holy Thursday. It penetrates the believer's forehead and symbolizes the Spirit, which must from now on be the guiding force behind everything he does. At the same time, the celebrant (generally a bishop, who can be accompanied by priests or can delegate to them) pronounces these words: "[Name], be sealed with the Gift of the Holy Spirit," and the confirmed replies: "Amen." He is from that moment a fully fledged member of the People of God, a "layman" (from the Greek *laos*, "people").

217

The anointment is also a symbol of the strength that the Spirit gives. Chrism is similar to the oil that was used for massaging wrestlers' muscles to make them suppler for the fight and more difficult to grapple with.

Baptism, confirmation, and the taking of holy orders stamp a "character" on the soul, that is to say an indelible spiritual mark that allows different degrees of access to the Christian religion. That is why they are received only once, as opposed to the other sacraments that can be repeated.

The three sacraments of baptism, confirmation, and the Eucharist bring about "Christian initiation." In the early ages of Christianity, they were received together during a single ceremony (the Easter vigil was the most popular time for this), which introduced the "neophyte" ("new plant" in Greek) into the "divine" mysteries. This sequence is still followed today when an adult is baptized.

MASS

THE EUCHARIST IS THE RENEWAL OF CHRIST'S
SACRIFICE AND, THROUGH THE COMMUNION,
GIVES US ACCESS TO THE MYSTERY OF SALVATION

Through the ages, the Mass has perpetuated the unique sacrifice of the Son of God, which, as we have explained, is the key to our Redemption. It is a pacific offering that makes Christ's sacrifice a present reality, and it is at the heart of the Christian life. It consists of a spoken liturgy, along with songs, prayers, and several readings from the Bible, and an Eucharistic liturgy during which the bread and the wine are transformed on the altar (or "transubstantiated") into the body and blood of Christ.

It was in anticipation of the sacrifice of the New Covenant that, on the eve of his death, Christ wished to celebrate the Jewish Passover with his disciples.[1] With them, he then followed the normal ritual of the

Passover meal. The Christian Mass has adopted many Jewish prayers and practices, notably the blessings (*berakoth*) of the table, which are the origin of the eucharistic prayers, and reinterpreted them.

Since, according to tradition, the head of the Passover meal had to make a speech explaining the meaning of the ritual while the paschal-lamb was being served, which commemorated the escape from Egypt, so Jesus explains to his disciples that he is the true Paschal-Lamb, he that "takes away the sin of the world."[2] At the moment when the main meal was begun, the head pronounced a blessing (in Greek *eucharistia*, "act of grace") over the unleavened bread. That is why Jesus consecrates it by presenting it as his body: "This is my body given for you" (Luke 22:19). At the end of the meal a fourth cup of wine was normally blessed, so Christ too consecrates the wine, making it into his own blood: "This cup is the new covenant in my blood poured out for you." He then adds, "Do this in remembrance of me" (ibid.). This ritual of remembrance of Israel goes further than a simple commemoration. It brings the past into the present and even anticipates the future: it is as if these three temporal dimensions were telescoped into one another. When partaking of the Eucharist, Christians become contemporaries of the Crucifixion in the present of the Church, according to a ritual that will last "until he [the Lord] comes" (1 Corinthians 11:26). Ordination allows a priest to consecrate the bread and the wine and, by so doing, he effectively renews Christ's sacrifice, just as Jesus anticipated it on the eve of the Passion.

The Catholic faith professes that the bread actually becomes Jesus's body and the wine his blood. In this way, at the table of the Last Supper and on our altars, Jesus is in fact present in the symbolic and sacramental state of a sacrificial victim, whose body and blood have been separated. This brings us face to face with the entire mystery of our Redemption, since these tangible elements put the living, glorious Christ within our reach. At the end of the eucharistic prayer, the congregation of the faithful gives its assent to the mystery of the Covenant, which has been renewed on the altar, with a solemn "Amen." The Lord's Prayer can then be recited. This is the prayer of children reconciled to their Father through the sacrifice of his Son, who became man. The ritual of peace-giving then follows, manifesting the reconciliation of the brethren to one another.

The congregation then communes with this sacrifice at the eucharistic table. When, respecting the preordained steps, we receive the body and the blood of Christ, we gradually enter into close communion with the Son: "As the living Father sent me and I draw life from the Father, so whoever eats me will also draw life from me" (John 6:57). United to Jesus Christ, Christians can, through him, participate in the very unity of the Trinity itself.

Thus, of all the sacraments, the Eucharist is essential for the Church. According to an expression handed down by tradition: "The Church makes the Eucharist; the Eucharist makes the Church." Through the ministry of the priests, the Eucharist is a celebration of that unique sacrifice in all places and for a variety of different communities and religious assemblies. This celebration, which is a concentrated version of what God has done for us and what he continues to do, creates and maintains Church unity.

Accordingly, the faithful should take part in the Sunday Mass, for that was the day on that the Lord was resurrected. During the communion, a member of the Mystical Body of Christ is guaranteed "to receive that which he is," to quote one of Saint Augustine's telling phrases. Furthermore, it is highly recommended for priests to celebrate mass every day, and for the faithful to partake of it if they can. The office of Eucharist is also part of the daily routine for monks and nuns. Fervent Christians can repeat word for word what one of the martyrs of Abitena (Tunisia) said in February of the year 304: "We cannot live without the Lord's Meal."

An extremely ancient Church tradition accepts the offerings of the faithful, who ask the officiating priest to present their wishes at the altar during the course of the mass. This practice should by no means be interpreted as a pricing of the sacraments, administration of which for money (*simony*) was vigorously forbidden by the Holy See on numerous occasions during the Middle Ages and by the Council of

Trent. The mass is priceless and its universal implications surpass any personal intention. It is simply a matter of honoring the ministry of the priest who agrees to offer up a mass for a particular reason (one honorarium per mass is authorized).

1. "And he said to them, 'I have ardently longed to eat this Passover with you before I suffer'" (Luke 22:15).
2. He that was announced by John the Baptist, John 1:29-36.

HOLY ORDERS

THE SACRAMENT OF HOLY ORDERS CONSECRATES THOSE WHO HAVE BEEN CALLED TO TRANSMIT THE GIFTS OF GOD TO THE SERVICE OF THEIR BROTHERS

To guarantee the lasting authenticity of the communion of love that proceeds from his mystical body, Christ himself provided it with living signs of his presence and his deeds. After the Resurrection, he appeared to his apostles and gave them a mission to convert the nations:[1] they are thus vital witnesses of his humanity, while the gift of the Holy Spirit at Pentecost fills them with power from on high.[2]

Among these apostles was Simon, called Peter, whom Jesus designated as the foundation of his Church, even mysteriously identifying himself with him as the payer of the religious tax of the shekel.[3] This simple, generous man, originally a fisherman from Galilea, experienced a moment of weakness by denying Christ three times over during the night of the Passion. But having received three declarations of love from him, the Risen Lord nevertheless chose him to watch over his entire flock.[4]

Thus, by the will of Christ, his Church, which is a living body, was structured by Peter and the Apostles. In turn, they transmitted to the chosen, by the laying-on of hands, the dignity of being Christ's representatives, with the strength of the Holy Spirit that they needed.

Throughout the centuries, this mission has continued in the ministry of bishops, to whom the plenitude of the sacrament of Holy Orders has given the status of being the apostles' successors.

They are Christ's signs and instruments in each of their dioceses and their churches. Saint Augustine considered himself to be both a member of the Church, like the faithful of Hippo, as well as their living sign of the Lord, invested with the power to unite them in him. In the same way, the Second Vatican Council's Constitution of the Church presents God's People first and foremost, before specifying the Church's hierarchy based on the episcopate.

The bishops are subordinates of the Bishop of Rome, Peter's successor, who presides over the Church's mission. "The Servant of the Servants of God," the Vicar of Christ, he is the only one to receive the honorific title of "pope" (from the Greek *pappas*, a child's word for "father"). As a sign and reference of its unity, he is one of the Catholic Church's main symbols. He is generally assisted in his curia and unites the college of bishops around him for councils and synods. For the faithful of each diocese, the bishop fulfills the role of a pastor, of a priest, and of a doctor, and hence participates in Christ the Lord's own ministry. From the earliest Church onwards, he has been assisted by priests whom he ordains and who share his ministry; who, like him, can administer the Eucharist acting in *persona Christi* ("in the person of Christ"). He is also aided by deacons (from the Greek *diakonos*, "servant"), to whom he gives a participation in the Order, not in the ministry itself but for certain sacramental "services." The diaconate had long been a preparation for the priesthood and has, since the Second Vatican Council, become a permanent order once more.

Bishops, priests, and deacons thus represent the three levels of the sacrament of Holy Orders, which is conferred by the laying of hands on the head of the ordinand and then by the prayer of ordination. Bishops are the only ministers (in the Latin sense of the term minister, "servant") of ordination. But, during the ordination of priests, any priests present also lay on their hands. Anointment of the head for bishops and of anointment of the hands for priests are complementary rituals. Bishops are given their pontifical insignia, the miter and the crook; the priests receive a stole and a chasuble, as well as the bread and wine for the mass; deacons are presented with the book of the Gospels, before being clothed in a stole and a dalmatic. When not officiating at ceremonies at which the ecclesiastics have to wear their liturgical vestments (which will be explained further on), their official dress is a black soutane tightened round the waist by a wide belt, or, since 1963, what is called the "clergyman": a black or gray suit with a small cross on its lapel, over a dark shirt decked with a white dog-collar.

The Pope is the only one to wear a white soutane; a white cape covers his shoulders and chest. On his finger, he wears "The Fisherman's Ring," in memory of Saint Peter's origins, which was used for sealing letters (*sub annulo piscatoris*). On his head, he wears a white calotte and a pectoral cross hangs from a chain around his neck.

The Cardinals—Bishops who are closer to the Pope—first exercised their ministry in the different quarters of Rome (in Latin *cardines*) and they constitute a sort of pontifical senate. They receive a red biretta (a type of square cap) and are entirely dressed in red (soutane, cape, and calotte); they wear a ring on their fingers and their pectoral crosses hang from a red cord. The color red (also called "cardinal's scarlet") symbolizes the fidelity that they pledge to the Pope, going as far as to shed their blood for Christ and his Church. The Bishops' and Archbishops' color is violet (soutane, cape, and calotte); they also wear a ring which symbolizes their marriage to the Church (they constitute the sacrament of "Christ the bridegroom"); their pectoral cross hangs from a green cord (violet during Advent and Lent). Certain other ecclesiastical dignitaries, such as the protonotaries apostolical, also wear violet vestments.

RELIGIOUS PROFESSION

The expression "to take holy orders" is well known, though it does not actually mean the taking of the sacrament of Holy Orders, but corresponds to the choice of making a religious profession. Apart from the "secular" clergy, so called because they administer the sacraments to the *saecularia* (that is to say, to the faithful of the People of God in "this world"), the Church also includes what are called "regular" orders, because their members are committed to obeying *regula* (written rules governing their lives). The men and women belonging to these orders are not part of the hierarchy we have just described, even if some of them do become bishops, priests, or deacons (they even include several Popes), but are living symbols of the holiness of the Church.[5]

Religious life is not a sacrament, but a state of consecration to God that a novitiate prepares for: before the Church, which is to receive them in the name of God, the candidate professes perpetual vows of poverty, chastity, and obedience (and other vows appertaining to certain religious communities), which are known as religious vows.

This is a spontaneous act, a "promise made to God" according to Saint Thomas Aquinas, a lifelong commitment to the path of perfection. Baptism has made the Christian a son of God, and Confirmation has invested him with the Holy Spirit; here he is called to holiness, that is to say he must become absolutely open to the inward movements of the Spirit of Love. From this personal, intimate reaching out on the part of all Christians evolves the purity of the entire Christian community, that divine Bride whom Saint Paul calls "holy and faultless" (Ephesians 5:27).

The grace of God inspires a particular calling in those men and women who have left everything to follow him, leading many disciples with them and, above and beyond anything else, the People of God. Such is the origin of monastic and religious orders, which are successors to the early Church's communities of hermits. There are contemplative orders, often inspired by the Rule of Saint Benedict, including the Benedictines, the Cistercians, and the Carthusians. Later on came other orders that mingle prayer with a variety of apostolic works: the Dominicans (from Saint Dominic), the Franciscans and the Poor Clares (from Saints Francis and Clare of Assisi), the White Friars and the Carmelites (reformed by Saint John of the Cross and Saint Theresa of

Avila). Other charitable or teaching orders are still being created today.

The superiors of monks' abbeys are called Father Abbots, which is to say "father" twice over, since *abba* in Armenian means "papa." Abbots wear the ring and the pectoral cross (with a green or violet cord), but they are dressed in cowled robes, which are black for Benedictines and white for Cistercians ("black friars" and "white friars"). The rule of prayer and of joyful self-denial, which those in orders have chosen in order to live their faith out to the full, reminds all baptized Christians that they, too, should "prefer nothing to the love of Christ," as the rule of Saint Benedict demands.[6]

1. "Go, therefore, make disciples of all nations; baptize them in the name of the Father and of the Son and of the Holy Spirit" (Matthew 28:19).
2. Acts 1:8
3. "You are Peter and on this rock I will build my community." (Matthew 16:18) Cf. also Matthew 17:27 for the shekel.
4. "Jesus said to him, 'Feed my lambs'" (John 21:15-17).
5. Dogmatic Constitution of the Church in the Second Vatican Council, N°44
6. "No one who prefers father or mother to me is worthy of me. No one who prefers son or daughter to me is worthy of me" (Matthew 10:37).

MATRIMONY

THE CELEBRATION OF MARRIAGE DIGNIFIES WITH DIVINE LOVE THE SOLEMN UNDERTAKING MADE BY THE SPOUSES

The requirements of Catholic marriage are based on the fundamental principles of unity and indissolubility, together with a commitment to the bearing of children. The changes in contemporary society, in a world in which the importance of spirituality is decreasing, make such a doctrine difficult to accept. This phenomenon seems to manifest itself in the fragility and instability of modern society, and people can quite often suffer disastrous effects from it in their private lives. In this way, the Church's message is often misunderstood, as what it tries to do is serve the honor of God and the dignity of mankind.

All religions have, in one way or another, made the conjugal union sacred, for the mystery of life and of childbearing generally inspires a sense of divinity. As a reaction against pagan practices, which often were degrading, the Judaeo-Christian Revelation gives matrimony a powerful symbolic dimension, for one of the most important currents that run through the Bible is that of the marriage between God and his People.

From the moment of their creation, a man and a woman, united in life, form together an image of God; the man leaves his father and his mother to join himself with his wife, and they become one flesh.[1] Moses went to Egypt to fetch the People of God, like a fiancée, and lead them through the desert to Sinai, the mountain of their nuptial Covenant with Yahweh. The *Song of Songs* chants the mutual love of Yahweh and Israel. Finally, the New Testament reveals that Jesus is the Bridegroom of the new People of God, the Church.

Christian matrimony is the sacramental sign of the union between Christ and his Church. According to the teaching of Saint Paul: "This mystery has great significance, but I am applying it to Christ and the Church" (Ephesians 5:32). The spouses who exchange their vows before God and in front of the priest who represents him—and who blesses the couple in his role as a sacramental witness, according to the ancient rules, which were codified in the sixteenth century by the Council of Trent—participate in the fullness of this holy unity.

The spouses are said to give themselves the sacrament of matrimony; indeed, their mutual "yes" given to one another in their human love is the sign and instrument of that very love that God bears for them. Those that live out the joy and depth of love realize that the force that moves them also inspires them: it comes from outside them and leads them to excel themselves. For them it can be a true revelation of divine love, which nourishes their mutual feeling and guarantees its permanence.

1. Genesis 1:27; 2:24

PENANCE

DISTANCED FROM GOD BY SIN,
THE PENITENT FINDS THE PEACE HE IS LOOKING
FOR IN REPENTANCE AND ABSOLUTION

Throughout history, man has realized that he is sinful. While he aspires to the untainted life that divine teaching shows is available to him, he is subjected to numerous and various temptations and sometimes succumbs to them. All religions, therefore, have their rites of purification: ablutions, baptisms, or even public penance, which can, at times, take aberrant forms.

As far as the Catholic faith is concerned, there exists an original sin, which is explained in allegorical terms in the opening pages of the Bible. In his Incarnation as the Redeemer (from the Latin *redimere*, "to buy back," notably to pay the ransom for a captive in order to buy back his freedom), Jesus Christ came to deliver us. But a principle of evil is at work in this world,[1] that "devil" who divides us. The world and its history—that of the twentieth century, for example—clearly shows how perverse mankind can be, and how this perversion makes us suffer.

Baptism washes away original sin, and penance (or reconciliation) cleanses us of later personal faults. In the Gospels, Christ affirms, while curing the paralyzed man, that he has the divine privilege of forgiving sins.[2] On the evening of his Resurrection, this power was transferred to the apostles[3] and, beyond the apostles, to those whom they have chosen to continue their work. Before his sins are forgiven, the sinner must make an act of contrition, that is, to express regret for having committed them. He then specifies the nature of his sins by confessing them to a priest, who gives him absolution, on the condition of a symbolic restitution, which generally takes the form of a few prayers. Contrition, confession, and restitution are the necessary steps to obtaining absolution.

The Church invites its faithful to receive this sacrament at least once a year, at Easter. "Doing one's Easter duty" consists of confession and communion. As in our daily lives, so in the life of the spirit we also eat, drink, and wash. The eucharistic communion feeds us, while confession cleanses us. Both should be performed frequently.

In most churches, the sacrament of penance is administered in confessionals, the wooden boxes that stand in the side-aisles. But custom also allows penitents to be received in small rooms, in which a longer dialogue is possible.

1. "The mystery of wickedness is already at work ... And therefore God sends on them a power that deludes people so that they believe what is false, and so that those who do not believe the truth and take their pleasure in wickedness may all be condemned." (2 Thessalonians 2:7, 11-12)
2. Matthew 9:1-8
3. "Receive the Holy Spirit. If you forgive anyone's sins, they are forgiven; if you retain anyone's sins, they are retained" (John 20:22-23).

ANOINTING OF THE SICK

FOR THE SICK, ANOINTMENT ALLEVIATES SUFFERING BY BRINGING PEACE TO THEIR SOULS

The Gospels report that Christ cured the sick and brought them to their feet by the laying-on of hands.[1] He even familiarized the apostles with this sort of contact, and added to it an anointment with oil.[2] This is an expression of humanity and divine tenderness. Above and beyond this symbolic gesture, which constitutes the sacrament of Anointing the Sick, God and the Church support and gently care for those with bodily suffering, as well as for the old and dying. This tangible sign of solicitude is the last of the seven sacraments, which accompany us throughout our lives.

From the earliest apostolic times (first century), the practice of the laying-on of hands on the sick became widespread. "Any one of you who is ill" wrote Saint James in his Epistle, "should send for the elders [*presbuteroi* in Greek, hence "priests"] of the church, and they must anoint the sick person with oil in the name of the Lord and pray over him. The prayer of faith will save the sick person and the Lord will raise him up again; and if he has committed any sins, he will be forgiven" (James 5:14-15). It is thus a sign of physical as well as spiritual healing, which is concluded by absolution. The administration of the sacrament by a priest involves the silent laying-on of hands, and anointment with the oil for anointing the sick (blessed by the bishop on Holy Thursday during the chrism mass) on the forehead and the hands, accompanied by these words: "[Name], through this holy anointing, may the Lord in his love and mercy help you with the grace of the Holy Spirit. May the Lord who frees you from sin save you and raise you up."

The expression "Extreme Unction" is better known than the "Anointing of the Sick," although the latter is a more exact description. Extreme Unction was given only when death was imminent, when the sick were *in extremis*. Superstitiously, the family waited for the last possible moment before calling in the priest with his oils and *viaticum* (the last communion), because his visit was generally considered to be a sign of death. The Second Vatican Council reintroduced a custom of anointing the sick, which is more consistent with its beginnings.

It is, therefore, not necessary to wait until the last moment before asking for anointment; a serious illness, any major operation, or simply the onset of old age, are reason enough to receive it in faith, with the alleviation of the body and soul, which it always brings.

1. Mark 6:5; Matthew 8:3-15
2. Mark 6:13

SONG AND MUSIC

A S   H I G H E R   E X P R E S S I O N S   O F
H U M A N   F E E L I N G ,   S O N G   A N D   M U S I C   U N I T E
O U R   H E A R T S   I N   P R A Y E R

Personal prayer is made in silent concentration, from a simple attachment of love. The liturgy which unites a community, is a symphony, which presupposes that its various instruments are tuned together. As the Old Testament puts it: "Praise him with fanfare of trumpet, praise him with harp and lyre, praise him with tambourines and dancing, praise him with strings and pipes, praise him with the clamor of cymbals, praise him with triumphant cymbals. Let everything that breathes praise Yahweh. Alleluia!" (Psalms 150:3-6). As in many religions, which make song into a higher register of human expression, the voice is the most beautiful instrument of divine praise, and the organ, which is a sort of orchestra all on its own, is its best accompaniment for sacred music. "Whoever loves singing," said Saint Augustine, "and who sings well, prays twice over."

Derived from the Greek word *psalmos*, "the plucking of a string," a psalm is a poem sung to God, accompanied by a cithara or a lute. For both Jews and Christians, the Book of Psalms is the perfect expression of personal and communal prayer. There are 150 psalms, attributed to King David, which express to God the full range of human feelings when "touched" by misfortune or happiness, persecution, fear, or tenderness. In turn, when we sing them in a choir they are filled with our experiences and expectations. They are a sort of love song from the Bride, who tells the Bridegroom of her joy, and her sufferings.

Different centuries and cultures have left us with many forms of religious song and music, among which Gregorian Plainsong remains "specially suited to the Roman liturgy."[1] Attributed to Pope Gregory I, who was responsible for establishing the texts, this repertoire adapts and extends the psalms with the strength and the beauty of a profound interior knowledge. The origins of the chants are extremely ancient, and they flourished between the Loire and the Rhine in the eighth and ninth centuries. After that, they spread across the whole of the Christian West, where they are still sung by numerous monastic communities.

In order to unite the faithful in a single prayer, there are also many other songs, whose force depends on their biblical inspiration, and are sung in our various mother tongues (the chorales in German and English for example). Even today, music and song, when linked with different cultures, are a part of any religious celebration. They are a beautiful homage to God, which also honor those who sing them.

1. Constitution of the Sacred Liturgy of the Second Vatican Council, N°116

GESTURES AND POSTURES

WHETHER ALONE OR GATHERED TOGETHER,
PEOPLE SPEAK TO GOD THROUGH
THE MOVEMENT OF THEIR BODIES

Rather than a concerto, in which a solo instrument is set off against the orchestra, the Catholic liturgy is a symphony: each instrument is an essential element of the overall work, playing its own part and playing it to its fullest extent. But this musical metaphor is not quite adequate, for, apart from the voices and instruments, the liturgical act also demands the participation of the whole of man: his soul, his spirit, his heart, and his body. A better image would be that of an opera, which also figures the actors' movements and postures. This is no easy comparison, for the notion of *Opus Dei*, which has been spread by the rule of Saint Benedict, means "the Work of God," that is to say both the work he consecrates to us and that which he accomplishes through us and for us; it should not be forgotten that the word "opera" comes from the Latin *opera*, "works," the plural of *opus*.

Even though Christian liturgy cannot be said to be choreographed, it nevertheless demands the precise organization of the move-ments of its various participants. Its ceremonial side is necessary for the liturgical rites to take place in absolute peace and communicate a sensation of sacredness to the faithful, that is to say God's active and loving presence.

According to the context, liturgical celebrations ask us to adopt four different stable positions of the entire body: standing, sitting, kneeling, and, more rarely, prostration.

The standing position is the most noble because it characterizes mankind, who was created in God's image. It is also a sign of the respect that man bears for the sacred and is appropriate, for example, to the reading of the Gospels. We stand upright before God when praying, generally turned towards the East—that is to say towards the rising sun, the symbol of the resurrected Christ. That is why the choir in churches is generally "orientated" towards the East. The sitting position represents peaceful openness, more fitted to listening to read-ings or sermons. We kneel down to show a more intense supplication, or for humbler and more intimate prayers, such as in the mass during the consecration, and also for the adoration of the Holy Sacrament.

Prostration consists in lying stretched out on the ground. It is reserved for solemn moments. Thus, during the singing of the litany of the saints, the ordinand is prostrated before receiving the sacrament of Holy Orders, as is the person who is about to pronounce his religious vows. On Good Friday, after the reading of the Passion according to Saint John, which tells of the death of Jesus, the lector stops for a moment and the whole congregation prostrates itself.

The hands and the arms of the celebrant play a very important part in the carrying out of a liturgical rite, in blessings, anointments, and particularly in consecrations. As a symbol of the purity he requires the priest washes his fingers after the offertory and after the communion. Hands are put together in a gesture of supplication and they are kept together when a priest is officiating during a ceremony and when he has nothing to do or to hold. Sometimes the celebrant stretches his hands and arms out, as in the recitation of the Lord's

Prayer in the mass. This is the ancient posture of the Orant, which has been found depicted in the catacombs from the earliest Christian times. The hands are the best instruments for the administration of the sacraments, and the bishop lays them on the candidate during ordination.

The liturgy also requires the faithful to make several gestures with their hands: they cross their foreheads, stomachs, and shoulders. At the moment of the announcement of the Gospel, the thumb traces a small sign of the cross over the forehead, mouth, and heart. When the faithful shake hands, which commonly replaces the kiss of peace, which is mutually given before the communion, it is a sign of the chaste affection that they have for one another.

There are also other rites that involve other parts of the body. The mass on the evening of Holy Thursday includes the washing of feet, which reenacts Christ's gesture during the Last Supper.[1] The faithful bow their heads before the symbols of the divine presence: the altar, the cross, and the book of the Gospels. Monks bow down low at the end of each psalm when they chant the "Glory be to the Father and to the Son and to the Holy Spirit" during the celebration of their offices. It is required in all churches that one genuflect when passing in front of the Holy Sacrament, whose presence is indicated on the altar by an ever-burning light.

During a funeral, the body of the deceased is sprinkled with holy water as a sign of purification and thurified as a sign of respect because, according to Saint Paul, our bodies are the members of Christ and temples of the Holy Spirit.[2] They are called upon to enter, transfigured, into the heavenly liturgy.

During certain ceremonies, the entire congregation walks towards the Lord, just as the Bride goes to join her Groom. The best-known examples of these processions occur on February 2, after the blessing of the candles, on Palm Sunday, and at the moment of entering the church at the beginning of the Easter Vigil, after the blessing of the Paschal Candle. On Corpus Christi Day, the processions of the Holy Sacrament are even more important. The frequency of such processions varies according to the country or region. There are, for example, more of them in Lourdes, where processions with torches are extremely popular.

1. "No one who has had a bath needs washing, such a person is clean all over. You too are clean... " (John 13:10).
2. 1 Corinthians 6:15-19

SACRED VESTMENTS

WHEN OFFICIATING IN THE NAME OF GOD, CELEBRANTS WEAR CERTAIN SPECIFIC ORNAMENTS

Earlier in the book, a parallel was drawn between Catholic liturgy and an opera. Such a comparison may be extended to the use of costumes, as celebrants are obliged to wear particular vestments when carrying out sacred rites.

The Book of Revelation often talks of the heavenly liturgy, with its instruments, songs, processions, and assorted movements. Saint John saw: "a huge number... standing in front of the throne and in front of the Lamb, dressed in white robes and holding palms in their hands. They shouted in a loud voice, 'Salvation to our God, who sits on the throne, and to the Lamb!'"(Revelations 7:9-10).

The white robes of the chosen, a symbol of the purity they need in order to meet God, is also reminiscent of the dress of the angels who announced the Resurrection of Christ to the holy women. Equally, the newly baptized receive a white robe, which is the sign of their inner rebirth. During the solemn communion, the communicants wear white albs, which is also the primary vestment of all ministers during liturgical rites, whatever their function; a variant of these robes are worn by those who have received the sacrament of Holy Orders.

– Alb (from the Latin *alba*, "white"): the alb is a white robe with long sleeves that covers the entire body, and which is gathered at the waist by a cord. When the alb has neither a hood nor a collar, an amice is worn around the neck. The alb is the basic vestment of all those who take part in liturgical ceremonies: bishops, priests, deacons, acolytes (servers), and lectors. Some servers also wear white surplices over red or black soutanes.

– Stole (from the Latin *stola*, "long robe," which became a liturgical vestment during the eighth century): worn above the alb, it is the minimum vestment that ordained ministers can wear. It consists of a long strip of cloth made up of two equal bands. Bishops and priests wear it round the neck and the two bands hang down in front parallel to each other. Deacons wear it across their chests, coming down from the left shoulder. A stitch or a small knot at the bottom joins the two parts together, so that the stole forms a diagonal all round the body, in front as well as behind, like a bandoleer.

– Chasuble (from the Latin casula, "small house"): the chasuble is a generous upper vestment, put over the head like a poncho. It completely envelops the wearer and protects him like a small house, or a tent. It is the vestment that the bishop or priest wears when celebrating the mass; in the chasuble they "put on" the presence of Christ to act in his place during the eucharistic sacrifice. The voluminousness of the early chasuble, has been reintroduced, but we can still find "violin-case" chasubles of the baroque period (so called because they are rectangular at the back, while at the front they are shaped like a violin case), which allow the priest free use of his arms. Chasubles are generally ornate, and are sometimes even richly embroidered.

– Dalmatic (from Dalmatia, now Croatia): in solemn ceremonies the dalmatic is the vestment worn by deacons (that is to say "servants," symbols of Christ the Servant) over the alb and the stole. As far as Christians are concerned, "to serve is to reign." This voluminous tunic, which is split under the arms, ornate like the chasuble, and with short sleeves, was originally part of the dress of Roman emperors and of certain Popes in the High Middle Ages.

– Cape (from the Latin *cappa*, "hooded cloak"): a long ceremonial cloak covering the entire body, the cape consists of a semi-circular piece of cloth, with its two folds held together at the front by hooks and eyes. The cape is worn during solemn offices outside the mass. The celebrant wears it over his alb and stole, and assistants and cantors can also wear it.

– Liturgical colors: liturgical vestments (and ornaments) are colored according to a set of rules. White signifies the time of Christmas and Easter, as well as festivals of saints who were not martyrs. Violet is worn during Advent and Lent, which are times of preparation or penance. Pink is for the third Sunday of Advent and the fourth Sunday of Lent. Red is for Good Friday, Pentecost, and the festivals of martyrs. Green is for ordinary periods. In certain regions, gold is worn for solemn rites, blue for the Virgin Mary, and black for the deceased.

These highly symbolic vestments are set aside for the celebrant and those who surround him, because they are the representatives or servants of Christ. This should not create the impression that a celebration of the liturgy is a show put on in front of an audience of the faithful; there is only one congregation in which each person fulfills his role and participates in the celebration of the mystery of the Eucharist, in perfect harmony with, and as complements to, all the others. The faithful, too, can put on the clothes of Christ, as is witnessed by the white vestment that they receive during baptism and religious profession.

PONTIFICAL INSIGNIA

THE MITER AND THE CROOK,
THE PASTORAL HEADDRESS AND STAFF,
MAKE UP THE BISHOPS' INSIGNIA

A pontiff is someone who acts as a "bridge" between two people (from the Latin *pons*). Jesus Christ is the finest example of a pontiff: at once God and man, he unites God to man in the New Covenant. By virtue of their ordination, bishops, the successors to the apostles, exercise this mediating power in the name of Christ, the High Priest. In their midst, the Pope, as the successor of Saint Peter, and as a result the Vicar of Christ, is called the "Sovereign Pontiff."

The insignia that the Pope and the bishops generally wear are the pectoral cross and the ring. During solemn offices, they make use of pontifical insignia, the miter and the crook, which they received at their ordination into the episcopate.

The miter is a "headdress." The original Greek *mitra* was a headband, or a diadem. In the Old Testament, the High Priest and the priests wore a turban, decorated with a golden flower, a sign of consecration.[1] The Christian miter, originally a headband with a veil, has changed during the ages, but was from early times reserved for bishops. It is triangular in form and points upwards. Early miters were lower. During the baroque period they were heightened and have now returned to more or less reasonable proportions.

The crook, or pastoral staff, is the most typical sign of those who represent, for their church or for their community, the presence of the Good Shepherd. The word comes from "crochet" because of the hook at its tip. In early times, the shepherd's crook was bent at the top into a hook, with a sort of groove that allowed shepherds to throw earth or stones at sheep that had strayed, as well as the predators who came near them. Since Paul VI, the Pope has carried a crook that is topped with a curved cross, which symbolizes his mission to bring together God's scattered sheep.[2] The crook and the miter are reserved for bishops, but they are also given to father abbots (heads of monastic abbeys) during their abbatial benediction, for they take the place of Christ in their communities.

The pallium, a legacy from the dress of certain Roman dignitaries, is the badge of the Pope and of the archbishops. It is a strip of white wool that is worn round the neck, over the chasuble, like a collar. Two flaps hang down from this broad collar, one in front, the other behind. Six black crosses are embroidered at intervals on the strip of wool.

1. Exodus 39:28, 30-31; Leviticus 8:9
2. John 11:52.

SCRIPTURE

Holy Scripture is made up of the Old Testament (common to both Jews and Christians) and the New Testament, which includes the four Gospels, the Acts of the Apostles, Epistles written by apostles, and the Revelation of Saint John. This priceless gem, a superbly detailed history of the People of God culminating with the mystery of Christ, is venerated by all Christians. Yet, while the Protestants consider reading the Bible enough to nourish their faith in salvation, the Catholics gain access to Scripture only by means of the Tradition that created it and has carried it down the ages, according to the Church's living teaching and especially thanks to the liturgy.

There are, then, numerous editions of the Bible, which vary according to different confessions. Catholic editions always include notes of explanation, inspired by the living Tradition of the Church. During the last two decades, some marvelous ecumenical translations have been made, with notes that point out, when necessary, the different churches' interpretations; this is an important step towards Christian unity.

Roman Catholic liturgy is extremely biblical, perhaps even more so than the liturgy of the eastern churches, whose large number of long prayers are still inspired by the Scriptures. We have already seen how the Book of Psalms is the great inspiration behind the celebration of the "Hours." The liturgy of the Word, the first part of the mass and of other offices, consists of readings taken from the Bible, and the most important among them is always a passage from the Gospels.

These readings, which are essential for a true understanding of the liturgy, must be done with skill and respect; the lector is an officially appointed minister. The proclamation of the Gospel is reserved for the celebrant, or for the assisting deacon, and is accompanied by various rites.

The evangelistary is a book worthy of its role, beautifully but soberly bound and decorated. It is laid on the altar at the beginning of the mass, then carried in procession to the ambo (one of two raised stands from which parts of the service are chanted or read, from the Greek *anabaino*, "to go up"), the place of the Word. The cathedra (a chair or throne), positioned near the middle of the nave, has also performed this function.

Nowadays, the ambo is placed in the sanctuary, not far from the altar, so that both parts of the mass work together in the best possible way. It consists of a slightly raised platform, equipped with a lectern, from which the lectors and the cantor, the deacons and the celebrant address the congregation. The oldest churches in Rome have preserved magnificent ambos, such as Saint Clement's, that dates to the twelfth century.

THE ALTAR

AT THE CENTER OF THE CHURCH, THE ALTAR IS BOTH THE PLACE OF SACRIFICE AND THE COMMUNION TABLE

The altar is the meeting point between God and mankind, the true center of all religious buildings, positioned at the heart of the sanctuary, raised up on a few steps so that the architecture is drawn towards it. The word "altar" is derived from the Latin adjective *altus*, meaning "high." Mankind has always been led to put his places of worship on high—Mount Olympus was the dwelling-place of the Greek gods. When no natural heights are available, the sanctuary is placed on the top of an artificial structure, as can be seen in the ziggurats of Mesopotamia. When man wanted to force his way into the holy kingdom, he thought up the Tower of Babel. Jewish tradition considers that mountains—where heaven and earth touch—are the natural places to meet God. It was at the summit of Mount Sinai that Yahweh spoke to Moses.

As a sign of respect for divine transcendence, the smoke of offerings was first made to "go up" towards God who "smelt the pleasing smell" (Genesis 8:21). This is the tradition of sacrifice by fire, the holocaust (from the Greek holokaustos, "entirely burnt"). In the rite inspired by the Covenant on Mount Sinai, Moses shared the blood of the victims between the altar he had just built, which represents God, and the people whom he sprinkled with it. Yahweh and Israel thus became "of one blood."[1] The New Christian Covenant continues this "consanguinity" and makes us God's table guests, since the sacrifice of the communion feeds the congregation with the very body and blood of Christ himself. The altars in our churches are tables where these offerings are laid out. They are symbols of God, who receives the gifts that are offered by the congregation of the faithful. But the altar is also a communal table at which the guests share the sacred meal. Christ is at once the altar, as God who receives the sacrifice, the priest, and the victim, as the man who offers the sacrifice by offering himself.

During the dedication of churches, the first thing is to seal up relics of saints—or, originally, of martyrs—inside the altar in order to mark the continuity between Christ's sacrifice and that of his faithful. The altar is then consecrated with an anointment of holy chrism. After that, it is illuminated by the burning of incense, which is the sign of the Holy Spirit's taking possession of it. Finally, it is laid with altar cloths.

The altar is, then, the most elevated symbol of Christ in the church. Even before the cross, it is the first object that we venerate when entering. The priest kisses it at the beginning and the end of the mass as a sign of respect.

1. Exodus 24:4-8

BREAD AND WINE

THE BREAD AND THE WINE,
TRANSFORMED RESPECTIVELY INTO THE BODY
AND BLOOD OF JESUS, MAKE THE RISEN
CHRIST PRESENT AMONG US

Bread and wine are universal symbols of that which brings us life: food and drink. The psalmist thanks God for satisfying mankind's needs: "for cattle you make the grass grow, and for people the plants they need, to bring forth food from the earth, and wine to cheer people's hearts" (Psalms 104:14-15).

Thus Christ chose the simplest of elements as the sacred signs of his grace. Christians nourish themselves with bread and wine, which have become the body and blood of the Lord Jesus. As far as the Catholic and Orthodox churches are concerned a real transformation of substance occurs during the consecration: the "transubstantiation." This belief is shared by High Church Anglicans and certain Lutherans, but for most Protestants the bread and the wine are nothing more than symbols (in the broadest sense of the term) of Christ and not his actual presence.

The separation of Christ's body and blood is obviously a symbol of his death on the Cross. Their actual presence is witness of the renewal of the sacrifice of the Eucharist, inaugurated by Jesus himself during the Last Supper. This body and this blood must be given as nourishment to the faithful, following Christ's words: "Anyone who does eat my flesh and drink my blood has eternal life, and I shall raise that person up on the last day. For my flesh is real food and my blood is real drink ... As the living Father sent me and I draw life from the Father, so whoever eats me will also draw life from me" (John 6:54-57).

Whoever receives the communion of the Eucharist is truly given the life of Jesus, through the Father, and thus also through the mystery of the Trinity, which unites in love the Father, the Son, and the Holy Spirit. We are invited to the "holy table" and are received there as

241

guests to share with Jesus his life as the Son at the heart of the Trinity.

The bread of the Eucharist consists of a small wafer of unleavened bread, which is called the host. This word is a link between the Christian communion and sacrifice, for the Latin word *hostia* means a sacrificial victim, and this is the sense in which Saint Paul uses it when talking of Christ.[1] Unleavened bread is the only bread permitted in the Jewish ceremony of Passover,[2] which is why it was consecrated by Jesus during the Last Supper. For this reason, the Roman Church does not permit the consecration of ordinary bread (as opposed to the Orthodox churches, which celebrate the Eucharist with leavened bread). During the last few centuries, the disputes that were once caused by these diverging customs have fortunately lost their bitterness.

In the West, a distinction is made between the small hosts for the faithful (which are easy to distribute and to receive) and the large ones for the priests (so that they are easily visible when raised after consecration). Nowadays, thicker ones are produced and their baking sometimes gives them a color that is more golden than white.

At the beginning of the mass the hosts that are to be consecrated are placed in one or more patens (from the Latin *patena*, "a shallow dish"), which are convex, circular, and made of precious metals plated with gold or silver. They can also be made of other fine materials and some patens are masterpieces of the goldsmith's art. The same is true for the ciborium (from the Greek *kiborion*, "the fruit of the water-lily" and, by extension, a cup shaped like this fruit) in which the hosts are placed for the assembled faithful. The ciborium is a hemispherical cup, closed with a cover, which is often topped by a cross. Outside the mass, it is kept in the tabernacle to hold "the Reserved Sacrament," which are the consecrated hosts that have not been distributed during the communion. It is then covered by a "canopy," a piece of cloth in the shape of a round tent.

During the adoration of the Holy Sacrament, the consecrated host is presented to the faithful in a monstrance (from the Latin *monstrare*, "to show"). It consists of a piece of gold or silver plate, decorated with an ornamental motif, centered on a circular base (the "lunette" or "little moon," decked with two glass discs) on which the host is placed. The monstrance often creates the effect of a gleaming sun around the Holy Sacrament.

When the Holy Sacrament is not being displayed it is kept in the tabernacle in a metal box called a custodial (from the Latin *custodire*, "to keep") or a pyx (from the Greek *pyxis*, "a box"). Pyx is also the name for the small circular boxes that are used for taking the communion to the sick.

The Code of Canon Law gives a precise description of communion wine: "The wine must be natural, made from grapes of the vine, and not corrupt" (canon 924). It must therefore be the result of the fermentation of pure grape juice. During the Last Supper, it was the "fruit of the vine" that Jesus transformed into his own blood at the end of the meal. The traditional Passover meal includes four cups of wine and it was the fourth one, the cup of *Hallel* (the adulatory praise of Psalms 114-117), which Christ consecrated.[3]

Since the time of the Old Testament wine has been one of the fundamental symbols of the messianic feast at which, according to Isaiah, must be served "well-strained wines" (Isaiah 25:6). The eucharistic sacrifice and communion make the Last Supper and Calvary a present reality for us, by giving the faithful a foretaste of the feast of the Kingdom to come.

For the consecration of the wine during the mass, the Roman Church generally uses white wine, which will not stain any vestments with which it may come into contact. The celebrant pours it into a chalice (from the Greek *kylix*, in Latin *calix*, "drinking-cup"), which is generally a, fine piece of goldsmithery that is often decorated with eucharistic symbols or phrases from the scriptures, although the style has changed during the ages.

The way in which they are produced means that the bread and the wine are also symbols of the unity of the believers who partake of them. This is explained in one of the most ancient Christian texts, the *Didache*, or "Teaching of the Lord to the Gentiles," which dates to the end of the first century A.D.: "Even as this bread that we break was once scattered through the hills and has been gathered and molded into one, may thy Church be gathered together from the ends of the earth in thy Kingdom! For thine is the glory and the power for ever and ever." The same can be said for the multitude of grapes: pressed together, they become one single wine. Thus, the faithful who break the bread and drink the cup of salvation, who, in other words, eat the body of Christ and drink his blood, grow up into adult members of the Mystical Body of Christ,[4] which is his Church.

While discussing the Eucharist, we should mention a custom that should be revived: the *Benedicte* at the beginning of a meal, and grace at its conclusion. This is also a Jewish rite, derived from the numerous blessings or *berakoth* which mark different moments of the day. In family ritual the ancient blessing of meals, the *Birkat-ha-Mazon*, was of central importance. Here is an extract: "Blessed art thou, Lord God, King of the Universe, thou who feedest the whole earth from thy bounty, grace, tenderness and mercy... Day after day, thou takest care to do us a multitude of good things. It is thou that multiplieth us for ever in thy grace, tenderness, spirit, mercy and all that is good." During the offertory of the Catholic mass, the two prayers of presentation of the bread and the wine are blessings of this sort. Even more profoundly, the blessing of a meal lies at the root of the Christian Eucharist.

Christians must keep the benefits that God's love gives them permanently in mind, and thank him constantly, even if the path they have been given to follow is beset with a variety of difficulties. These acts of grace (which is, in fact, the original meaning of the word "Eucharist") pass through Jesus Christ, even as, according to Saint Paul, grace comes to us through him: "Blessed be God the Father of our Lord Jesus Christ, who has blessed us with all the spiritual blessings of heaven in Christ" (Ephesians 1:3).

Through respect for bread and for what it signifies in the Church —the person into whom it is transformed by the Eucharist—it is a Christian custom not to throw any of it away and, before slicing a loaf, a cross is first traced over it with the knife.

1. "… and follow Christ by loving as he loved you, giving himself up for us as an offering and a sweet-smelling sacrifice to God [*tradidit semetipsum hostiam deo in odorem suavitatis*]" (Ephesians 5:2).
2. Exodus 12:8
3. Matthew 26:29
4. Ephesians 4:12.16; Colossians 2:19

THE TABERNACLE

THE TABERNACLE, WHERE THE CONSECRATED HOSTS ARE KEPT, IS THE "TENT" IN WHICH GOD DWELLS AMONG US

The original meaning of the Latin *tabernaculum*, from which tabernacle is derived, was "a tent." In the history of salvation, the presence of God amidst his people in exodus was symbolized by the "Tent of Meeting," where Moses went to converse with Yahweh in the name of the People, "as a man talks to his friend" (Exodus 33:11). In the New Testament, Saint Paul compares the very humanity of Christ to a tent that was not made by human hands.[1] The Greek text of the prologue to the Gospel according to Saint John contains these very words: "The Word became flesh, he lived [in the Greek *eskenosen*, "pitched his tent"] among us" (John 1:14).

The tabernacle in our churches is that small, ornate, locked cupboard on a wall or a side-altar in which the Holy Sacrament is kept. Hosts consecrated during a mass were originally kept for the sick or dying (the viaticum), which is still the case today. During the last few centuries, thanks to an increase in Eucharistic devotion, the Reserved Sacrament has also become an object of long, silent adoration.

Two signs show that the tabernacle is inhabited. Firstly, it is covered by a canopy (from the Greek *konopion*, "a mosquito net"), whose color is determined according to the liturgical calendar (violet, white or green). When the tabernacle is cylindrical, this canopy or "grand pavilion" really does make it look like a tent. The other sign of the Lord's actual presence is the lamp that constantly burns beside the tabernacle, the symbolism of which goes back to the Old Testament.[2] Rather than an electric night-light, what should be used is an oil lamp with a live wick, which is generally placed in a red glass. This is also a symbol of the soul, which is invited to burn itself up before God by consuming its time for him.

In order for there not to be a confusion between signs and symbols the tabernacle must not be kept on the main altar, which is, as we have already explained, an essential symbol of Christ. It must therefore be kept free and clear, with or without its cloths and light. The Lord Jesus, who is actually present in the hosts kept in the tabernacle, must be worshiped, but not on the main altar. For this reason, the tabernacle is fixed on the wall of the sanctuary, or better still on the altar of one of the church's side-chapels, such as the cathedral's axial chapel, which opens out on to the middle of the ambulatory.

1. Hebrews 9:11.
2. Exodus 27:20; 1 Samuel 3:3

CANDLES

AS WARM AND HUMBLE LIVING FLAMES,
CANDLES SYMBOLIZE, ACCOMPANY,
AND EXTEND OUR PRAYERS

Originally, candles were simply a means of illumination, in the catacombs, small oil lamps were used, which the Lord alluded to in his parable of the ten virgins,[1] who are symbols of the watchful anticipation of the faithful. Going beyond any practical need for light, Christians have continued to use candles for symbolic purposes. Immediately after an altar has been consecrated by anointment, it is covered with cloths, then candles are arranged around it. Almost all liturgical ceremonies make use of this warming light, which is a familiar part of Catholic celebrations (it is also used by Orthodox Christians, Protestants, and Jews).

Light is inextricably linked with Christ, who declared: "I am the light of the world" (John 8:12). The Credo speaks of him as being "light from light." Christians are "children of light" (Ephesians 5:8) who no longer want to live in the shadows. When giving a lighted candle at the end of the rite of baptism, the celebrant illustrates this by saying: "Receive the light of Christ."

A blessing of candles, followed by a procession, takes place before the mass on February 2, during the celebration of the Presentation of the Lord at the Temple, which is called Candlemas. In the Gospel reading of that day, old Simeon, in his Nunc Dimittis, sees in the child he is holding in his arms "a light of revelation for the gentiles" (Luke 2:32). The best-known example of a sacred light is the Paschal Candle, a symbol of the risen Christ. The Easter Vigil, the high point of the entire liturgical year, begins by the solemn blessing of the candle. This is an adaptation of the Jewish rite, which ordered the lighting of lamps on the Friday evening at the beginning of the Sabbath. It became the lucernarium (from the Latin *lucerna*, "lamp") of the early Church.

The celebrant engraves several symbols of Christ on to the Paschal Candle: the Cross; alpha and omega, which are the first and last letters of the Greek alphabet;[2] and, finally, the four digits of the number of the year. Five grains of incense are then melted into the center and the four extremities of the cross, as reminders of the five wounds of Christ crucified: in the hands, the feet, and in the side. The candle is lit from a freshly kindled light and carried into the church in procession, while the deacon proclaims three times "The Light of Christ." The candle burns only during the fifty days of the Easter period but, in the hearts of the baptized, it must never be allowed to go out. During funeral ceremonies, the Paschal Candle is lighted near the coffin as a sign of hope.

1. Matthew 25:1-13
2. " 'I am the Alpha and the Omega,' says the Lord God." (Revelations 1:8)

INCENSE

THE PLEASANT SCENT OF INCENSE
FILLS THE CHURCH WITH THE FRAGRANCE
OF GOD'S PRESENCE

Incense is an aromatic gum from the East, which, when burnt, gives off a perfumed smoke (from the Latin *incensum*, "something that is burnt"). Aromatic substances, such as benzoin, are often added to incense. It has also been burnt in order to purify houses or tents, as in joss sticks.

Religions make great use of incense, which creates a particular atmosphere, and a sort of welcoming presence in holy places. God himself told Moses to offer it twice a day in front of the sanctuary.[1] The smoke from incense is clearly visible and ascends in soft whirls, which symbolize prayers mounting up to God: "May my prayer be like incense in your presence" (Psalms 141:2). It was while he was making this same offering that Zechariah was told by the Archangel Gabriel about the birth of John the Baptist at the very threshold of the New Testament.[2] This part of the liturgy is closely related to heavenly liturgy: "Another angel, who had a golden censer, came and stood at the altar. A large quantity of incense was given to him to offer with the prayers of all the saints on the golden altar that stood in front of the throne; and so from the angel's hand the smoke of the incense went up in the presence of God and with it the prayers of the saints" (Revelations 8:3-4).

Incense is thus an homage of adoration given to God, like the gift, offered by the Wise Men to the infant Jesus: through frankincense, they recognize that he is God, through gold, that he is a King, and myrrh foreshadows his sepulture.[3] Given firstly to God, incense is also received by everything that it touches, and everything that belongs to him: the Cross, the altar, the book of the Gospels, the bread and the wine before and after consecration, but also the celebrants and the faithful, even the deceased. During a funeral, their mortal remains, which were the temple of the Spirit, are thurified.

For the burning of incense, a censer is used. This is a portable fragrance-burner suspended from three chains, with a cover that can be moved by means of a fourth one. Censers with only one chain can also be found. With the help of a spoon, the celebrant takes some incense from an incense-boat and places it on the burning coals contained in the cassolette. The smoke is then spread by swaying the censer. The server in charge of this delicate, complex instrument is called a thurifer, "a carrier of incense" (from the Latin thus, "incense" and ferre, "to carry"). In Eastern Orthodox churches, incense is very often used in front of icons and is normally highly perfumed (often with roses).

1. Exodus 30:7-8
2. Luke 1:9-11
3. Matthew 2:11

WATER

THE WATER THAT WASHES AND
PURIFIES, ALSO RESTORES IN THE SOUL
THE FRESHNESS OF ITS YOUTH

As a vital and familiar element in human existence, water has always been full of significance, in ancient views of the world, it was considered to be at the origin of all things and, in order to serve life, it had to be made fertile by the Breath of God.[1] If left to its own devices, water could carry everything away into death and primeval chaos (the flood and the sea). Thus, it is an ambivalent symbol that simultaneously evokes life and death, purification and sanctification.

The various ablutions and sprinklings of water in religious rites, like the blessing and the asperges at the beginning of Sunday mass, or the washing of the hands during the offertory, are first and foremost acts of purification, that is to say that they wash away any faults or stains that would be improper to the celebration of the liturgy.[2] In its positive aspect, water is the basis of life and a symbol of birth and rebirth.[3]

Liturgical rites are effective only if they involve the action of God. Baptism with water that of John the Baptist was merely a preparation for the baptism with water and the Spirit which the Son of God instituted.[4] When enlivened by the Spirit, water becomes one of its finest symbols. It received this consecration during the baptism of Jesus in the Jordan, becoming that "living water" which is a "gift of God," that is to say the Spirit itself which, being at the heart of the life of the Trinity, can alone come "welling up for eternal life" (John 4:10-14). When plunged into the life and death of Christ through baptism, the sons of God receive the Spirit as a "pledge," which waters and quenches them, while they wait to be immersed in the River of Life which flows from between the throne of God and the Lamb.[5]

The rivers of living water began to flow at the moment of Christ's death on the Cross, at the very hour when Jesus "gave up his spirit" (John 19:30) and let the blood and water spring out of his pierced heart as symbols of the sacraments that would henceforth operate through the force of the Spirit.

The blessing of water, to which holy salts can be added (a symbol of preservation and flavor), is a church tradition. The sprinkling of holy water is performed during many rites of blessing. It is sprinkled on the mortal remains of Christians, on their coffins, and on their tombs. At the entrance to churches, the basin of holy water is an invitation to the faithful to cross themselves after wetting the tips of their fingers in it. Holy water can also be requested and taken home: This is an act of faith, linked to the mystery of the Cross, which freed us from the Evil One.

1. Genesis 1:2
2. Ezekiel 36:25
3. Ezekiel 47:1-2; Revelations 22:1-2
4. John 3:5
5. 1 Corinthians 12:13; Revelations 22:1

HOLY OILS

WHEN AN ANOINTED OIL PENETRATES
THE FLESH, THE SPIRIT OF GOD DESCENDS
INTO THE MIDST OF OUR HEARTS

In every age, mankind—men often as much as women—have adored perfumes and unguents. The Scriptures talk about oil as a true symbol of joy, which sets faces shining.[1]

As it penetrates and fills the flesh, an anointment with oil symbolizes the consecration of a person by God in the role of being a king, priest, or prophet. Objects and buildings can also be consecrated by anointment. Our greatest example of the Anointed is the Messiah, or Christ, both of which are names in Hebrew and Greek respectively for Jesus, the King, High Priest, and Prophet. His strength and beauty is celebrated thus in one of the psalms: "You love uprightness and detest evil. This is why God, your God, has anointed you with oil of gladness, as none of your rivals" (Psalms 45:7).

Oil is a symbol of joy and beauty, and hence of consecration, but it is also a balm (or an ointment as we would now say) that relieves pain and strengthens wrestlers, making them suppler and less vulnerable. From this varied symbolism, the Church has concentrated on three types of oil, known as the "holy oils": the oil of the catechumens gives the strength of the Holy Spirit to those who are going to be baptized and become the wrestlers of God, beside Christ, against the spirit of Evil; the oil of anointing is the outward sign (the substance) used in the sacrament of the anointing of the sick as unction for the forehead and the palms of the hands and it relieves the sick with the presence of the Holy Spirit; the holy chrism is a fragrant oil used for anointment during consecrations. After baptism, it marks the top of the head of the new son of God. During confirmation, it crosses the forehead. After an Episcopal ordination, it is rubbed into the top of the new bishop's head; similarly, the hands of a new priest are anointed with it. During the dedication of churches and altars, it is spread over the crosses of consecration and all across the table of the altar. On each of these occasions, anointment with the holy chrism symbolizes the intervention of the Holy Spirit, which takes possession of beings or objects according to their mission or function.

It is during the "chrism" mass on the morning of Holy Thursday that the bishop solemnly blesses the oil of the catechumens and the oil of anointing before finally consecrating the holy chrism. The priests who celebrate this mass with him extend their hands during the consecration of the holy chrism. The holy oils are then kept in silver or golden ampullae, or altar-cruets, which are often topped by a small cross.

1. Psalms 104:15

THE ROSARY

IN THE CONSTANT REPETITION OF THE
"HAIL MARY," WE ENTER INTO THE MYSTERIES
OF JESUS THROUGH THE MATERNAL
TENDERNESS OF THE VIRGIN

Devotion to the Virgin Mary, the mother of God, is a characteristic of the Catholic and the Orthodox Churches. Protestants consider that giving to the Mother is to take away from the Son, and that turning to Mary is an offense to Christ's universal power as mediator, even though Our Lady is entirely dependent on Our Lord.

The most widespread form of Marian devotion is without doubt the rosary, which can be found in any Catholic's hands until the day he dies. This "rose-garden" (from the Latin *rosarium*) is a crown intended to honor the Virgin Mother. The rosary consists of five sets of ten beads, which are separated by individual beads, and are an invitation to fifty recitations of "Hail Mary," five of "Our Father," and five of "Glory be to the Father." The rosary also has a sort of tail, finishing with a cross, which carries three successive beads with two individual beads, one at each end. On the cross, which is in fact the starting point, we recite the "I believe in God"; on the first individual bead the "Our Father," then three "Hail Marys," and finally a "Glory be to the Father." The rosary thus honors the Trinity, the Cross, and the Virgin at the same time, which are all fundamental Catholic truths.

This lesser rosary is only a part of the full rosary. To tell the Rosary is to offer Our Lady a garland of roses made up of three lesser rosaries. The Feast of the Holy Rosary, on October 7, is related to the naval victory of the Christians over the Turkish fleet at Lepanto in October, 1571.

The "Hail Mary"—or the *Ave Maria*—is also known as the "angelic salutation" because it recalls the salutation of the Angel Gabriel to Mary at the Annunciation, to which can be added Elizabeth's salutation during the Visitation.[1] The second part of the prayer is not taken directly from the Gospels: "Holy Mary, Mother of God, pray for us sinners now and at the hour of our death. Amen." When recited privately or with a group certain variants exist, in particular the addition of "petitions," which dwell on the mysteries that are meditated on in the first part.

Saying the rosary is a way of entering into the mysteries of salvation through the proximity of Mary's heart.[2] The three crowns of the rosary are consecrated to the joyous mysteries, the sorrowful mysteries, and the glorious mysteries. Like the 150 psalms, these 150 *Ave Maria* are a study in contemplation. They allow us to enter, through the heart of a Mother entirely given over to the Spirit of Love, into the designs, which, through her Son, the Father has conceived for us.

1. Luke 1:28,42
2. Luke 2:19,51

THE LITURGICAL CALENDAR

WITHIN THE TEMPORAL CYCLE OF DAYS,
WEEKS, AND YEARS, THE SUCCESSION OF
FESTIVALS AND SAINTS' DAYS BRING US
EVER CLOSER TO GOD

Even if the ancients did not correctly understand the movements of the stars and planets, and believed that the Earth was the center of the universe, they were perfectly familiar with the rotation of the seasons, dividing the year into twelve months and observing the close proximity of certain planets, which they linked with their mythological gods.

When the Roman Empire abandoned its old system of dating by means of the Kalends, Nones, and Ides, replacing it with a seven day week, which they took from the Egyptians, these gods were used to name their days: Sunday was the Day of the Sun (*solis dies*, in German *Sonntag*); Monday was the day of the Moon (in French *lundi*); Tuesday was the day of Mars (in French *mardi*), who in English has been replaced by his Norse equivalent Tiw, the god of war; Wednesday was the day of Mercury (in French *mercredi*), in English replaced by his equivalent Woden; Thursday was the day of Jupiter (in French *jeudi*) replaced by Thor, the god of thunder; Friday was the day of Venus (in French *vendredi*), who was replaced by the goddess Frig; and Saturday was Saturn's day. Hours were counted according to the solar day, which breaks down into four groups of three hours.

The Bible has put its own understanding of the cosmos in the place of these polytheistic religions. According to Genesis, the sun and the moon are nothing more than instruments intended to divide light from darkness; the stars and the planets are the armies of the Lord of Sabaoth, and they cannot be worshiped in any way. The first six days of the week correspond to the successive stages of the creation, and the seventh is that of divine rest. That is why, for the Jews, Saturn's day is the Sabbath (from the Hebrew *shabbath*, "rest"; a Greek variant of this word turned it into *sambati dies*, hence the French *samedi* and the German *Samstag*).

The Christians called the first day of the week, Sunday, the "Day of the Lord" (*dies dominicus*, hence the French *dimanche*) in honor of the Resurrection. It also perpetuates certain ancient symbols, for the shining of the sun, which is born again each morning, is associated with the image of the Risen Christ; this metaphor was derived from the Old Testament.[1] The Virgin Mary who is not, like her Son, "light from light" (*Credo*) but reflects his brightness, therefore her role of mediator is symbolized by the moon. Numerous painters from all periods have represented her with her feet resting on a crescent moon.

From a delicate interweaving of this succession of different beliefs and symbols, as well as the different way in which time was measured, the three cycles of Catholic liturgy finally emerged: the daily cycle, the weekly cycle, and the yearly cycle. The daily liturgical cycle of "Hours" is made up of prayers, psalms, and readings that sanctify the various moments of the day: Lauds in the morning, the noontide office, Vespers at the end of the afternoon, and Compline before going to bed. The "Books of Hours," of which superb examples come down from the Middle Ages, are collections of prayers which allow laymen to follow these rituals. There are also nocturnal vigils (or Matins) for monks and nuns, and the "Little Hours," inspired by the Jewish tradition, which still follow the divisions of the day that were used in antiquity: tierce (about 10 a.m.), sext (about 1 p.m.), and nones (about 3 p.m.).

The weekly cycle starts on Sunday,[2] which is at once its source and its peak, hence the importance of Sunday mass for Catholics. From Monday to Saturday, each day follows its own liturgy from the second to the seventh *feria* (in Latin, "feast," for each and every day is sacred; this liturgical nomenclature goes back to the Later Byzantine Empire during which a vain attempt was made to ban the old pagan names for the days of the week). Friday, the day on which Our Lord died, is a day of penance and abstinence, which has made it unlucky in popular superstition.

The yearly cycle is more complicated, because it is simultaneously made up of the celebration of various liturgical moments in time (the "temporal") and the festivals of saints, which have been increasingly multiplied by popular devotion. But the mysteries of the Incarnation and Redemption are celebrated in the temporal cycle, which is thus of more importance. The Second Vatican Council made sure of re-establishing its primacy.

The temporal consists of two important cycles, Christmas and Easter, the celebration of which allows us to explore the entire mystery of our salvation in Christ. They both start with a time of preparation, Advent and Lent, are centered on the Feast of the Nativity and the Paschal Triduum, respectively, continue with "Christmastide" and "Eastertide," before finishing with the Feast of the Baptism of Our Lord and with Pentecost. The rest of the year consists of thirty-four weeks of "Ordinary Time."

Here then, in chronological order, are the main festivals of the temporal cycles, with explanations of their meanings:

I. ADVENT (from the Latin *adventus*, "coming"): the liturgical cycle begins with a time of preparation for Christmas, starting on the fourth Sunday before December 25. Advent is, for us, a time of joyous waiting (particularly on the third Sunday, which is called *Gaudete*, "rejoice," from the first word of its introit) for a triple coming: the humble birth of Jesus in a stable in Bethlehem, the grace that is still today given to us by celebrating his liturgy, and Christ's return in glory on the last day. The first Sundays of Advent are focused on the third event, while the week immediately before Christmas concentrates on the other two.

II. CHRISTMAS (or Noël, from the Latin *natalis dies*, "the day of birth"): nine months after the Annunciation (March 25), December 25 celebrates the birth of Christ and the mystery of the Incarnation, the basis of all Christian symbolism. Christmas is also the festival of the Holy Family of Joseph, Mary, and Jesus, and so of all families, a celebration of life which comes from God before returning to him.

The solemnity of Christmas christianized the pagan festival of *Natalis Invicti* ("birth of the unconquered Sun") at the winter solstice. On that date, the sun starts to climb back up the sky, like the Child who is destined to grow up. Reciprocally, the summer solstice, on June 24, corresponds to the festival of Saint John the Baptist, the Precursor, who said of Jesus: "He must grow greater, I must grow less" (John 3:30).

III. EPIPHANY (from the Greek *epiphainein*, "to show, or reveal"): in the East, the feast of the Epiphany was the celebration of Jesus's birth and revelation as the Messiah and Savior. Fixed on January 6, it is the festival of the True Light, that of the star, which appeared to the Wise Men and guided them to Christ.[3] The feast of the Kings remains popular. In every crib, three "Magi" come to adore the true King and give him gold, frankincense, and myrrh. Twelfth-night cake, which is blessed at the mass, symbolizes Christ, bread, and life (in Hebrew, "Bethlehem" means "the house of bread"). The Wise Men have rather eclipsed the two other "revelations," which Epiphany also celebrates: the baptism of Christ in the Jordan by John the Baptist (a feast day is consecrated to this on the Sunday after Epiphany, which concludes the Christmas cycle), and the Wedding at Cana, where his first public action took place.

IV. CANDLEMAS: on February 2, forty days after his birth, the Lord's Presentation at the Temple of Jerusalem is a complement to the Christmas cycle. This was an old Jewish custom, which the Holy Family respected.[4] It is a celebration of light, in connection with the words of old Simeon, who saw in the child "a light of revelation for the gentiles." It consists of a blessing and procession of candles before mass. The faithful, who hope to become "children of light," generally carry holy candles with them. These are then burnt beside the dead, as a sign of hope for eternal life.

V. LENT (from the Old English *lencten*, "the spring"): this "holy quarantine" of forty days is a time of penitential preparation for Easter. The period of forty days is the same as that which preceded the meeting with God on Mount Sinai for both Moses and Elijah.[5] Jesus himself prepared for his public ministry by fasting in the desert for forty days. Lent lasts for six weeks, but, since penance is not performed on Sundays, it begins on the Wednesday before the first Sunday, that is on Ash Wednesday.

Ash Wednesday's "ashes," normally obtained from burning the previous year's palms from Palm Sunday, symbolize mankind's worthlessness when faced with God. Following original sin, dust is the image of death, linked with sin: "For dust you are" God said to the first man, "and to dust you shall return" (Genesis 3:19). The practice of fasting also allows us to explore the limits of our human condition. As an antidote to overeating, it asks us to realize that we are beings dependent on our Creator's goodness.

In the middle of Lent, the fourth Sunday, which is called *Laetare* ("rejoice," the first word of the introit), marks a pause. The Church invites us to a joyful break before Easter. The great festival's white vestments are still to be donned, but the violet of penance brightens into pink.

The sixth Sunday of Lent is Palm Sunday, which starts Holy Week. It commemorates the solemn entry of Jesus into Jerusalem, a few days before his Passion and death on the Cross.[7] The congregation meets somewhere outside the church. Here, the celebrant blesses the palms (or branches of boxwood or bay, according to different regions) and a procession sets off towards the church for a mass, during which one of the Gospel accounts of the Passion is read. The faithful take home these branches, which have been blessed, and use them to decorate their crucifixes.

VI. EASTER (from *Eastre*, a goddess whose festival was held at the spring equinox; the adjective "paschal" comes from the Hebrew *pasach*, "to spare," hence *pesach* "paschal-lamb," in Latin *pascha*; the sacrifice of the paschal-lamb being the prelude to the escape from Egypt): the Easter festival is the most important of the entire liturgical year and includes the three days of the paschal *Triduum*. It begins with a mass on the evening of Holy Thursday, which commemorates the Last Supper, during which Jesus instituted the Eucharist. On the next day, Good Friday, we celebrate his Passion and death on the Cross, particularly during the afternoon office.

Apart from the liturgy itself, we also perform the ritual of the way of the Cross, with its fourteen stations that go from Jesus's condemnation to his burial; it can also be followed from the Last Supper until the Resurrection. Easter Saturday is a day of silence, of waiting, and of hope. The celebration of the Resurrection begins with the Easter Vigil on Saturday evening, with the blessing of the newly kindled fire and of the Paschal Candle, followed by some lengthy readings and a mass. It inaugurates the Solemnity of Solemnities, which constitutes the Easter festival, bearing witness to Jesus's victory over death in token of our own resurrection.

Easter is a movable feast, the date of which is not fixed by the civil calendar. According to the rules, which were established in the fourth century, it is celebrated on the first Sunday after the fourteenth day following the new moon in March; that is to say, between March 22 at the earliest and April 25 at the latest. Each year, the entirety of the Easter cycle is fixed according to the date of Easter Day, which is introduced into the succession of the thirty-four ordinary Sundays.

The fifty days of the Easter period, which continue up to Pentecost, do not in reality contain more than one day of celebration, which is a time of joy and gladness, dominated by the chanting of Alleluia (from the Hebrew *hallelujah*, "praise Jah," that is to say "praise be to Yahweh, praise the Lord"), an acclamation that can be found in the Psalms.

VII. THE ASCENSION: forty days after Easter, the Ascension celebrates the final going up to heaven of the risen Lord. According to the Acts of the Apostles, Jesus, now victorious over death, appeared to his disciples for forty days during which he would "tell them about the kingdom of God" (Acts 1:3). As it is expressed in the creed: "He ascended into heaven and is seated at the right hand of the Father. He will come again in glory to judge the living and the dead, and his Kingdom will have no end."

VIII. PENTECOST (from the Greek *pentekoste*, "the fiftieth [day]"): the fiftieth day after Easter, Pentecost is the festival that concludes Easter-tide and, with the gift of the Spirit, it is the culmination of its mystery. The apostles were together with Mary in the Upper Room when they were filled with the Spirit, which came down on them as a violent wind and as tongues of fire that came to rest on their heads.[8] The fire of divine love could henceforth be spread by them, according to the mission that Jesus had given them. Pentecost is the day of the inception of the Church, which was born in their preaching concerning the marvels of God (Acts 2:11).

IX. TRINITY: the Sunday after Pentecost is the Festival of the Trinity, which comes late in the liturgy because the mystery of the unity of the Father, the Son, and the Holy Spirit is the beginning and end of the entire Christian life. It is constantly being celebrated (cf. the chapter dealing with the Trinity).

X. CORPUS CHRISTI DAY: on the Thursday after the Festival of the Trinity (or on the Sunday in certain countries and regions), Corpus Christi Day celebrates the Eucharist. It is a popular festival, marked by the worshipping and procession of the Holy Sacrament. The route that the Lord is to take is strewn with foliage and also decorated with designs made from dyed sawdust. Several towns throughout the world are famous for their magnificent processions.

XI. THE SACRED HEART: this festival is celebrated on the second Friday after Trinity Sunday. It is based around the idea of Christ's human love, and was suggested by the episode during which his heart was pierced after his death on the Cross.[9] The water and blood that flowed from that wound symbolize the sacraments, which spring everlastingly from Jesus's open heart.

XII. THE ASSUMPTION: the Virgin Mary's ascent into heaven, where she rejoins her Son in both body and spirit, is celebrated on August 15. As opposed to Christ, who ascended into the sky on his own, the Virgin was borne up by angels in the glory of God. This explains the word "Assumption" (from the Latin *assumere*, "to lift up, to raise").

XIII. ALL SAINTS' DAY: since the ninth century, November 1 has been a celebration of the memory of all the saints, and it is a joyous anticipation of our own salvation. The next day, November 2, is consecrated to All Souls, which is sometimes mistakenly confused with All Saints' Day. This commemoration of the dead was founded by Saint Odilon, Abbot of Cluny, at the beginning of the sixth century.

XIV. CHRIST THE KING: since 1925 we have, on the thirty-fourth and last Sunday of Ordinary Time, celebrated The Feast of Christ the King, a solemn homage to him who gave himself completely for us, even to death. It is a preparation for the new liturgical year, which begins with Advent on the following Sunday.

Throughout the year, we also celebrate saints' days, whose memorials, feasts, and solemnities are part of a different cycle. Each day is thus the occasion to remember different saints from various periods, whose merits can be a guide to Christians on the path towards perfection. Some of these days are more important than others, depending on the country or church; particularly the celebrations of "patron saints" of different churches or regions. There are also many firmly established popular traditions such as, in France, les *feux de Saint Jean* on Midsummer's Day, or the various sayings that have become attached to saints' days.

These different cycles that interweave and follow one another should not create the impression that Christians go round in circles. On the contrary, each year, each week, and each day, they enter more fully into the essential mysteries of religion. Our nature as human beings means that we need these sorts of reminders, which let the grace and great love of God dwell more deeply in our hearts.

Liturgical cycles are signaled by the ringing of bells, which hence have an important place in the life of Christians. When they sound a baptism, marriage, or funeral, the daily or Sunday masses and, in monasteries, the hours of the divine offices, the pealing of bells from a church is a sign of its vitality. Bells symbolize God calling to his people to celebrate the Covenant and also, traditionally, the voices of angels;

this explains the veneration they have always received and the solemnity that surrounds their blessing, which is, in a way, their baptism with an ablution, anointment with holy chrism and burning of incense.

1. "But for you who fear my name, the Sun of justice will rise with healing in his rays" (Malachi 3:20).
2. "On the first day of the week, at the first sign of dawn, they went to the tomb" (Luke 24:1).
3. Matthew 2:1-12
4. Leviticus 12:2-4; Luke 2:22-38
5. Exodus 24:18; 1 Kings 19:8
6. Matthew 4:2
7. "The great crowd of people who had come up for the festival heard that Jesus was on his way to Jerusalem. They took branches of palm and went out to receive him..." (John 12:12-13).
8. Acts 2:1-13
9. John 19:32-34

SYMBOLS OF TIBETAN BUDDHISM

BY CLAUDE B. LEVENSON

THE WHEEL OF TIME

TEMPORAL CYCLES CADENCING
THE TIMELESS GESTURES OF EVERYDAY LIFE

Tibetans anchor human beings in their physical, spiritual, and universal dimensions through the wheel of time. It is created in colored sands for initiations, or represented on embroidered or hand-painted cloth scrolls.

The Wheel of Time is a sumptuous multicolored diagram of the initiation of the *Kâlachakra,* one of the *Vajrayâna*'s most complete teachings, at once the opening up of the road to knowledge and the path that leads to harmony. This harmony grows out of a subtle resonance between the human body and mind and the outer universe, which encapsulates them within its astrological and cosmic dimensions. Yet the Tibetans have done it with their special genius, marrying the ephemeral and the eternal. In the rigorous and complete practice of the *Kâlachakra,* the Himalayan sages glimpse the possibility of attaining Enlightenment in a single lifetime. Hence its complexity.

According to Tenzin Gyatso, the present Dalai Lama and the fourteenth of the line, the symbolism of the Wheel of Time is closely associated with our world and era: "We firmly believe in its ability to reduce tension," he explains, "we feel that it can create peace, peace of mind, and thereby promote peace in the world. Some day, in centuries to come, the Kingdom of Shambala might well reappear in the reality which seems to be our own, and contribute to the overall task we still need to accomplish in this world."

The spiritual leader has himself conferred this great initiation on more than twenty occasions, between 1954, at Lhasa in his native Tibet, and 1995 at Ulan Bator in Mongolia. Among his destinations were Bodh Gaya and Sarnath, the spiritual centers of Buddhism; Rikon in Switzerland; Madison, Wisconsin, in the United States; Barcelona in Spain; Leh in Ladakh; and Mungod in southern India.

To attend such an initiation—to observe the preparation of the stupa, listen to the teaching, visually penetrate the universe of colors and symbols, survey the sacred cosmogram, and banish all else from view—sows the seeds of a forthcoming happy rebirth.

By attuning the human being to the cosmos, the *Kâlachakra* activates the internal and external forces illustrated by the *mandala*, the medium of meditation and diagram of the universe, with all the associations it engenders. At the heart of the *stupa*, in the innermost sanctuary of the deity, within the palace of the primordial conscience represented by the blue *vajra*, *Kâlachakra* symbolizes the moon, while his consort *Vishvamata* personifies the sun in the form of an orange yellow point. Wisdom and compassion unite here in an embrace in which all contradictions dissolve, a void that harbors all possibilities.

But the Wheel of Time is also the mechanism that regulates the daily calendar based on lunar cycles. It is no surprise to find a dual root, Indian and Chinese, in the calculation of Tibetan time. It appears that Indian influence was preponderant, although the designation of the years preserves a strong Chinese imprint. To distinguish between these two influences, the Indian computation is qualified as "white mathematics," and the Chinese manner as "black mathematics," this latter also overlapping divinatory practices. Almanacs and astrological tables are frequently used in daily life, highlighting the outstanding events of the year.

The days of the week are named after the planets, and form thirty-day months, their names strictly ordinal: first month, second month, etc. Each month begins on the new moon, so that the full moon marks the mid-month. The Tibetan year is thus lunar, and begins on the new moon in February, preceded by a day called *Gutor*, during which one rids oneself of all that was negative in the previous year. The eve of *Lo-Sar* (New Year) is usually spent doing a thorough house—or tent-cleaning.

Both good and bad days are accounted for in everyday activities, the eighth day of the month being dedicated to the Buddha of medicine, the fifteenth to the Buddha Amitâbha, and the thirtieth to

Shâkyamuni, the historical Buddha. On these special days, the effects of any action, positive or negative, are multiplied by one hundred. To restore the concordance between the solar and lunar years, a day is simply skipped from time to time, and the necessary adjustments regularly made to avoid inextricable problems.

Twelve animals—mouse, cow, tiger, hare, dragon, snake, horse, sheep, monkey, bird, dog, and pig—order the duodecimal cycle, of which five complete repetitions constitute in their turn a sixty-year cycle. To avoid confusion, an element is added to each of these symbols (earth, metal, water, wood, fire), a gender (masculine or feminine), sometimes even a color, which actually corresponds to one of the elements: yellow ocher for earth, white for metal, blue for water, green for wood, and red for fire. Astrological calculations, still practiced in medicine and horoscopy, make extensive use of these data, with an accuracy that our sober dispositions would find astonishing. By way of example, the Tibetan year 2123, of the fire mouse, began on 19 February, 1996.

THE WHEEL OF LIFE

EACH INDIVIDUAL IS ATTUNED
TO HIS OWN SPIRITUAL AWARENESS

The Wheel of Life is a visual depiction of the various states of being. It is found in every monastery, usually painted directly on the wall, but also on paper or cloth supports. The Wheel of Life reminds all sentient beings that the supreme aim is ever and always Enlightenment. Ceaselessly reproduced or recreated through the centuries, it has accompanied generations of rough nomads and refined scholars on the many roads of the quest and of devotion, recalling to each person the passing of time and the Four Noble Truths: the existence of suffering, its origin and causes, its ending and the way to achieve this.

Traditionally, the Lord of Death, with the wrathful mien, projecting fangs and forehead wreathed in a macabre crown, holds firmly between his powerful arms a large disc in which four concentric circles of codified dimensions are inscribed. Complete with clawlike nails and a tiger's skin of which the tail and hind paws can be seen, this terrifying personage wears rich serpentine jewels. He is thought to personify destiny, what is ordinarily called karma, and symbolizes the transient nature of all phenomena.

This existential breviary is best interpreted by starting at the center. The first circle contains the three spiritual poisons responsible for the evils to come: a black pig for ignorance, a green snake for hatred and envy, and a red cock for lust and greed. A second circle surrounds it, half white, half black. Whoever is ensnared by these evil drives takes the path of darkness (*ngan gro' i lam*) which leads to unhappy rebirths and the fires of hell. The others take the path of light (*de gro' i lam*) which leads to better rebirths and to the fields of liberation.

A dozen smaller tableaux, all explicit, make up the outer circle of the great disc. They unfold the steps of human existence, with easily understandable symbols. Starting at the lower left, the old man seeking his path remains in the grip of ignorance, which is a spiritual blindness. Then, continuing clockwise, the potter turning a pot shapes his destiny by his own acts; the monkey leaping from branch to branch refers to the uncontrolled awareness of the ignorant, which must be disciplined in order to be mastered; the coracle and its two passengers represent name and form, or the energies—physical and spiritual—that are inseparable in the stream of life; the five-windowed house of the fifth vignette evokes the five senses and the faculty of thought, without which there is no perception of the outside world; and the man and woman in intimate union signify contact, the consequence of perception.

Emotions come next. Thus the woman offering drink to the man arouses desire, the symbol of the thirst for life nourished with perceptions. This leads to sensual attachment, the tendency to cling to the object of desire: a man gapes at the fruit of a tree. In the next image, the attractive young woman suggests procreation, new life developing. Next comes the actual birth, a new life. Finally, the last earthly step is sanction by death, and the preparation for rebirth in one of the six worlds that make up our universe.

Between the outer circle of the human seasons and the double white or black road extend the six worlds where the being must be reborn according to his own acts of body, speech, and mind. First, in the center of the upper section, is the paradise of the gods (a temporary paradise, fleeting, even if it lasts for centuries, because gods also die when they begin to believe in their own immortality), where they listen to the melody that the Buddha plays for them on the lute, without hearing his implicit warning against the vanity of pleasures. Sometimes echoes of distant combats reach them from the neighboring empire of the Titans, who savagely battle to satisfy irrepressible ambitions. Among them, the Buddha bears his sword.

The bottom half contains three spaces where it is unwise to return: ominous places where evil spirits relentlessly multiply torments. On the right, greedy monsters tortured by thirst and hunger are unable to assuage their desires due to prohibitive physical deformities. Yet their sky is illuminated by a Buddha bearing a casket overflowing with jewels of the mind. Slightly lower down are the infernal regions, where fire and ice punish the guilty for evil deeds perpetrated under the domination of hatred or anger. This nightmarish world is surveyed by an acolyte of the Lord of Death, who measures the weight of each of the actions of his victims. Yet only he who has committed them is the real artisan of his own doom. The Buddha here carries a flame, the flame of hope, because no life in any of these worlds is eternal.

The last lower level, on the left, is populated with animals, slaves of the goodwill of other beings, and here the Buddha attests his presence by a book. Between this animal kingdom and the home of the gods, lies the realm of men in all their diversity. It is the human being who ultimately enjoys the greatest privilege, because, in this infinitely

271

variegated kaleidoscope, he alone can consciously make the choice to lend an ear to the teaching of a begging monk who shows him the way to end suffering. By awaking from his hallucinated dream, he sheds all chains, be they of gold or of iron, but it is he who must walk on the path.

THE WHEEL OF LAW

HELP OTHERS, DO NOT HARM THEM

The Wheel of the Law is present in every Tibetan sanctuary. It generally has eight spokes, and is pictured, flanked by two gazelles or deer, on the main façade of all monasteries, whether large or small. It symbolizes above all the doctrine preached by the historical Buddha, and the graceful animals that accompany it represent his first two listeners or disciples. Yet Buddhism leaves nothing to chance; behind the apparent simplicity of this first explanation, upon continued reflection, a deeper meaning of the symbol unravels and it must be followed like Ariadne's thread.

The Wheel, or *chakra*, is the endless cycle of birth and rebirth, samsâra pullulating with the multitude of beings ensnared in the nets of illusion. The Law as spoken of here is—to be sure—what is implied in its association with "true nature," underlying the natural law of the universe: the ethics and morals of human beings. The supreme truth of the whole diversity of worlds and universes, it was perceived, understood, and defined by Prince Siddhartha Shâkyamuni, as the Enlightened One, who formulated it so as to make it intelligible to the generations of the present cosmic cycle.

The eight spokes of the Wheel of the Law symbolize the Eightfold Path, the eight ways of liberation that lead to Enlightenment. The four-spoked wheel evokes the four crucial "moments" in the life of the Buddha, and his disciples considered it an all-conquering weapon to control the passions. It is also the constant reminder of the Four Noble

Truths of suffering, its cause, its ending, and the way to achieve this.

According to Tibetan tradition, the Wheel of the Law was set in motion on three occasions: during the first teaching dispensed by the newly enlightened sage in the deer park, near Sarnath; on the appearance of the *Mahâyâna*; and when the *Vajrayâna* or *Tantrayâna* appeared.

The Wheel of the Law also symbolizes the Middle Way. It is the path followed by Shâkyamuni, who warned his followers to shun extremes—rigorous asceticism and unbridled debauchery alike—in order to attain supreme knowledge, which is the fulcrum midway between the reality and the non-reality of things. This shows how important the Wheel of the Law is as a fundamental symbol on which many interpretations are founded, even though these various facets are so many reflections of a single essence.

The legend of Siddhartha relates that, after six years of rigorous asceticism, the Buddha in the making replenished his energies with a bowl of rice and undertook to meditate beneath a sacred tree, on the west bank of the Lilajan River (some ten kilometers south of Gayâ, in Magadha), the modern-day Bihar. He had decided not to leave the spot until he had attained Enlightenment, *Bodhi*. In the course of a famous night, he achieved the goal he had set for himself, despite the temptations of the legions of Mâra, master of death and of illusion. And the new dawn brought him omniscience.

For seven weeks, Shâkyamuni tasted this unprecedented happiness in the immediate confines, now sacred, of Bodh Gaya. Near the tree of Rajyatana, he met with Tapussa and Balluka, two merchants from the Indian province of Hutkala (modern-day Orissa), who became his first two disciples, and are symbolized by the two animals that accompany the wheel. Some sources claim they are deer, others find gazelles, and yet others insist that they are actually unicorns.

The Wheel of the Law, the foundation of human existence, is inseparable from the concept of *karma*, the act: every act is the fruit of a previous act, bringing a consequence in its wake. This sequence embodies the law of causality. Yet it does not imply a blind or implacable determinism, because, while *karma* shapes present situations according to previous acts, the individual retains the ability to devise his own response to the conditions of the moment. He has the choice between persisting in the direction conditioned by his past acts, or, on the contrary, taking a path that alleviates his evil tendencies.

Another aspect is that intention generally prevails over actual performance of the act. In the eyes of Buddhists, it is therefore important to avoid any harmful intention, because merely forming the idea gives rise to karmic consequences, good or evil. On the other hand, performed without hatred, without envy or confusion, any act whatsoever remains devoid of karmic results. Acts are physical, but also psychic or verbal: hence the need to preserve the purity of body, mind, and speech, which are the basis of an existence according to the law.

The Wheel of the Law stops turning only at the precise moment when the bonds of causality are forever loosened, when the individual is released from illusion and attains the omniscient wisdom of Enlightenment.

RED HATS AND YELLOW HATS

UNDER THE PROTECTIVE WING OF THE THREE JEWELS

The hat, an attribute of certain rites, has become the emblematic sign of the so-called schools of the Ancients (red) and the Moderns (yellow). As Buddhist doctrine evolved locally, four main orders emerged in the Tibetan Land of the Snows. After a first wave of translation of the founding texts, the seventh century witnessed the birth of the *Nyingma* school, whose adepts are generally called the Ancients and claim the heritage of the sage Padmasambhava.

After the bloody political religious conflicts in later centuries, almost annihilating the Good Law and restoring earlier beliefs, the renewed flourishing of the doctrine gave birth to the *Sakya* and

Kagyü schools. Other currents blossomed in turn around spiritual masters who based themselves on a personal interpretation of the texts, enriched philosophical reflection, and trained their disciples in the exercise of particular paths of access to Enlightenment.

Forming and disbanding in a random pattern, often rooted in a remote spot due to the local presence of a hermit or an ascetic, certain minor orders lasted the space of a human lifetime—the master's. Always more or less sticking to the Eightfold Path, others survived and spread along the byways. Such were the Kagyü order, which had many avatars, and the Kadampa school, originally associated with the Reting Monastery, the influence of which persisted in the Gelug order.

A final wave on the colorful scene of Tibetan Buddhism, the school of "those who practice virtue," owed its birth to the great erudite reformer Tsongkhapa, who founded the famous Ganden Monastery in 1409, after having powerfully contributed to the creation of two other monasteries, Sera and Drepung. These three great monastic universities are in fact still considered as the "three pillars of Tibet." The *Gelugpa*, the vehicle of transmission of knowledge and wisdom generated by the reform of Tsongkhapa, ultimately prevailed over the others (*Nyingmapa, Sakyapa,* and *Kagyüpa*) chiefly through the political ascendancy of the Dalai Lama.

It is nevertheless important to discard the impression of a perpetual antagonism between these different orders. Undoubtedly conflicts occasionally arose between them, due to personal rivalries and diverging interests, often inspired by temporary outside allies. In terms of doctrine, however, Red Hats and Yellow Hats acknowledge each other as faithful servants of the Law of the Buddha. Besides, while the former are associated with the Ancients and the latter are closer to the Gelug order, either hat is sometimes used for specific rituals.

The first indispensable step for the Buddhists of the Land of the Snows is an unreserved commitment to the way, implied by *kyabdro,* that is to say "seeking refuge" in the Triple Gem. For Tibetan Buddhists, this is a normal prerequisite to any initiation into the Good Law, inasmuch as concrete practice is indissociable from text learning. And besides, to perform meditation exercises correctly, it is necessary to have a master able to direct this dual apprenticeship.

From this requirement stems another, the mutual and judicious choice that seals the relationship between master and disciple. Wherever it may be, the foundation of the Buddhist vision remains the Triple Gem or the Three Gems, which are the Buddha (the Enlightened One), his teaching (the *Dharma* or the Law), and the monastic community (the *sangha*). With the evolution of the *Mahâyâna*, which advanced the notion of the universality of Buddhahood beyond the historical personality of Shakyâmuni, the development of the *Vajrayâna* enhanced the pre-eminence of the master/teacher who incarnated its principle while living among men. Moreover, the term "lama" is not employed for each and every monk, but is a title reserved for the most accomplished and the most scholarly, sages authorized to teach doctrine and to perform rites, to train others and to guide them to Enlightenment in accordance with their own aptitudes.

For the strict practitioner, the Tantrayâna tradition is to place one's whole existence under the complementary yet capital protection of the "Three Roots": the lama, the source of benediction during the quest; a meditation or tutelary deity (*yidam*), as a token of accomplishment; and the protectors of the Law and the female deities (*dâkinî*), the pledge of enlightened activity. The "taking of refuge" is generally accompanied by prostrations, the physical expression of humility, which is also a way of honoring the teaching.

THE STUPA

A MATERIALIZATION OF THE INTERIOR QUEST

The *stupa* is a monument of Indian and pre-Buddhist origin, primarily intended to mark the important places of the doctrine consecrated by the historical Buddha's passage on earth: in Lumbini, the village of his birth; in Bodh Gaya where meditation opened the doors to Enlightenment; in Sarnath where he gave his first teaching. A *stupa* also stands at Kushinagar to accommodate the Buddha's mortal remains after his physical departure from the land of man (his *parinirvana*).

Adjusting to the vagaries of Buddhist doctrine, the *stupa* went through many metamorphoses in different latitudes: in Ceylon it became the *dagoba*, in Siam the *chedi*, and in Tibet the *chörten*. Examples both admirable and varied are found in the Royal Singhalese cities, in the sumptuous Shwedagon pagoda in Rangoon, not to mention the marvel of Borobodur in Java, and the countless *chörten* disseminated in the sanctuaries along the pilgrim trails in Tibet.

The perfect proportions of the Buddha's body served as a model for the erection of these distinctive monuments, which were built according to strictly defined rules. The foundation stands on a square base denoting the earth, surmounted by a dome symbolizing water, prolonged by a flight of stairs betokening the steps of Enlightenment and representing fire. A stylized umbrella, emblem of the wind, caps the overall structure and culminates in a crescent moon on which the solar disc rests, the expression of the cosmic supremacy of the Buddhist Law.

In the *chörten*, which frequently serves as a receptacle for offerings or a tomb for great spiritual masters, the Tibetans see the figuration of the body, speech, and mind of the Buddha. Architectural variants sometimes include a five-petalled lotus flower crowning the parasol and symbolizing the five lines of Buddhas in the *Mahâyâna*. Other interpretations embody the high points in the spiritual quest, occasionally with the statue of a deity at the center of the reliquary.

Small or large, the *chörten*, or *stupa*, built amid sanctuaries or standing alone among the mountains, is honored by the faithful, who donate offerings, prostrate themselves before it, burn incense, and circumambulate it in a sunwise direction. Alone, in groups, or in series, *chörten* always imply the presence of the Buddha, and are indissociable from the reading of the world given by Tibetan tradition.

THE PRAYER WHEEL

In a "country of shepherds and monks, isolated from the world and so close to the sky," of which Jacques Bacot said at the turn of the century that "the natural occupation of its inhabitants is prayer," the *khorten*, commonly called the "prayer wheel," is undoubtedly the Buddhist ritual object best known to the profane, as well as being the pilgrim's dearest companion. Another name for it is the *chos-kor*, which means "to turn the doctrine" and refers to the first teaching of the Buddha, when he set the Wheel of the Law in motion.

From the smallest to the largest, the prayer wheel always consists of a hollow cylindrical body, usually of metal, engraved with mystic emblems or prayers. It is penetrated along its axis by a rod provided with a handle, if portable, or with two clips if it is fixed to a stand. This applies to all prayer wheels that are placed at hand height, along the outer walls of sanctuaries.

Enclosed in the *chos-kor* are sacred texts or invocations (*mantra*), written on paper or parchment. The cylinder of the wheel is rotated in the same direction as the sun, and each turn is the equivalent of a reading of the prayers enclosed within. Set in motion, the wheel emits a gentle ticking sound in pace with the walker's rhythm. According to the faithful, this attests to the flight of the prayers thus scattered to the four winds. The portable prayer wheel is fitted with a ball at the end of a small chain fixed midway along the metal body; with a flick of the wrist, the person carrying the wheel sets its twirling rhythm.

Many materials can be shaped to form the body of this singular instrument, not only coarse metal, but also more precious alloys, sometimes even enhanced with mother of pearl, coral, or turquoise. Thus certain prayer wheels are genuine works of art.

At the monastery entrance, the *chos-kor* may be of impressive size, protected from the weather by a roof, or even installed in a sort of watchtower with a door. An unencumbered space is provided all around to enable the devotee to accompany the turning wheel which is adorned with sacred *mantra*. It is driven by one or more handles, which serve to turn the wheel. In the greener lands of the Himalayan valleys, nestled in the faults of the mountain ramparts, a rudimentary but highly effective system is used to harness waterfalls and running streams to turn the prayer paddle wheels, which ceaselessly give voice to pious murmurs, cadencing and echoing with an incantatory and rhythmic regularity.

Tibetans also have a custom of erecting prayer flags, mounted in garlands, on the roofs of their houses, or in the case of nomadic shepherds, on top of their tents. Prayer flags ornament the bridges that straddle torrential streams, and they accumulate at mountain passes. These beneficial formulas are printed on small pieces of cloth in the five basic colors (yellow, white, red, green, and blue), which stand for the five elements (earth, water, fire, air, and ether), the five senses, and the five wisdoms. Prayer flags are a means of spreading the good word to all beings, both in populated regions and in the vastness of deserted spaces. But their function is also to attract good luck, to preserve health by warding off disease, the evil eye, demons, and evil spells, and finally, to manifest one's gratitude for a wish fulfilled or an unexpected beneficial occurrence.

Near monasteries, prayer flags become victory banners. Mounted on tall poles, they indicate places worthy of attention. They mark the location of sacred caves, and the high points of mountain passes, where the traveler may thank the gods for their protection.

At sowing time, these small colored cloths are placed on the foreheads of farm animals, to ensure good harvests. The yaks that accompany pilgrims also wear them, which serves as a signal that they are not to be sacrificed but should be allowed to die a natural death.

In the middle of the most common model of prayer flag stands the *lungta*, or wind-horse, the bearer of the precious Wish-fulfilling Jewel. It can be inscribed with the name of the person for whom the wind-borne wishes are intended. The remaining space is filled with sacred or magical formulas, and the four corners usually contain a tiger, a lion, a dragon, and the mythical bird, the *garuda*. All these animals are symbols of power and energy. A victory pole can be mounted, or garlands of prayer banners assembled, for ceremonial occasions: the presence of monks then confers a sacred character on the act, which becomes commensurately more beneficial by being part of a ritual.

SACRED MANTRA

"OM MANI PEME HUNG"

This millennial litany is both the symbol of Buddhist life in Tibet and the expression of a way of being. It has been the subject of hundreds of exegeses, of thousands of interpretations. The Tibetans pronounce it *om mani peme hung*, and its simplest translation would be "om jewel of the lotus om." For the common believer, its incantatory recitation suffices to ensure his spiritual well-being. For the advanced adept, the complexity of the successive layers of meaning of each of the sounds, taken individually or as a whole, unveils the thousand and eight facets of reality—or illusion. The origin of this *mantra* is associated with Chenresig-Avalokiteshvara, the Great Compassionate One. He is the supreme Protector of Tibet, and is incarnated in the Dalai Lama, who thereby remains the spiritual and temporal leader against all comers.

For the *Vajrayâna* or *Tantrayâna* practitioner, the first and last syllables are believed to be charged with power, and must be handled with infinite precaution. *Om* is the body, the speech, and the mind of the disciple, at the same time as those of a Buddha: it symbolizes their metamorphosis, or the attainment of Enlightenment. *Mani*, the Jewel proper, grants all wishes and signifies the supreme goal to which one aspires. *Peme*, the lotus flower, embodies wisdom, particularly that of the perfect void. And *hung* expresses the indivisibility, the indissociable unity of method and wisdom.

Roughly speaking, the Great Tibetan Mantra states that the practice of a way, by the inseparable union of wisdom and appropriate means, can serve to transform a common body, speech, and mind into the perfectly pure equivalence of a Buddha: a whole program of life based on discipline and reflection, pushed to absolute limits, until the attainment of full Enlightenment.

Everywhere in the Land of the Snows, the presence of the Great Mantra is proclaimed on prayer flags, engraved on roadside stones, or inscribed on the mountainsides in monumental displays. It is found on scraps of paper pinned onto the doors of homes and monastery thresholds; or woven into khata, traditional scarves of praise and happiness. All of Tibet is embodied in these few words that ring out from moment to moment, from one life to the next. The Great Mantra is the land's favorite protector, replete with inner meaning. Inextricably associated with the Dalai Lama, it is the most powerful of all utterances.

THE ROSARY

THE MÂLA

The *mâla* is a rosary in the Buddhist manner, one of the essential attributes of the pilgrim and of many deities. It has 108 beads, and is used to recite prayers, but, above all, to count the number of repetitions of a particular formula, intoned to a select deity. According to the school and deity, and according to whether the faithful are monks or laymen, they generally keep to the deity to whom they feel closest, to the *mantra* which they received during a particular initiation, or to the invocation indicated by a lama for a precise purpose, such as protection, cure, or gratitude.

The *mani* happens to enjoy the greatest favor. A widespread practice, which may be individual or collective, is to repeat this *mantra* a million times, for purification, or to increase one's merits. The exercise also helps to calm and clarify one's thoughts, which is the indispensable preparatory phase for meditation.

When the *mâla* is used to intone the recitation, the right hand tells the beads. At rest, it is usually worn as a bracelet, wound around the left wrist. Since Tibetan believers are not at all intimidated by the most astronomical figures, nor put off by the incantatory intonation of the same formula, to avoid getting lost in their counting, they insert four markers called *chaturmaharâjâ* between the beads of the *mâla*. These are larger beads, or symbolic double pendants (thunderbolt scepter and bell), attached to the body of the *mâla* by a twist of red strings. Ten small rings, mobile or fixed, are threaded above each charm to make counting easier. Tibetan *mâla* normally terminate in three larger beads, which represent the Three Jewels.

Mâla are most commonly made of wood, but can be made of any material, including seeds, glass, precious or semi-precious stones, ivory, jade, coral, turquoise, and mother of pearl. The beads vary in size, but are designed for ease of handling. Color is also important: those who have the means often prefer a color directly associated with a particular divinity for their devotions.

For certain secret rites, Tantric masters formerly used chaplets composed of beads carved out of bone, sometimes even—it is alleged —out of 108 skulls. This was seen as a proclamation on the part of the initiate of his mastery of fear, if not the enigma of death. The *mâla* is also the distinctive sign of famous teachers and of certain divine manifestations.

THE ALTAR

NOTHING IS TOO BEAUTIFUL FOR THE ENLIGHTENED ONE

For home and sanctuary altars alike, the four images that are indispensable to the believer in his daily practice are usually present: a representation of the Buddha, whether sculpted or painted; Avalokiteshvara, the Great Compassionate One; Târâ, the incarnation of the Buddha's activities; and Achala, the deity who removes obstacles. To these basic emblems other deities may be added, objects of personal devotion, the *Bodhisattva* of loving benevolence, or *Maitreya*. A sacred text, or sometimes a miniature *stupa*, symbolizes the word of the Buddha.

Offerings are placed before these emblems: food, fruit, and flowers; clear water in the seven ritual bowls; and light shed by candles placed in small dishes. As modest as they may be, the offerings must be prepared with the greatest possible care, and presented with the best intentions. This instruction is without exception, because, if not respected, even the finest things lose their value.

The Dalai Lama repeatedly says "Do not pay too much attention to external things, the accent must be placed more on interior development." It must never be forgotten that the intention behind the offering is even more important than the gesture itself.

Still today, despite destruction, vandalism, and theft, the altars of Buddhist sanctuaries display a joyful mélange of objects: small coins, or miscellaneous ritual objects of gold or silver set off with gemstones. A vast range of items can be found laid down in front of the deities: ewers for nectar or lustral water, fans of peacock feathers, crafted conch shells, pairs of thunderbolt scepters and bells (*vajra* and *drilbu*), magic daggers (*phurba*), miniature wheels, *mâla*, *cintamani* (the wish-fulfilling jewel, which represents knowledge and the liberated mind), flower vases, fly whisks, three-dimensional *mandala*, mirrors, swords, spears and tridents, axes and choppers (defensive

283

weapons that protect the Buddha and his Law, as well as the sign of victory over the forces of evil or ignorance).

Ex-votos are offered beneath brocades and *thangka*. Between these laid-out riches and the penury of the ascetics of bygone ages, are these words of the Dalai Lama: "People like us depend so much on external things, like having statues, incense, butter, lamps, and so forth; but if these things bring about no effect in the mind, they are not much help."

MUSICAL INSTRUMENTS

AT THE SERVICE OF THE GODS
FOR THE BENEFIT OF BEINGS

Music and song play an important role in Tibetan daily life, accompanying work in the fields, as well as dance and entertainment. Formerly the warm season was the occasion for picnics at the water's edge, and Lhasa once had a theater and opera season.

Like all traditional art of the Land of the Snows, music is essentially religious. Dance itself is strongly marked by the influence of the *cham*, or sacred dance of monastic origin. Tibetan liturgical music is rich in fascinating sonorities, where unsuspected echoes can be perceived, and it is said to engender awe. In the most rigorous sense of the term, these sonorities were constructed to foster receptiveness to singular vibrations, a door opening onto a reality beyond perceived reality.

Tibetan sound masters enjoy the reputation of having used the human voice to achieve a rare and profound skill demanding years of practice, in which exercise is treated as a veritable yoga. According to expert practitioners of this art, it contains, amplified and magnified, the interior melody of the human body, which can be heard by stopping the ears to shut off outside noises. It is a music of transition, of uncommon strength and purity, expressing at once suffering and compassion, a tireless quest and a soothing serenity.

Many wind and percussion instruments also lend their support to this ritual. Perhaps the most impressive of these is the *radong*, a telescopic horn requiring one player and several carriers. Made of three tapering sections fitted one into the other, it can be as much as fifteen feet long. Usually constructed out of *repoussé* metal, it is lined with wood in places, and often very skillfully decorated. This horn, with its extremely low-pitched sound, is used to announce the start of ceremonies or to inaugurate public festivities. It is played in pairs, so as to keep the sound continuous, and when in use, its bell-shaped mouth rests on the ground, on a stand, or even on the shoulders of sturdy monks. For the sound to resonate in all its fullness, the musicians are generally positioned on the monastery roof.

The *gyaling*, similar to the oboe, is present in nearly all ceremonies, except for rituals of exorcism. It provides the high notes of the melody and is often richly ornamented. The conch shell is also very popular, its mouthpiece usually silver-plated and its mouth decorated with a cloth pendant. It reminds the faithful of their daily duties but is also used for emergency calls; in the east of the country, for example, it is used to warn off an approaching hailstorm or blizzard. During certain rites, the initiation of the *Kâlachakra* for instance, the conch shell is used to distribute lustral water to the participants.

A special ritual trumpet, the *kangling*, normally holds the attention: it is made from a human thighbone, or otherwise a similar animal bone, polished and sometimes artistically crafted. It seems to have emerged in Tibet for the performance of esoteric rites, in the footsteps of the great Tantric masters, such as Padmasambhava (eighth century). It is also often found among the distinctive attributes of the wrathful deities.

Cymbals of various sizes are employed during the services, the largest in the worship of the "wrathful" deities, and the smallest for the benevolent ones, the presentation of offerings, or certain Tantric ceremonies. Their desired sonority is determined by the proportions of metal alloy from which they are made.

The large prayer drum is carried on a single pole stand and struck to measure the rhythm of the procession or ceremony, by means of a long rod curved at the end and fitted with a leather or cloth ball. The monks use it to assemble the community or for Tantric services.

The omnipresent *damaru*, native to India, is a tambourine made up of two wooden hemispheres joined back to back and covered with cloth or leather, each one provided with a small ball at the end of a cord. The rotation of the wrist that holds the handle produces the instrument's characteristic sound. Tantric masters sometimes prefer an object made of two half-skulls, set with precious stones. The *damaru* cadences the mantric recitations or stresses their important passages. The combined sounds of the *damaru*, the ritual bell (*drilbu*), and a bone trumpet are used to invoke rain.

Other instruments are also found in the Land of the Snows: the yak horn is used by magicians and sundry casters of spells, always feared by the populace. In their travels, wandering musicians and bards are often accompanied by a rudimentary lute with one or two strings, probably of Chinese origin.

Musical skills and the difficulties of their apprenticeship have never been the subject of any rigorous transcription, and they are learned in performance. The only indications given are in the form of lines, more or less dense or fine, with the peaks marking fortissimo, and the hollows representing piano.

THE SACRED SCARF

THE KHATA

The *khata* is, first of all, the sign of a simple civility, a gesture of offering, of welcome, and of courteous exchange. It is present in all ceremonies, large and small, public and private. It is usually white, sometimes orange or golden yellow, and sky blue in Mongolia.

Since Tibetans are well known for their pragmatism and for a subtlety bordering on perversity, the giving of the *khata* obeys a code that is richer in meanings than may first be apparent. In a society where etiquette has always been important—to the point where it was formerly possible to ascertain a person's precise rank from the level of the rugs on which he was posed—the ritual of the *khata* casts a special light.

The handsomest scarves are made of the finest silk, supple and fluffy, slightly *moiré*, with long fringes. The sacred formula of the *mani* and eight auspicious symbols are woven into the fabric. This *khata* is a substantial piece of cloth, about four yards long and nearly one yard wide, and is nearly exclusively reserved for the highest religious dignitaries and important figureheads. The *khata* of the affluent, though slightly less sumptuous and more widespread, are still made of silk, but are smaller in size (less than three yards long and one yard wide). The most common scarves are smaller again, and are symbolic more than anything else. Today they are rarely made of silk but instead, when possible, of quality lightweight cotton, but more often of some synthetic material: they have become merely the symbol of a symbol. Nevertheless, *khata* continue to pile up with the same fervor at the feet of the divine effigies, attesting to the vigor of the faith.

The exchange of the *khata* is governed by a code. In the higher ranks of the hierarchy, for a Grand Lama or a high civil dignitary, for example, the scarf is given with the hands joined at the level of the forehead, with a ceremonious inclination of the upper body. This gesture is a testimony of respect and good intentions. If the *khata* is given back, its owner keeps it all the more preciously, because henceforth it becomes the bearer of benedictions, like a talisman. If the interlocutor offers another scarf in return, it is considered as a token of protection, accompanied also by auspicious wishes.

THUNDERBOLT SCEPTER AND BELL

DORJE AND *DRILBU*
MEANS AND WISDOM

Thunderbolt scepter and bell, *vajra* and *ghanta*, *dorje* and *drilbu*, are the most frequently encountered objects on the Diamond Path (*Vajrayâna*). Together they represent both the most ordinary and the most complex symbol of Tibetan Buddhism. Whether present in solitary meditation or in the vast gatherings that mark monastic life, their role is essential; without them rites and ceremonies are hardly conceivable.

Unified, they form a symbol which is associated with the incorruptible purity of the diamond, with the truth that no force, no weapon can destroy. Simultaneously, but in another register, they represent the victory of knowledge over ignorance, the mastery of spirit over the "poisons" that tarnish existence.

The thunderbolt scepter, held in the practitioner's right hand, is a token of stability of the method, while the bell, in his left hand, is a reminder of the wisdom of impermanence. Equilibrium between the two is established through ritual gestures, the *mûdrâ*. In the hands of the masters of esoteric interpretation, this inseparable pair signifies the unity of masculine power and of feminine energy, or the emblem of the dual unity of absolute and relative truths.

The *vajra* originally stood for lightning, and is the attribute of the Hindu god Indra. Having been adopted and adapted by Buddhism, in reaching Tibet and becoming the *dorje*, it assumed a dominant place among Tantric symbols. Of metal or of stone, with one to nine points, the commonest thunderbolt scepter generally has three, representing the Three Jewels. With a single double point, the *dorje* stands for the union of the spiritual and material worlds; with two double points (seldom seen), the duality of appearances; with four double points it is associated with the great moments in the life of Çâkyamuni; five points make it a crown; and four points around a shaft symbolize the five elements, the five wisdoms, the five primordial Buddhas. Thunderbolts with nine double points are exceptional, even in Tibet, and are linked to secret interpretations. In all forms, it is a symbol of the absolute beyond all opposites, or of the fundamental unity achieved by meditation.

The double *dorje*, or intersected *vajra*, is sometimes interpreted as the Wheel of the Good Law. Consisting of two thunderbolt scepters joined at the center, it denotes the indestructibility of the essence of all phenomena, the most complete understanding of the adamantine truth.

The *dorje* very often adorns the handle of the bell, of which it is the pendant, a sign that their functions are indissoluble in daily practice. The prototype of this emblem par excellence of Tibetan Buddhism is closely guarded at the Sera Monastery on the outskirts of Lhasa. It is accessible to the public only once each year, on the occasion of a major ceremony. It is thought to have belonged to Padmasambhava himself, and was found in his meditation cave at Yerpa by his disciple Dacharpa.

The bell, *ghanta* or *drilbu*, is at once the opposite and complement in this symbol of transcendental knowledge. Its handle may terminate in a *stupa*, a *cintamani*, or a single- or many-pointed *dorje*. It represents not only sound, but also void and impermanence: its crystal tinkle dies no sooner than emitted, recalling that all is fleeting. It is thus the symbol of the immediate wisdom of intuition, which instantly grasps and understands the void without reflection or reasoning. Endowed with creative power by the attendant vibration of the *mantra* or *dhârani* which it accompanies, the ritual bell also has the function of inspiring and activating the enlightenment of the heart.

In a world ruled by opposites, where there is no day without night, no nadir without zenith, no north without south, no sunrise without sunset, the symbolic pair *dorje* and *drilbu* mirrors the image of interdependent opposites, indissolubly united: it is the original essence of the Diamond Path, the seed of the double unity of contradictory appearances through which it is manifested. In this sense, the diamond scepter expresses the perfect clarity of the void, veiled by the endless diversity of its masks. For the needs of certain rituals, *vajra* and *ghanta* represent the two fundamental diagrams, virtually inseparable in the Buddhist universe, which are the *mandala* of Garbhadhâtu and of Vajradhâtu, or the world of appearances and the world of spiritual energies and forces. The combination of these two aspects is always indispensable for the attainment of Enlightenment.

RITUAL BOWL AND DAGGER

TRIUMPH OVER INTERIOR ENEMIES

This is perhaps one of the most striking paradoxes of the Tibetan way of Buddhism: on the one hand, the masters and practitioners owe their universal reputation to their peaceful strength, to the quality of their listening, and to their serenity—and, on the other, representations of fierce, wrathful, and terrible deities abound, at first inspiring a feeling of repulsion, rejection, and even fear. It must be borne in mind, however, that these allegories are merely other facets of the benevolent and protective deities, projections of the mind, one of the functions of which is to fight the enemies of the doctrine, while also, by transmuting them, to annihilate the spiritual "poisons" that pose obstacles to Enlightenment. Thus these fearsome effigies are accordingly furnished with weapons of all sorts, and these are freely used by the adepts of Tantrism in their practices.

Three objects from this well-stocked arsenal are relatively common. The *kapâla* is a bowl, often mounted on a carefully crafted support, made of a delicately worked skull and fitted with a lid. It is used by the ascetic during secret solitary practices, or during monastic services in honor of the protective deities. In the latter case, it is filled with beer or tea, signifying ambrosia or blood. Its use is not accorded to all, since it implies authorized transmission. He who employs it must have a clear understanding that it is a reminder of the transient nature of existence.

The *phurbu*, or ritual dagger, was originally a simple nail. Today, it consists of a small triangular blade (usually of metal and sometimes of wood), which is surmounted by a short hilt, often in the effigy of a deity or in the form of a *dorje*. Widespread, the *phurbu* is ascribed magical qualities. It is used to keep bad vibrations and diseases at bay, to expel evil spirits, to combat the enemies of the Law, and even to control the clouds in the science of weather-making. The *phurbu's* effectiveness is enhanced when it is used in a trio. Its role is essential to the sacred masked dances and in the sanctuaries of the tutelary divinities, where it may even have its own altar. Joined in a ring, 108 *phurbu* form a protective circle that wards off harmful influences.

The third of the common weapons, the *trigug* (or *kartîka*), is closer to a semi-circular cleaver with a central, solid handle. Its sharp blade serves to "cleave the bonds of ignorance."

THE AUSPICIOUS SYMBOLS

EIGHT EMBLEMS TO BRING GOOD LUCK
AND SECURE PROTECTION

These eight emblems, or *tashi tag gye*, which are omnipresent in Tibetan spiritual life, originated at a crucial moment in the life of the historical Buddha. Some say that when the Prince-ascetic finally obtained his goal, in the dawn that followed the famous night under the Tree of Bodh Gaya, joy and gladness spread to all the kingdoms of the universe. And to manifest this great happiness, the celestial beings flocked to the site, loaded with myriad gifts for the Enlightened One. The memory of the centuries and of mankind has retained some of these presents, which were judged essential and became emblematic of the veneration shown to the Master.

These symbols adapt to all fantasies of expression. They may be fashioned into jewels, sculpted in wood, printed on paper or parchment, or even reproduced in simple decorations on everyday objects

and ritual instruments. They are found at public and private meetings, at major ceremonies, or when welcoming high-ranking dignitaries. Ascribed the reputation of bringing luck when applied to tents
and the thresholds of houses, they appear at the entrance to monasteries and prayer rooms, but are also inscribed on mountainsides and
on roadside rocks. On feast days, they are depicted in white or red
powder on the paths taken by the guests or processions. They sometimes adorn *mandala*, and the finest *khata* display them, subtly
woven into the silk.

The precious umbrella, *chatra* or *rinchen dug*, is the sign of royal
dignity and offers protection from all evils. The two golden fish,
matsya or *sergyi-na*, the insignia of the Indian master of the universe,
here express spiritual liberation. They stand for the beings saved from
the ocean of suffering of earthly existence. The treasure vase or bowl,
kalasha, or *bumpa*, contains spiritual jewels, and can serve as a
receptacle for lustral water, considered to be the nectar of immortality. The lotus flower, *padma* or *pema*, symbolizes original purity. It is
found in various colors and forms, and is a privileged attribute of the
Buddhas and *Bodhisattvas*.

The white conch shell, *sankha* or *dungkar*, which is even more
revered if its spiral winds towards the right, signifies the word that
proclaims the glory of the Enlightened Ones, and sometimes bears
the name of victory trumpet. The endless knot, *srîvasta* or *pälbeú*, is
a token of love or eternity, representing infinite life. The great banner, *dhvaja* or *gyältsen*, is in fact a wound flag, testifying to the
power of Buddhist teaching or the victory of the Good Law. And the
golden wheel, *chakra* or *khorlo*, is naturally the wheel of teaching
(*Dharma*), to be practiced assiduously to attain Enlightenment. It
represents the unity of all things and remains the quintessential
symbol of Buddhist doctrine.

In Tibetan tradition, it is not uncommon to associate the eight
auspicious emblems with the seven jewels, *saptaratna* or *rinchen
nadün*, which are attributes of the *chakravartîn*, or ruler of the
world. This mythical personage is impartial and fair, magnanimous

and literate, and, like all legendary princes, the protector of widows and orphans. These exceptional qualities are, quite logically, also ascribed to the Buddha.

This indispensable suite to the glory of the universal monarch naturally includes the wheel, *chakra* or *khorlo*; the precious jewel, *ratna* or *norbu*, which grants all wishes, and which is also one of the names given by the faithful to the Dalai Lama; the magnificent queen, *rani* or *tsunm*; the best civil minister, *mantrim* or *lönpo*, a peerless administrator without whom there cannot be a great king; the best white elephant, *hâti* or *langpo*, whose strength is invaluable at the hour of combat; the fastest horse, *ashva* or *tamchog*, that works miracles at festive tournaments and leading troops into battle; and the best of military commanders, *senapati* or *magpon rinchen*, to preserve the empire. An eighth emblematic personage is sometimes added to these seven royal insignias: the best great treasurer, *khyimdag*, who holds the purse strings in complete justice and ensures the well-being of the sovereign's subjects.

The eight auspicious symbols and the seven jewels, which are extremely popular and widespread, may appear alone or in groups, or even in a random order, as dictated by the needs of the moment. At special events, such as weddings, the eight auspicious emblems are united into a single composition, called *tag gye pünzog*, rich in all the meanings which they convey.

OFFERINGS

SACRED AND PROFANE OFFERINGS, AN HOMAGE TO THE DEITY

The offering, an integral part of meditation and liturgy, is always a gesture to the deity: humility, praise, obedience, prayer, or gratitude. It is a sort of direct relationship betokening the respect or devotion of the faithful. Offerings of light and water are the most common: a lamp burns permanently on every Tibetan altar. Legend has it that the Precious Master himself, Padmasambhava, declared more than twelve centuries ago that the water of the Land of the Snows was so clear that it was pure enough even for the gods.

These do not necessarily, however, satisfy the faithful, who swell their gifts with money, incense, flowers, and fruit, *khata*, as well as cakes prepared explicitly for the purpose. These include *torma* and *tsog*. The former are made on the spot, in the courtyard of the sanctuary or on the parvis, with *tsampa* (barley flour, the Tibetan staple) and butter. Monks and laity usually partake in the operation, which i s conducted with vivacity and good humor. The most skillful then decorate the traditional shapes in bright colors. These ritual offerings are placed on the altars to be imbued with good vibrations, and are then shared among the participants when the ceremony is over.

Festive offerings, called *tsog*, are more elaborate and intended to be consumed by those who have prepared them. This once led the Dalai Lama to say, "When we talk of *tsog*, we think of something delicious to eat, whereas when we talk about a ritual cake, we think of something to be thrown away. This is a mistake. When you make offerings, you should do it as best you can." The monks of the Three Pillars of Tibet, namely the three monasteries of Sera, Drepung, and Ganden, formerly assembled in Lhasa in the second month of the lunar year (March) for a great meeting of festive offerings.

At certain ceremonies, the offering may consist of 108 lamps, 108 bowls of rice, 108 ritual cakes, and 108 tea bricks. What really counts is the sacred number. In the olden days, at exceptional festivities, astonishing offerings were prepared, sculpted in butter, and richly decorated, then proudly displayed by their authors and admired by spectators. During private meditation, it is also possible to offer oneself, body, speech, and mind, to the deity.

THE SCRIPTURE AND THE TEXTS

TREASURES TO PRESERVE MEMORY

By royal will and as part of a deliberate plan to become instructed and to instruct. This occurred in the time of the great King Songtsen Gampo of the Yarlung dynasty, who unified various principalities into a formidable empire for the first time. History credits him not only with having transferred his capital to Lhasa by leaving the Tsetang Valley, but also for having sired a large family, as two distant princesses, one Nepalese and the second Chinese, arrived to join his three Tibetan wives. The two beautiful foreigners were pledges of alliance with neighboring courts fearful of the military power of the conquering sovereign. Yet it was based on this dual influence that the monarch adopted the doctrine of the Buddha, and, since that time, despite the hazards and vicissitudes of passing centuries, the Good Law has remained the touchstone of Tibetan civilization.

Around the year 640, the King felt the need to record the teachings which the wandering monks and missionary pilgrims had disseminated for some time through mountains and valleys. However, as the monarch admitted, the Tibetans had hitherto been little concerned with spiritual matters, and notably lacked any means of written expression. Songtsen Gampo accordingly decided to send a group of trusted young men to India, the land of the Buddha, with the specific assignment of studying and bringing back whatever was needed to accord to the royal wish. Among these was Thönmi Sambhota, whose title of Minister promised him a great future.

The trip was not easy, and out of the group of emissaries that bravely departed for Kashmir, at that time the brilliant home of Buddhist thought, fifteen succumbed to the diseases and obstacles on the way. Thönmi Sambhota pulled through, studied assiduously, and returned home armed with sufficient knowledge to construct an alphabet inspired by Sanskrit and a grammar adapted to the peculiarities of the Tibetan language. Both are still current and offer an uninterrupted view of the evolution of the written tradition, which is essentially religious.

The Tibetan alphabet has twenty-seven consonants and five vowels. While the spoken language has changed throughout the years, the classical written language has hardly been modified at all: capitals are still used in printing (by xylography), while cursive or running hand is supplemented by ornamental variants, reserved more specifically for ritual texts.

With these new tools, added to the formula for an indelible ink, also brought back from Kashmir, Tibet witnessed a period of dizzying intellectual effervescence. Indian pandits, assisted by their local pupils, supported by masters and reputed scholars, were invited to share their knowledge. They were actively seconded by outstanding translators, and busied themselves for years, indeed centuries, in explaining, interpreting, and commenting on the basic texts, brought back from India at such a terrible price. Every monastery had its own library, and many ascetic sages inspired new streams issuing from the same central idea.

Two collections of works, translated from Sanskrit into Tibetan in the course of about six centuries of sustained and exemplary efforts, formed the foundation of this religious literature. The *Kanjur*, in 108 volumes, is composed of the teachings of the historical Buddha as gathered by his disciples, while the *Tanjûr*, in 227 volumes, contains the commentaries on these founding texts. Copied identically by meticulous scribes, they were piously preserved on loose sheets, between wooden boards, enveloped in protective cloths, stacked on hundreds of shelves nestled in chapels, and revered at the same level as statues and other sacred objects. The most precious copies were made by hand, in gold ink.

It needed the destructive folly of the cultural revolution of the twentieth century to scatter, burn, and annihilate the main part of this heritage of humanity; the loss is especially tragic because many antique Buddhist treatises had already disappeared elsewhere, especially in India and China, swept away by local historical upheavals.

The Tibetan translations were often the last remaining testimony of a wisdom threatened by human folly. Today, it is in the cellars of the Russian museums, the hiding places of the desecrated former sanctuaries of Mongolia, the keepsakes of émigré families, and the entrails of the libraries of Europe and America, that the surviving treasures, retrieved by intrepid explorers and coated with the dust of time or oblivion, are exhumed.

Fortunately, the inflexible monastic custom, which demanded that the ancient texts be learned by heart, has helped save this knowledge from another era, and the texts gathered scrupulously from the monks of the Tibetan diaspora have been set down so that they can be safeguarded for future generations.

Since thousands of Tibetans have been forced to go into exile, even popular songs and traditional epics belonging to a living and eternal oral tradition have been compiled and set down, so that, even under threat, one can be sure that these roots will some day bear fruit again.

THE MUDRAS

SIGNS FOR THE EXPRESSION OF INDESCRIBABLE FORCES

The word itself means "seal" or "sign," revealing the intention to both seal and to demonstrate, in other words to "translate" words by different means. In short, a species of visual alphabet that serves to attain the essential beyond speech. Here also, the heritage is Hindu, but the interpretation varies with the latitudes, and, as very often in the vast Buddhist panorama, the Tibetan variant has its singularities. These sacred gestures flourished with greater exuberance in the schools of the Great Vehicle, while those of the Small Vehicle generally restricted themselves to the distinctive seals characterizing the rigorously precise and codified "moments" in the life of the Enlightened One.

Among these myriad gestures some are pre-eminent, in that they permit the immediate identification of an effigy by associating it with a family or school. They are routinely used in religious ceremonies. The most widespread throughout the Buddhist world is the *anjali mûdrâ*, the hands joined vertically at the height of the breast. Greeting and veneration alike, it is characteristic of the praying figures of certain minor deities, but, above all, it remains, still today, the ideal way to greet a person in India, Thailand, Burma, and Tibet.

Obviously, the commonest way to pay tribute to the Enlightened One is to join the hands above the head, which is inclined at the same time. Its religious interpretation refers to the cardinal notion in the *Mahâyâna* of the True Nature of all things, of the attainment of Enlightenment, which integrates object and subject.

The *dhyâna-mûdrâ* is widely known: the hands one upon the other and resting in the lap of the meditator, palms upward, fingers extended, and thumbs touching at the tips to form a triangle. It is a characteristic *mûdrâ* of meditation, of concentration on the *Dharma*. It clearly symbolizes Enlightenment, the privileged moment when opposites are transcended, and the road to omniscient wisdom opens. When the personage represented in this posture has a bowl in his hands, the Tibetans refer to him as the Buddha of Medicine.

The gesture of touching the earth, in other words left hand on the knee in the lotus position and right hand downward and turned inward, is the gesture of Çakyamûni at the dawn of Enlightenment: the earth bears witness to his spiritual accomplishment. This is the *bhumisparsha mûdrâ*, found everywhere in the Buddhist geographic area. It also specifically indicates an unshakable solidity, as personified by the Buddha Akshobhya and the historical Buddha.

The two hands in front of the breast, thumbs and forefingers forming two touching circles, right hand turned outward and left hand either upward or inward, indisputably express the *Dharmachakra*, the setting in motion of the Wheel of the Law. This is naturally the distinctive gesture of Çakyamûni, but also of Maitreya, the Buddha of the Future, and sometimes also of Amitâbha, Buddha of Infinite Light, very popular in all variants of the *Mahâyâna*.

The *vitarka mûdrâ* is the gesture of teaching, or of explanation that convinces: right hand upward, palm outward, left hand downward, also palm outward, with the thumb and forefinger of each forming a circle, thus referring to the perfection of the Buddha's Law. In Tibet, this *mûdrâ* is often reversed and is characteristic of the effigies of Târâ and of the *Bodhisattvas*.

The upright hand, generally the right, at shoulder height, palm opened outward, and the left hand alongside the body, or both hands making the same gesture, offer protection and goodwill, while also indicating the lack of fear: this is the *abhaya mûdrâ*, Çakyamûni's first gesture immediately after Enlightenment. It is mainly found among standing or walking Buddhas, particularly in representations that are common in Southeast Asia. But it is also a gesture of protective power or appeasement, which refers to the need to shed fear in order to advance on the path of knowledge. Amoghasiddhi, one of the five Great Buddhas, is often depicted in this way.

The *varada mûdrâ* symbolizes welcome, giving, generosity, and compassion: right hand turned outward and downward, this gesture is often associated with the *abhaya mûdrâ* of protection and serenity. It denotes the wish to devote oneself to human salvation and to strive to lessen the sufferings of men so that they may finally attain the perfection of Enlightenment. It is also the reputed seal of the granting of wishes.

Buddhist iconography contains many variants of these *mûdrâ*, generally associated with the recitation of the *mantra*. During ritual exercises, they induce certain states of mind which help advance on the path of the interior quest. The esoteric schools make considerable use of it, usually strictly codified with respect to a precise Buddha or a particular energy harnessed in the pursuit of a predetermined goal. Some *mûdrâ* must be used with the greatest caution, especially if associated with the propitiation of fierce or wrathful deities, whose formidable powers might be invoked incorrectly by seekers of the absolute incapable of controlling them.

THE GREAT PRAYER

MONLAM CHENMO
THE ANNUAL INVOCATION FOR THE
WELL-BEING OF BEINGS

This ceremony is associated with the new year festivities. Tradition attributes its codified institution to Tsongkhapa the reformer, the spiritual father of the youngest school of Tibetan Buddhism (the *Gelugpa* or Yellow Hats, or, more precisely, "those who practice the way of virtue"). With the establishment shortly thereafter, in the sixteenth century, of the line of the Dalai Lama, largely founded on these teachings, political power was the privilege of the adepts of the reformed branch, and of the three great monasteries: Ganden, Sera, and Drepung, near Lhasa. Created on the impetus of Je Tsongkhapa, they have since then been considered as the "three pillars of Tibet."

Just as everywhere else in the world, the new year has always been the pretext for festivities and revelry, including jousting tournaments among the good-natured Tibetans, who like to indulge their pleasures and rarely forego entertainments. The patronal festivals of the monasteries also provide the opportunity for colorful encounters, marked first by the recitation of epics and performance of sacred dances for two to three days, followed by equally popular profane entertainments.

Custom has it that, on New Year's Eve, everyone should do their housecleaning, to expel the evil spirits and harmful influences due to the faults and negative actions of the previous year. Nomads do likewise in their tents, and whole families set off on pilgrimage to monasteries and sanctuaries, in order to secure solid protection for the coming months. In Lhasa, the capital, it is customary for a scapegoat, generally a vagrant or some unlucky creature, to be loaded with all the evils, and solemnly conducted outside the walls, accompanied by a tremendous rolling of drums and blaring of music to dispel all dangers.

In the past, this was also the time when the keys to the city were put into ecclesiastical hands, and throughout the ceremonies and festivities the monks took charge of law and order in the "city of the divine." Honors went to the *dob-dob*, guardians and experts in the martial arts, who were responsible the rest of the year for ensuring compliance with the discipline of daily life in the monastery. About three weeks of the first month of the lunar year (which begins with the new moon in February according to the Gregorian calendar) were devoted to these community activities, marked on the fifteenth day of the month by a public teaching of the Dalai Lama. Special rites were performed three times daily in the most venerated sanctuary in Tibet, Jokhang, which houses the statue of the Jo-Wo (an effigy of Çakyamûni preciously guarded in the holy of holies of the temple since the seventh century, when it was brought there by the Chinese wife of the great King Songtsen Gampo). Tens of thousands of monks participated in these ceremonies, and in the weeks marked by alternating prayer and festivity, Lhasa was swollen with a floating population at least three times larger than usual, a crowd as immense as a hundred thousand people according to historical documents.

This tradition is scrupulously observed in exile: Tibetans and neo-Buddhists of Tibetan schools throng each year to Dharamsala, in Himachal Pradesh in India, for the occasion. Dharamsala is where the spiritual leader resides and is the administrative center of a government in exile that strives to address the interests of a small community, scattered chiefly throughout India and in a few other more or less distant countries. For some of the participants, the occasion offers the possibility of replenishing their energies in confirmation of the communal cohesion, which unfailingly amazes them, and for all, it is the chance to share precious moments of what may be called communion. In fact, during these always exceptional festivities, the religious and the profane are intimately linked, conferring an unusual vividness to daily activities.

The *Monlam Chenmo* ceremony bears the mark of this fervor. Instituted around 1408, the great prayer for the well-being of all beings perfectly reflects the key idea of the *Mahâyâna* and the ideal of those who travel its path. It was also the biggest monastic gathering in the "city of the divine." This is in fact still true, except for a period of some twenty years, when it was purely and simply prohibited by the Chinese occupation authorities. Although celebrated anew since the eighties, due to the absence of the Dalai Lama, and the surveillance to which it is subjected, it certainly lacks its former luster; this was true even when the ceremony was conducted by the Pänchen Lama, authorized by Beijing to spend a few days among his own.

It was precisely during the preparations for this ritual in 1989 that the second hierarch of Tibetan Buddhism died in circumstances that many Tibetans still consider suspect. The test of strength, initiated in 1995 between the Dalai Lama and the Chinese government, concerning this succession leaves uncertainties clouding the future and line of the Pänchen Lama and of the Great Prayer, as formerly known and practiced by generations of Tibetans in Tibet.

THE MASTERS OF KNOWLEDGE

FROM MAGIC TO PHILOSOPHY, THE MIDDLE WAY FROM SCIENCE TO KNOWLEDGE

Although it did not all entirely begin with Padmasambhava, he nevertheless stands out as the founding figure of Tibetan Buddhism. Responding to a call from Trisong Detsen, on the urging of the philosopher Santarakshita, the great sage came to Tibet to pacify the opposing forces, which hindered the consolidation of the Good Law. Born in the semi-mythical kingdom of Orgyen, which some locate in northeastern Kashmir and others in the confines of Bengal, his real existence is nonetheless established, albeit embellished by legend in the intervening centuries. Guru Rimpoche, as he is still named today throughout the Himalayan arc, was a "Precious Master" in many respects.

A century after King Songtsen Gampo had embraced the doctrine of the Buddha, it had steadily advanced, but clashed with the resentment of the supporters of the pre-Buddhist religion of Bön and the persistent power of shamanistic deities. Around 760, Trisong Detsen, grandson of Songtsen Gampo, decided to erect the first Tibetan monastery at Samye, not far from Lhasa, so that Santarakshita, the great Indian wise man who had renounced his position as abbot of the famous University of Nalanda to teach in Tibet, might ordain the first native monks. Operations, however, were hindered, because whatever the men built by day, the genies tore down at night. In the understanding that knowledge and erudition were not sufficient to overcome these harmful influences, Santarakshita advised the king to hand over the task to Padmasambhava, "the Lotus-Born," whose reputation as a highly accomplished *yogin* and master of the *Tantra* (esoteric instructions) had spread far and wide.

By harmoniously blending supreme wisdom and extraordinary powers acquired thanks to a peerless native intelligence, inflexibly shaped by rigorous discipline, Padmasambhava soon brought the adversaries of the doctrine to heel. Not content with pacifying them, he made them protective guardians of the Buddhist Law, and unremittingly strove to teach them until the end of his life in Tibet.

Padmasambhava traveled the land to its remotest corners. His many caves of solitary meditation, still piously maintained to our day, dotted the vast expanses of the Tibetan plateau. He is greatly revered, in particular by practitioners of the school of the Ancients, the Nyingmapa. Through the centuries, its adepts have discovered valuable *terma* (hidden treasure texts) that he had carefully concealed here and there, awaiting a time when they might be understood. Gifted with the exceptional powers characteristic of sages, Padmasambhava is also credited with prophesying a number of events that actually occurred later in history.

Padmasambhava is commonly represented in the lotus posture, holding a *dorje* in his right hand and a ritual cup in his left. He is often accompanied by his consort, Princess Mandarava, and his principal feminine disciple, Yeshe Tsogyal, an accomplished *yogini*, who wrote the master's biography. Mandarava was given to him by her father after a miracle: outraged to find the guru dispensing his teachings to five hundred nuns and to his own daughter, the king of Zahor ordered that the presumptuous sage be burned alive. He changed the fire into a lake of pure water, from which he emerged enthroned on a lotus. The king was so impressed that he immediately adopted the *Dharma* and gave the sage his daughter as a pledge of loyalty. Yeshe Tsogyal was one of the wives of Trisong Detsen before devoting herself to the quest for Enlightenment, which she attained in a single life under the wise direction of Padmasambhava. Some call her "the celestial dancer," considering her a *dâkinî*, an emanation of the inspiring energy of awareness, leading to the perfect understanding of supreme reality.

Among Tibet's other significant figures, Nägârjuna has a special place. This Indian guru, who lived in the second or third century, and whose name connects him to the *Nâga* who instructed him in their aquatic kingdom, was never actually in Tibet. Yet the philosophical system that he constructed, the *Mâdhyamika,* or middle way, became the cornerstone that led Tsongkhapa to the reform that later gave birth to the school of the *Gelugpa.* He therefore enjoys special renown and is highly venerated.

The vicissitudes of Tibetan history led Buddhism through many ups and downs. Years of royal protection were followed by periods of destruction, which failed to thwart the renaissance and rooting of the Good Law. After the era of persecution of Langdarma, reconstruction began in Amdo in northeastern Tibet, where a handful of faithful found refuge and succeeded in keeping the tradition alive. They regained the monastery of Samye, settled there, and resumed the broken thread of translations.

Among these faithful and determined intermediaries, Rinchen Zangpo accomplished much that was decisive. To satisfy the desire of the king, who wished to separate the good grain of the *Dharma* from the chaff that the historical upheavals had engendered all around, he set forth to seek one of the wisest of Indian pandits, the high priest of the monastic University of Vikramashila, the master Dipankara Srîjnâna, whom the Tibetans call Atisha, the "great saint."

A youth spent in wandering had enabled this aspirant to wisdom to receive the most diverse teachings available at the time from Râjagriha in Bihar all the way to Orgyen. The Buddha Çakyamûni himself is said to have appeared to Dipamkara in a dream and commanded him to become a monk, which he did, subsequently dispensing the instructions of the Law in Java and Sumatra. Returning to India, he continued his studies and teachings in the great Buddhist universities, ultimately reaching Tibet when more than fifty years old, in the year 1042. After settling in Thôling, he set himself to work with the team of Rinchen Zangpo, translating the basic texts illuminating the doctrine.

Atisha himself wrote many commentaries and sets of instructions, of which the best known, "The Lamp on the Road to Enlightenment," is still authoritative. It is to Atisha that the Tibetans undoubtedly owe their deep attachment to Târâ Drölma, the master's tutelary deity. Her sanctuary near the capital, which also contains the tomb of Atisha, was one of the few to escape the destruction by the Red Guards. Historians consider Atisha to be the founder of the *Kadampa* (oral teaching) school, which stressed the intense practice of meditation to release the spirit from the impurities that plunge it into darkness.

In the fourteenth century, Tibetan Buddhism was enjoying a climate that allowed it to explore the most varied routes, without necessarily renouncing the central path—though temporary personal rivalries sometimes tended to discard the principles of tolerance and integrity preached by the Enlightened One. A man of great ability then undertook the restoration of respect for the rules and of preaching by example, revising all the major texts, the *Kanjur* and the *Tanjur*, which he subjected to close scrutiny. "The man from the valley of the onions" was born in 1357 in Amdo, a rugged and backward province which gave Tibet some of its most luminous personalities.

Precocious and persevering, Tsongkhapa was initiated in monastic rule from the age of three by the fourth Karmapa, chief of the Karma Kagyü line.

Of the eighteen works of explication and commentary written by Tsongkhapa, which served to train generations of monks, two still enjoy the widespread favor: the *Lam-rim Chenmo*, or "Gradual Path to Enlightenment," and the *Ngagrim Chenmo*, or "Great Explication of the Secret Mantra." His disciples were held to strict observance of monastic rules, particularly celibacy, and Tsongkhapa exercised extreme caution in the transmission of the *tantra*, especially of the esoteric practices.

Je Rimpoche, as the Tibetans devotedly call him, died in his monastery of Ganden in 1419, at the age of sixty-one. Duly embalmed and placed in the *chörten*, his mummified body was the object of unflagging adoration until its destruction during the cultural revolution. Some claim that the Red Guards who assailed it literally became mad with terror on discovering the serene smile of their victim.

MASTER AND DISCIPLE

AN UNSHAKABLE TRUST

All schools combined, Buddhism abounds with anecdotes demonstrating that finding a master is no easy matter. Already in the time of Çakyamûni, when the Enlightened One was preparing to leave his companions for *nirvana* and his disciples wept at the loss of their spiritual guide, the Buddha commanded them to be "their own torch." More so even perhaps than in other countries, in Tibet and in the *Ch'an* and *Zen* schools, the guru's role is cardinal: it is upon him that rests the duty of leading the pupil by the most appropriate path to the threshold of knowledge, wisdom and Enlightenment.

Nor, similarly, may the candidate for spiritual adventure pick just anyone to guide him on its narrow path. Besides, many famous masters have repeatedly warned against excessive haste in attaching oneself to a guru. This quest and relationship are ideally illustrated by the famous story of Milarêpa and Marpa, the lama with the pitiless requirements who made his pupil pay dearly for youthful misbehavior before granting him the keys that made him not only a famous ascetic, but also a poet whose songs enchant readers and listeners to this very day.

The "man from Mar," as his name indicates, lived in the eleventh century in southern Tibet. Born into a prominent family, he decided to study Sanskrit with the intention of traveling to India for training at the school of the wise. The sale of his personal property enabled him to undertake the voyage, and, for sixteen years, he followed the instructions of Nâropa, one of the great scholars of the time, a contemporary of Atisha, and also a teacher in Nâlanda. After returning to Tibet, Marpa led a family life, dividing his time between his lay obligations and translating and interpreting the texts brought back from India. History has preserved a very accurate record of this and the Tibetans call him "Marpa the translator." It was on his return from another trip to India that Mila begged him to accept him as a disciple.

Marpa spared no trial for the aspirant, and only the remonstrances of his wife, Dagmema, dissuaded him from extinguishing the pupil's enthusiasm. While his fame as a translator is not at all diminished, the "man from Mar" also symbolizes the intransigence of the true guru, who, before granting instruction, exacts from his disciple a total gift of himself. In this sense, he is the image of the supreme trust that Tibetan Buddhism places in a master seen to be fully enlightened—even though this means sometimes overlooking the fact that he happens to be human.

The Marpa/Milarêpa relationship was also tumultuous because, when he arrived at his master's, the seeker brought with him a weighty past. Having lost his father in infancy, the future ascetic became an expert in black magic to avenge his mother for the humiliations suffered on account of the greed of an uncle. Becoming aware of the villainy of his acts, he then sought forgiveness and applied to Rôngtôn, a renowned *Nyingma* master, who sent him to Marpa. Approaching the age of forty, Mila placed himself at his service and suffered whims and insults with hardly a murmur until his despair drove him to the edge of suicide. He failed to accomplish this fatal gesture, and, on the strength of this drastic purification of the past, Marpa finally agreed to initiate him into the arcana of supreme knowledge. He taught him the most taxing exercises, including the *tummo*, or inner heat, which Mila practiced for many years in the solitude of the Himalayan caves, particularly at the foot of the sacred mountain of Kaîlash. There he earned the nickname of *rêpa*, "he who wears the cotton robe of the ascetics," and once he had agreed to congregate with men, he attracted many faithful followers. One disciple, Rechungpa set down his exploits and related his life to the great joy of wandering bards and story-tellers, who have passed it on from generation to generation.

The example of the perfect *yogin* who travelled the hard road from the misdeeds of a turbulent youth to the most demanding ordeals, Mila composed *The Hundred Thousand Songs*, one of the brightest jewels of Buddhist literature. He is often represented seated on a gazelle skin posed on a lotus, dressed as a hermit, holding his right hand at his ear, as he listens to the silence. He and his master are considered to be the creators of the *Kagyüpa* school, founded on the teachings of the Mahâmûdrâ, or "Great Seal" and the "Six doctrines of Nâropa," which Marpa brought back from India.

As revealing as the story of this uncommon relationship may be, extraordinary in the personality of its chief protagonists and through the light it sheds on the special bond that is forged between master and disciple, one cannot overlook the equally insightful words of the Buddha. He cautioned that when seeking a relationship with a guru to engage in the quest for knowledge: "You should not believe anything simply because a wise man has said it, because it is generally believed, because it is written, because it is presented as being of the divine essence, or because someone else believes it. Believe only what you yourself judge to be true after you have tested it in the flame of experience."

THE PROTECTOR OF TIBET

CHENRESIG – AVALOKITESHVARA

"Hears the Prayers of the World," "The Lord who Looks Down upon the Suffering of the World," is a figurehead of the Tibetan tradition. One of the most remarkable Enlightened Beings of the *Mahâyâna*, this *Bodhisattva* is the patron saint of Tibet, and King Songtsen Gampo was considered to be his incarnation. Like his peers, his essential characteristic is compassion, thus his widespread appellation as the Great Compassionate One, or Lord of Infinite Compassion.

Chenresig is represented in some 108 different forms, described in various texts. Among the thirty commonest, and particularly in Tibet, he is personified with eleven heads and a veritable aureole of arms forming a halo around him: this is Avalokiteshvara (his Sanskrit name) with the thousand arms, each hand adorned with an eye, the better to see the miseries of the world and fly instantly to the aid of the needy. His image is always particularly dynamic, although in smaller effigies he is content with four arms, that symbolize all the others he uses to soothe the pains of the world.

According to legend, the *Bodhisattva* looked at the world one day and was so impressed by what he saw that he temporarily despaired of the scale of the task he had set himself, and his head literally burst with the pain. His spiritual father, the primordial Buddha Amitâbha "of Infinite Light," of whom he is the emanation, gathered the pieces from which he made eleven new heads that Avalokiteshvara wears in three successive series of three faces each. The first reflects compassion, the second wrath with regard to the distress of the world, and the third, the joy engendered by good. The next to last face above these is surmounted by a final head, the head of the Buddha Amitâbha. According to other interpretations, these ten faces refer to the ten steps travelled by the *Bodhisattva* until he attains Buddhahood.

Chenresig is especially dear to Tibetans because he is believed to have started the historic Yarlung dynasty whose founder, Nyatri Sangpo, grandfather of Songtsen Gampo, is believed to be his incarnation. In the classical canon of representation of this figure, six of the eight arms attached to his shoulders each bear a specific symbol: rosary, lotus, wheel of the Law, jar of nectar, while the last two form the *anjâli mûdrâ*. The remaining 992 arms all have the eye of mercy in the open palm, open to the suffering that is to be soothed. His sacred *mantra* is *om mani peme hung*, probably the first *mantra* to have made its appearance in Tibet, and, for practicing Buddhists, it is still the most popular.

Very often shown upright on the traditional lotus throne, like most Tibetan deities, whether peaceful or wrathful, Chenresig often holds a lotus flower in one of his hands: hence his occasional appellation of Padmapâni (Lotus Bearer). Moreover, Avalokiteshvara is directly associated with certain lines of wisdom throughout the Buddhist world, where he assumes rather striking local traits in the different latitudes. Thus, in China and Japan, the *Bodhisattva* of Compassion has been feminized and is the object of popular worship under the features of Kuan-Yin and Kwannon respectively.

Because of his thousand arms, Chenresig is also credited with a singular power of influence in favoring good and in lessening the suffering of being in the six realms of existence. In various forms, he dispenses comfort and aid, both to animals and to famished spirits, and naturally to human beings. These last are in fact privileged, in so far as, since they possess self-consciousness, they alone enjoy the incomparable fortune of being able to open their eyes to their condition of being, and even decide to take the path of Enlightenment that leads to the shedding of illusion. Besides, and by no means the least of his salient features, in Tibetan eyes the Dalai Lama is an incarnation of Avalokiteshvara, of the All Compassionate, and, as such, the veneration surrounding him is directed at once towards himself and towards the illustrious deity of whom he is the living representative in the world of men.

TARA DRÖLMA

GUARDIAN, PROTECTRESS, AND SAVIOR

Closely associated with Chenresig, Târâ Drölma is virtually inseparable from the *Bodhisattva* of compassion. She personifies the feminine aspect of his solicitude and actively assists him. Considered as the force, power, or energy of the deity, dynamism is her essence. It is thus not surprising to find her represented in twenty-one different forms, varying in color, posture, and attribution, although she remains first and foremost the "Savior."

Various legends, always closely linked to Chenresig, are attached to her birth. Some say that Târâ Drölma was born of a tear shed by Avalokiteshvara, momentarily dismayed at the vast scale of his mission, others that she was engendered by a blue ray emanating from the eye of the deity, and others still that, from a tear of Chenresig, sprang a lotus, on which Târâ instantly appeared. It is in Tibet that she has the largest number of followers, having been popularized by the devotion paid her by Atisha in particular, being his tutelary divinity. Her popularity persists with many believers who continue to invoke her in one or another of her many aspects.

Two of the many Târâs are of particular importance: the white and the green. Since it is not clearly known which has precedence, they are generally considered as equals. Both are clothed like *Bodhisattva* and richly ornamented, installed on lotus thrones, holding a lotus flower in the hand—in full bloom for the white and blue—half-open for the green. Moreover, so highly do the Tibetans esteem Târâ, that they made the two beautiful foreign princesses who married King Songtsen Gampo incarnations of the goddess—white for the Chinese Wencheng, green for the Nepalese Bhrikuti Devi. Both are benevolent aspects of the deity.

When endowed with a precise color, the Târâs are directly related to the five original Buddhas as the active power of the Tantric deities. Thus, in Tibet, the blue Târâ bears the name of Ekjatâ and was subjugated by the sage Padmasambhava, who made her an acolyte of the green Târâ. In this case she holds a cleaver and skull in the hand, and presents a ferocious aspect of the goddess. The yellow Târâ, "the Goddess of the Frowning Brows," born of a frown on the face of Avalokiteshvara, is another wrathful form of green Târâ, whose characteristic attributes she carries in her arms (*vajra*, rope, bow, and conch shell). Representing the power of love of the original Târâ, Kurukullâ the red has a gentle appearance, but the bow with which she is armed and her crown of skulls attest to the vigor of her acts.

The white Târâ, also sometimes called Sitatârâ, in bronze or any other uncolored sculpture material, is distinguished by her seven eyes: one normal pair, an eye in each hand, one on the sole of each foot, and one on the forehead. Whether depicted in paintings, on wall frescoes or embroidered on cloth (*thangka*), her many eyes are always carefully delineated. She is considered to be the country's supreme protector, both guardian of its Buddhist traditions and savior of the faithful, who never hesitate to call on her for help in even minor daily tribulations. Gifted with a variety of powers, Târâ is the guardian of all fear. She appears as soon as a follower calls. She arrives, ready to put to right the most terrible of situations. She protects the faithful from the threat of lions, elephants, poisonous snakes, and brigands. She also opens the door to impenetrable dungeons and loosens the chains that shackle prisoners. Healer of leprosy, she keeps the fear of death at bay, helps to overcome pain, and to lead pupils to the perfection of supreme accomplishment. She is attributed with unequalled power when faced with lightning, the fury of the oceans, or fire.

According to the *Tantra of Târâ*, during the era of the Victorious, known as the "Light of the many worlds," through her meritorious actions and her fervor, the princess Moon of Wisdom was encouraged to pray in order that she should be reborn a man in which state she might reach full Enlightenment. She replied: "In this life no distinction is made between 'masculine' and 'feminine,' any more than is made between 'oneself' and 'others,' to the extent that even to attach oneself to the idea is senseless. Beings of weak heart allow themselves to be trapped by this illusion. And as there are numerous people who wish to attain Enlightenment in masculine form, for my part I wish to proceed in a feminine body to the benefit of all being until the end of the *samsâra*." It was following this wish that the princess became the goddess Târâ.

It goes without saying that, like all the other emblematic expressions, the symbolic interpretations of Târâ and of her twenty-one aspects are intensified as the seeker advances on the path of knowledge. The close links between Chenresig-Avalokiteshvara and Târâ Drölma naturally make the latter one of the most powerful protectors of the different lines of wisdom, particularly of the Dalai Lamas.

THE GREAT PROTECTORS

MASTERS OF TIME, DEATH, AND NEGATIVE FORCES

These are the fierce guardians of the Law and faithful defenders of the Buddha. Often they are pre-Buddhist deities, unmitigating in their opposition to the messengers of compassion from beyond the Himalayas. Sages and mages strove vigorously to tame them, finally inducing them into service of the doctrine. They thus exemplify the metamorphosis of the disciple transforming aggressiveness and violence into forces for good. By an unfortunate misunderstanding, essentially due to fragmentary knowledge and hasty interpretations, the so-called ferocious deities have given the Tibetans a reputation as devil worshipers. Yet their spiritual masters had simply devised an original manner to signify the complementary polarities, positive and negative, gentle and wrathful, rooted in the human mind.

One of these is Mahâkâla, the "Great Black One," the lord of time and Transcendent Wisdom, whose physical appearance is revealing: with a powerful black warrior's body, protruding teeth and bulging eyes, he bears the sword, a skull cup, and a conch shell or a victory banner as he rides the snow tiger or lion, unless he is treading on a pig, snake, or cock, emblematic of the three poisons. He symbolizes the strength that destroys the illusion that hinders the attainment of Enlightenment. He is the other face of Chenresig.

Other equally ambivalent ferocious deities include Yamântaka, the slayer of the lord of death, and Pälden Lhamo, the only feminine expression among the great ferocious protective deities. She forms a couple with Mahâkâla, and her origin dates back to the Hindu goddess Shrî Devî. Carried on a red mule, her hair bristling ferociously around her head, she wears a necklace of skulls and her distinctive attribute is an umbrella of peacock feathers. A bloodstained head of an enemy of her religion often hangs from her saddle. In painting and embroidery, she often has an aureole of flames expressing her dynamic activity. A third eye normally adorns her forehead, and the grin she wears revealing two protruding teeth is far from reassuring. She has nonetheless been dubbed "the Glorious Goddess," often has a moon in her hair and a sun on her navel, and is considered as the guardian of Lhasa.

These three ferocious and powerful personages are the official protectors of the order of the *Gelugpa*, and their tutelary power makes them the privileged guardians of the Dalai Lama.

THE FIRE RITUAL

THE GREAT PURIFICATION

As in most civilizations, from earliest times until now, fire occupies a special place in Buddhism. A fundamental emblematic element, an unavoidable step on the path of knowledge, an integral part of offering because it is both heat and light, fire symbolizes, above all, purification and the flame of impermanence in development and change. In a country where wood is somewhat scarce, the funeral pyre was generally reserved for great accomplished masters, only the most revered being embalmed. The Buddha himself was cremated, and though his physical body left no ash, some bone fragments were recovered by the faithful and set in eight great *stupa*. Sometimes, as a trace of their passage, the great mystics leave behind multicolored beads, called *ringsel*, testifying to their spiritual accomplishments. Their followers regard these as precious talismans.

Today, as in previous times, fire still remains the most powerful purifier. In the case of sickness, sometimes to liberate a place or being from a harmful influence, or to assure that a location is propitious for building, a lama is summoned to perform the fire ritual, which is thoroughly codified and must be meticulously executed. If not, the perverse force may inadvertently prevail and wreak havoc that can only be overcome by a superior power. This also explains why, before starting the ceremony, its officiant must himself submit to prior exercises of perfect purification.

Juniper, incense, and all sorts of other aromatic woods can be burned. Depending on the extent of the evil to be countered or overcome, one or more monks are asked to exert their combined talents, generally accompanied by the recitation of *mantra* or *dhârani*, the making of specific gestures (*mûdrâ*), and the playing of the ritual tambourine (*damaru*) to enhance the effectiveness of the overall performance.

It is worth noting, although it should come as no surprise, that certain striking correspondences exist between the Tibetan fire ritual and ceremonies aimed at similar purposes in the Hopi Amerindian tradition. This shared practice forms a bridge across the Pacific, beyond time and human memory, standing as the reminder of a deep spiritual brotherhood, which, over the ages, has come to be forgotten.

MONKS AND LAITY

Until the Chinese invasion in 1950, Tibet was undoubtedly a world apart on a planet where social upheaval was causing sweeping changes. A still feudal society impregnated with theocracy, apart from and above all others, the Land of the Snows preserved the structures of another age. Yet the few eyewitnesses who went to Tibet all reported a primitive society, though not one lacking in refinement, and, above all, a harmonious social structure, with a population that was frugal but smiling and content with life.

Reflecting this equilibrium, monks and laity lived in symbiosis. Monks depended on the latter for food and accommodation, since it was the laity who cultivated the land and brought in the harvests. In return, monks were expected to guarantee the spiritual well-being of all. Tradition expected one child of each family to become a monk, which was considered an honor. The noviciate generally began at the age of eight, while monastic vows could only be taken after twenty.

As a rule, the entire lay population observed five basic precepts common to all Buddhists (not to kill, not to steal, and to avoid verbal and sexual misconduct, as well as the use of intoxicating substances). The obligations of novices were more restrictive: to abstain from destroying any living creature; from claiming what is not given; from erotic conduct; from liquor and drugs that lead to carelessness; from eating at undue times; from dancing, singing and going to shows; from wearing garlands and perfume; from sitting or sleeping on a couch or in luxury; and from accepting money. Lay persons could receive a so-called daily ordination from time to time in the eight precepts of the *Mâhayâna*, or the basic vows of the novices, provided they retake them whenever they wished to put them into practice.

THE MEDITATOR

MEMORY OF THE CENTURIES

The hermit and ascetic, often a wanderer, has been an essential component of Asia's religious tradition since time immemorial. Tibetan Buddhism is no exception, and the vastness of the Land of the Snows is particularly propitious to solitary reflection so dear to the great masters. It was, in fact, formerly the custom to prepare huts and caves lying outside the monastic enclosure to enable aspirants to practice retreats of varying length under the guidance of a guru, relying on the generosity of the community for a minimum of subsistence.

The classic retreat, common to all orders, traditionally lasts three years and three months in solitary, and can be repeated often during a lifetime. It cannot, however, be done without the consent or enlightened guidance of a master, who in some way shares the responsibility with the disciple in training. This was current in all the great monasteries of Tibet, and is perpetuated today in Tibetan Buddhist study centers that have sprung up throughout the world in the Buddhist diaspora. Some believe that this rigorous training tradition originated in the annual retreat made by the members of the *sangha* in the time of the Buddha during the three months of the rainy season. This tradition is still practiced in the Buddhist countries of Southeast Asia.

Nevertheless, while the full-time meditator may be in retreat from the world, he is not totally withdrawn from it—with a few rare exceptions. By training himself in this way, he prepares to put the knowledge he thus acquires at the service of others and of society when he returns among men. Inured to the ordeal of a rigorous discipline, he (or she) is presumed to have surmounted most of the obstacles (particularly the three poisons of ignorance, hatred, and desire) of daily life, thus enabling him to play a beneficial role for all.

In everyday life, he who meditates regularly without necessarily renouncing his routine obligations, seeks primarily to harmonize his interior life with the existence he leads. Yet, among all practitioners, on their own scale, it is their full and conscious participation in a multi-secular chain of an uninterrupted transmission of essential wisdom, which, in its most accomplished expressions, permits full detachment in the midst of universal bonds.

PILGRIMAGE

SIGNPOSTS IN THE
TERRITORY OF THE SACRED

All religions, from the rudimentary to the most expansive, have in common specific places of reference, which assume particular importance for their followers. In their eyes, this singular aura marks out a territory traveled mentally as often as desired, and physically as many times as possible, but, depending on the follower's means, at least once in a lifetime. A parenthesis—if not a break—a journey of pilgrimage, however long, provides an opportunity to leave daily contingencies behind in order to evaluate one's quest so far and devote oneself to reflection.

An inherently nomadic people, Tibetans are no exception. Born walkers, they are quick to break with the daily grind and depart on the trails of holy vagrancy, whether alone, in families, or even by whole villages or clans. Naturally, like all Buddhists of any school, the places directly associated with the life of the Enlightened One hold a special place in their hearts. Quite often, however, these places scattered within the confines of what was formerly the Kingdom of Magadha (approximately the Bihar of today's India) have been virtually inaccessible. Only wandering ascetics and the most demanding seekers of the absolute took the time to undertake this hazardous voyage from which they knew they might never return.

Bodh Gaya has been frequented for more than two millennia by adepts from all over the Buddhist world, who come to bow at the foot of the pipal tree where the historical Buddha crossed the threshold of full Enlightenment. Today, a sleepy little village, often oppressively hot, it keeps alive the memory of that exceptional moment, and hums with the serene activities of monks from all schools who are permanently established in its monasteries where study and prayer suffice to fill many a lifetime. Sometimes, on the occasion of a special event or particular initiation, the holy city swells with an unaccustomed human presence and becomes, for a few hours or days, a spiritual center vibrating with energy—an unforgettable event for those that experience it.

Sarnath, not far from the immemorial holy city of Varanasi, testifies, by the venerable *stupa* of the Emperor Ashoka, to the first teaching of the Enlightened One, the deer of its park recalling his first adepts. An enduring gentleness pervades this place where, upon the ruined foundations of ancient monasteries, others have sprung up to safeguard a heritage, which, despite all vicissitudes, has withstood the ravages of time.

In Lumbini, today in the Nepalese lowlands, near Kapilavastu, the capital of the Shakya Kingdom of which nothing now remains, clear evidence has been found, which indicates that this was Prince Siddharta's actual birthplace: Ashoka had a *stupa* erected there with tablets containing detailed information. Their authenticity has been corroborated by a year of intensive study since they came to light in 1995. And in Kushinagara, formerly a small village totally undistinguished from thousands of others, the Buddha stretched out on his side and, before entering *nirvana*, bestowed a final command to his tearful disciples: "Be a light unto yourselves."

So much for historical sites. The others, and there are many, dot the vast territory where the Buddhist light passed and was sometimes momentarily extinguished. In India itself, Sanchi boasted a magnificent *stupa*, while the Caves of Ajanta and Ellora bear witness to the sacred through beauty, and Borobodur in Java attests to the faith of its inspired builders by a unique stone *mandala*. The colossal statues of Gal Vihara near Polonaruwa in Sri Lanka are stunning in their timeless harmony, and ancient Siam, Burma, Afghanistan, Japan, Korea, China, and Mongolia have all, each in their own way, contributed their jewels to the edification of Buddhist art, transforming selected places into inexhaustible sources of replenishment. Nor did Tibet lag behind.

Since Buddhism has metamorphosed the deities of earlier religions into expressions of the Good Law, it is hardly surprising to find sacred lakes and mountains, the reward of a breathtaking natural beauty, upon the solitary vastness. Thus Amnye Machen in the east responds to the even more royal grandeur of Kailash, the mythical Mount Meru and axis of the world of Indian tradition, which became Kang Rimpoche (Precious Venerable of Snowy Peaks) for the faithful. This is one of Tibet's great places of pilgrimage, undoubtedly one of the most difficult of access with the passage of the Dölma Pass at an altitude of 21,882 feet, though also one of the most impressive. The Himalayan panorama unfolds in serene splendor, inducing in the traveler a physical awareness of his natural links with a world impregnated with the seal of an ineradicable and ubiquitous spirituality.

A place may become sacred even though fashioned by the labor of men. One such site is Lhasa, the capital of Tibet, which means "holy place." The Potala, the imposing red and white palace that towers above the city—until only recently the winter residence of the Dalai Lamas and the seat of government—bears the name of the celestial dwelling of Avalokiteshvara, the tutelary divinity of the Land of the Snows, whose ever-present incarnation on earth is the Dalai Lama. Nesting symbols that interlock with each other, multiple and myriad facets of a living legend of infinite duration, and footholds of a particular geography of the sacred.

THE PASSAGE OF DEATH

THERE IS NEITHER BEGINNING NOR END

Integrating death with life is an everyday fact for the Tibetans, or at least for many of them. One cannot exist without the other, and the cardinal notion of impermanence or rebirth reveals therein the touchstone of a way of life. "Sooner or later," says the Dalai Lama, "death will come. To think about it and prepare for it may prove useful when it arrives. If you believe only in this life, and disagree that life continues, being aware or unaware of death is irrelevant. If another life exists, however, it may be useful to be ready for death, because in this way one is less terrified of its process, and the situation is not complicated by one's own thoughts." For the Tibetan sage, meditation on death is equivalent to the exploration of a territory with uncertain landmarks.

In Tibetan tradition, the Lord of Death is a ferocious deity of wrathful mien. He is Yamantaka, "the Destroyer of the Lord of Death," a meditation deity peculiar to the *Gelugpa* school. He is the other face of Mañjushrî, the *Bodhisattva* of Peerless Insightful Wisdom, whose attributes are the volume of Perfection of Wisdom texts and the sword that cleaves the bonds of ignorance. Yamantaka is represented with several heads, the central one of which is that of a bull, and many pairs of arms and feet, dancing in union with his consort, Vajravetalî, upon a host of human, animal and demonic forms. This ambivalence expresses the Buddhist conception of perpetual metamorphosis that governs existence itself. The deeply anchored feeling that death is part of the natural order of things does not preclude its consideration by rites. On the contrary, the moribund is accompanied so that he or she might take the steps of this end of the road with serenity, and when the life principle has departed the body, prayers and ceremonies continue to convey him or her safely home upon the twisted trails of the limbo of the *bardo*. Either the officiating lama or an astrologer is consulted to determine the ordering of the rites and the most propitious moment for their performance.

For Tibetans, the world beyond life is peopled by unusual creatures, who are in fact simply projections of the human mind, and whose symbolism merely reflects its fears and anxieties. Thus the *citipati*, or pyre masters, are acolytes of Yama and are commonly represented in pairs or couples of dancing skeletons in the company of ferocious deities. In the eyes of the faithful, they illustrate the ephemeral nature of existence and are emblematic of the cessation of earthly attachments and suffering.

Feminine energies are personified by the *dâkinî* (*khandroma*) and, whether benevolent or wrathful, these always play an active role with the masculine deities. They guide the seeker in his quest, as well as the intermediary being in his passage through the bardo. Often represented by fine and well-proportioned female figures, but with slightly menacing facial expressions, only their attributes—*kapâla*, skull necklace, and sword—declare their nature, provoking the faithful to turn them into allies rather than adversaries.

Once abandoned by the breath of life, whose best point of exit is the apex of the skull, the corpse must be returned to one of its component elements: fire, water, earth, and air. Victims of infectious diseases, such as leprosy or smallpox, are normally buried. Inhumation is reserved for the great ones of this world (king to tomb, sage to *chörten*) after being embalmed and dressed in precious apparel. Some perfectly accomplished sages are thought to have the gift of literally "dissolving" at the ideal moment, into what is called "a rainbow body."

The lack of sufficient wood makes cremation an exceptional event. The custom of "celestial funerals" (*ja-gor*) is the most widespread and is practiced in a place often reserved near a monastery by the members of the *Ragyapa* corporation. They take charge of ritually dismembering the corpses in the presence of an officiating lama and a handful of relatives and friends of the deceased, and the pieces are then thrown to birds of prey. For the Tibetans, this action stands as the ultimate testimony of their non-attachment to a transient body, and of solidarity with other creatures who feed on its remains.

Just as Europe had its "Arts of Dying" in the Middle Ages, the Tibetans, too, have a guide to avoid the pitfalls on the narrow path leading from one life to another since Buddhists do not have the slightest doubt about reincarnation. This is the famous *Bardo Thôdol,* or "Tibetan Book of the Dead," which was a sensation in the West when it was first published in the nineteenth century. The book is read by the officiating priest into the ear of the dying person, explaining to him the steps of his travels and enjoining him to avoid succumbing to fear while crossing unknown realms, to undo bonds without returning to frighten the living, and to seize the opportunity presented and apprehend the luminous clarity when he encounters it. It is specifically for the success of this delicate passage that practitioners strive in meditation to chart a map of this territory strewn with pitfalls, in order to experience their death in full awareness, the indispensable prerequisite for good rebirth—unless they acknowledge the profound and real significance of the Great Light, thereby definitively breaking the circle of reincarnations. The person is thus freed from the chains of ignorance and attains Enlightenment.

THE DALAI LAMA

INCARNATION OF THE DIVINE

Ocean of wisdom, incomparable master, Yishin norbu or wish-fulfilling jewel, precious victorious or gyalwa Rimpoche, Lord of the White Lotus, or simply Kundün, the Presence: so many titles among a host of others express at once the power, knowledge, benevolence, and compassion the Tibetans use to evoke the most illustrious and the most revered among their number, the Dalai Lama.

An exceptional being, perennially surrounded by legend and mystery, the fourteenth of the line today, the acknowledged but exiled Holder of the Lion's Throne, Tenzin Gyatso, has shouldered the heavy burden for his people of being their spiritual guide in a period of impenetrable darkness, and their temporal leader at a turning point in history marked both by the cruel ordeal of foreign occupation and the necessity of opening up the country to the outside and to modernity. If he is today a thoroughly familiar symbol of Tibetan Buddhism throughout the world, it is this monk with his piercing gaze and infectious smile who represents his living faith as well as Tibet itself, the survival of which hangs in the balance. Whatever transpires, the Tibetans of the diaspora and of the interior continue to recognize in him their sole spiritual and temporal authority.

The historic institution of the Dalai Lama is rooted in Buddhism's fundamental concept of reincarnation: every being, whoever he may be, bears in himself the seed of Enlightenment, and will ultimately achieve it, even if his path is prolonged in time. Hence the inescapable necessity of the circle of births for its attainment. Yet some are more skillful than others, and, by working assiduously on themselves, they get there faster. In the course of successive lives, they choose and they affirm, thereby becoming capable of selecting the form in which they will return to complete this development. This is the privilege of a chosen few whom the Tibetans call *tulku* (literally, "bodies of transformation"), reincarnations of masters, who return in a renewed body to complete the task they have undertaken.

This tradition was consolidated in Tibet in the thirteenth century with the discovery of the second *Karmapa*, leader of the *Kagyü* school, and was subsequently confirmed for other great masters, thus guaranteeing the permanent transmission of knowledge from generation to generation, but also a much questioned political continuity. The actual line of the Dalai Lamas is a late phenomenon (dating from the sixteenth century) set up in the wake of the establishment of the *Gelugpa* order founded by the reformer Tsongkhapa. Yet the title itself, which means "Master of Wisdom Greater than the Ocean" (or Ocean of Wisdom), comes from *tale lama*, attributed by the Mongol Prince Altan Khan to his spiritual master Sonam Gyatso, at that time head of the school of the Yellow Hats. He retrospectively granted it to his two predecessors, of whom the first, Gendün Drup (1391-1475) was one of the closest disciples of Tsongkhapa.

It is with the Great Fifth Lobsang Gyatso (1617-1682) that spiritual and temporal powers became inextricably merged for greater effectiveness on the Tibetan national scene until the Chinese invasion of 1949/1950. The tradition of the *tulku* has survived in exile, despite obstacles posed by the difficult conditions of the moment, as testified by the dispute that broke out in 1995 between the Dalai Lama and the Chinese Government in Beijing concerning the reincarnation of the Pänchen Lama, the second religious hierarch of Tibetan Buddhism, whose fate is closely linked to that of the Dalai Lama and hence to the very future of Tibet.

There is no doubt that, to Tibetan eyes, the Dalai Lama is a being completely apart. Tradition, his education, his charisma, his power, his erudition, and the veneration he enjoys, certainly make him an outstanding person, but there is something besides: a subtle alchemy of uninterrupted exchange between his people and himself. For them, not only is he the protector, incarnation of the *Bodhisattva* of Infinite Compassion himself, but also the personification of a lost land and the token of its permanence, the promise of return.

It must be admitted that the life of Tenzin Gyatso, recognized fourteenth Dalai Lama at the tender age of two-and-a-half on a modest farm in a village in Amdo (eastern Tibet, today incorporated in the Chinese province of Qinghai), has been far from ordinary. "Simple Buddhist monk," as he calls himself, he is nonetheless a key personality of contemporary history, whose international role was acknowledged when of the Nobel Peace Prize in 1989 was bestowed on him.

Born in the village of Takster, on—according to the lunar calendar—the fifth day of the fifth month of the year of the wood pig (July 6, 1935), the fourteenth Dalai Lama was recognized by a mission of high religious dignitaries, and subsequently conveyed, in October 1938, to Lhasa where he was enthroned on the Lion Throne on February 22, 1940. For the lively spirited and turbulent boy this marked the start of a rigorous and virtually solitary training under the vigilant gaze of his two tutors, both outstanding scholars. Yet beyond the formidable Himalayan ramparts, events followed one another in quick succession, the Second World War brought the world into conflict, empires vanished and countries emerged, and China was torn asunder between nationalists and communists. Mao and his troops finally prevailed and the new power established in Beijing in 1949 immediately announced its intention to "liberate Tibet." This was quickly materialized as military invasion and occupation, a stranglehold that persists to this day, marked in 1959 by a popular anti-Chinese revolt that was quelled in bloodshed. This date also marked the exile of the Dalai Lama and some hundred thousand Tibetans, mostly refugees to India, but also scattered throughout every other continent. For Tenzin Gyatso, these years of ordeal opened up the world, but he has never lost sight of what he considers his essential mission for his people and his country in these difficult times: to save Tibet and its great civilization, to safeguard its spiritual wealth and unique heritage. Having, so to speak, renewed the secular tradition of the wandering monk, the Dalai Lama is undoubtedly no ordinary pilgrim. He is fully aware that his path is still strewn with many boulders, but the attention he awakens in his audience, the deference he enjoys, and the answers he offers to questions facing our world, encourage him to persevere in the hope of returning home and in a spirit of determined nonviolence.

Questioned about his own future, the Dalai Lama ceaselessly repeats that, like the Buddha himself, he is merely a man, and that his compassion and his profound understanding go to his fellows, all other human beings, and to their suffering. "We're just visiting," he says, "tourists making experiments, just passing through. Without tolerance or dialogue, we make our own lives unbearable, and, besides, we harm our environment. All we need is a small effort to make our world more livable for everyone, free from the violence that erodes and destroys everything."

And he continues: "Tibet is perfectly viable without a Dalai Lama. It thrived for centuries before the institution existed as such, and, theoretically, it's perfectly conceivable. Human institutions pass, and whether they continue or not is a matter of circumstances. In absolute terms, Tibet, its nation, its culture, and even Buddhism, are perfectly conceivable without a Dalai Lama. For the time being, the Dalai Lama is a symbol, a symbol of Tibet. This is why he is important. Later on, in thirty or forty years, who knows? Everything changes.

Incidentally, there will always be human beings who possess the requisite qualities to be a Dalai Lama. The incarnations of Buddhas or *Bodhisattvas* continue to be manifested whatever happens... And not only in human form."

THE LOTUS

DARKNESS AND LIGHT

The lotus flower, which is omnipresent in Buddhist representations, seems indissociable from the deities who populate this world where, closely intermingled, shadow and light relentlessly play hide-and-seek on the Eightfold Path to Enlightenment. The lotus has been a cardinal symbol from the beginning of Indian Vedic times, when the palette of its colors and the phases of its flowering were skillfully used to transmit precise meanings: blossoming or in bud, white, pink, red, or blue, it is associated with definite aspects of teaching, or of wisdom, of which it expresses a given revealing feature.

An implicit reminder of the true nature of man, the lotus refers to him by analogy: born in the mire of stagnant ponds, once it has traversed the perfidious sweetness of the water, like a miracle of harmony perpetually renewed, it emerges and blossoms in the air or on the surface. The fascination it has exerted on the human mind for so long led the artists of Asia to use it as the privileged seat for all Buddhas and *Bodhisattva*, while at the same time it is one of the most regular attributes of the protective and compassionate deities. Chenresig, the official Protector of the Land of the Snows, is incarnate among men in his emanation, the Dalai Lama, who bears the title of Lord of the White Lotus, a color which by itself embodies all others and symbolizes the spiritual perfection of the Buddha.

The pink lotus is the prerogative of Siddharta, the historical Buddha. The red lotus signifies compassion, or the original nature of the *Bodhisattva*, and is then directly associated with Avalokiteshvara-Chenresig. The blue lotus, always shown in bud, is a distinctive emblem of Manjushri, *Bodhisattva* of wisdom, he who is the image of the victory of mind over matter.

Its dual nature also makes the lotus a solar symbol, in so far as the variations of its blossoms are declinated in direct accordance with the power of the sun. Its eight stylized petals naturally refer to the Eightfold Path, and it accompanies the Tibetans in their solitary intonations. It may symbolize the Buddha himself, and even his dual aspect, masculine and feminine. Between the corolla and the stem, there is also a complementarity, expressed in the interrelationship between shadow and light that sculpts the highs and lows of daily existence.

SYMBOLS OF ISLAM

BY MALEK CHEBEL

ALLAH

AL-LAH, AL-ILAH, AR-RAB, DIFFERENT NAMES
FOR THE ONE GOD OF ISLAM.

In the Islamic consciousness, Allah is the Creator of the world
and the prime Motivator of its workings. As the God of monotheism,
there are 2,700 references to Him in the Koran: "Say: He is Allah,
the One and Only: Allah... the Absolute. He begetteth not, nor is He
begotten, and there is none like unto Him" (*The Purity of Faith*,
CXII, 1-4).

Historically, the notion of *Al-Ilah* ("God"), as He is called
throughout the Arabic world, existed in the Meccan pantheon long
before Islam, but He certainly did not occupy the place He was to
take in the Muhammadan mission. The Koran reinforces and hallows
His primacy and excellence. The omnipotence of Allah, (an idea
referred to in no less than 142 verses) and His mercy (evoked in 194
verses spread over 72 suras) eclipsed the peninsula's other gods.

How is Allah presented in the Koran? This is an important
question since Islam is defined both by its radical break with the
pre-Islamic pantheon and its vision of the future. The afterlife and
the resurrection of the dead are both involved. The Koran and the
traditions accept the existence of a final day of judgement when evil-
doers will be punished. Just as they are deciding factors in Judaism,
heaven and hell are fundamental facts in Islamic eschatology and
thought.

The Koran abounds in definitions of God. One of the most mysterious and poetic is the definition in the twenty-fourth sura, which
states: "Allah is the Light of the heavens and the earth. The parable
of His light is as if there were a Niche and within it a Lamp: the Lamp
enclosed in Glass; the glass as it were a brilliant star, lit from a
blessed Tree, an Olive, neither of the East nor of the West, Whose Oil
is well-nigh Luminous, though Fire scarce couched it: Light upon
Light!" (*The Light*, XXIV, 35).

Transcendent and omniscient, knowing all at every moment, Allah is both the guardian and the guarantor of leniency, of clemency (or forgiveness, *ghufrân*), and of mercy, as illustrated by this passage: "Allah is He, than Whom there is no other god—Who knows all things both secret and open; He, Most Gracious, Most Merciful. Allah is He, than Whom there is no other god—the Sovereign, the Holy One, the Source of Peace and Perfection, the Guardian of Faith, the Preserver of Safety, the Exalted in Might, the Irresistible, the Supreme; Glory to Allah! High is He above the partners they attribute to Him. He is Allah, the Creator, the Evolver, the Bestower of Forms. To Him belong the Most Beautiful Names: whatever is in the heavens and on the earth doth declare His Praises and Glory: And He is the Exalted in Might, the Wise" (*The Mustering*, LIX, 22-24).

The ninety-nine names of God evoked in these verses are intended to purify the souls of pious women and men and keep them away from the devil.

Their recitation, which is recommended in the Koran, is accorded an important place in meditation, especially by the mystics. At all times, in all places, they preserve the believer from evil by keeping it at bay. Seven names have a particularly evocative symbolism: *Allah, Huwa*: "He"; *Al-Haqq*: "The Truth"; *Al-Hayy*: "The Living"; *Al-Qayyum*: "The Subsistent"; *Al-Qahhar*: "The Invincible, the Victorious"; and *Al-Rabb*: "The Lord." But the following titles are also common: *Al-Rahman*, "The Merciful"; *Al-Rahim*, "The Compassionate"; *Al-Karim*, "The Most Noble"; and *Al-Tawwab*, which means: "He Who is near to His Creation (*tâb*)." Finally, in the last category of names of God, the faithful tell several attributes of Allah on the prayer beads: *Al-Wahab*, "The Generous Giver"; *Al-Majid*, "The Glorious"; *Al-Fattah*, "The Opener"; *Al-Razzaq*, "The Dispenser of Riches"; and so on. On this subject, Ibn-'Abbas recounts hearing the Prophet say: "God has ninety-nine names or one hundred minus one; he who memorizes them will enter into Paradise." [1]

The foremost quality of God in the eyes of Muslims is His goodness and His love. God is love. God is good. God is compassionate. These are the attributes to which the Koran and the Prophet refer to the most. Allah is the Giver (*Al-Muâz*), He Who answers the needs of mankind (*Al-Razzaq*).

Expressions such as: "Allah is most surely full of kindness, Most Merciful" (*inna Allaha lara'ufun rahimun*) (*The Cow*, II, 143) or "My Lord is... full of mercy and loving kindness" (*inna rabbi rahimun wadudun*) (*Hud*, XI, 90), punctuate many of the suras in which Divine Charity is mentioned. While the Koran is entirely devoted to the greatness and sovereignty of Allah (*jalalâti Allah wa 'udhmatihi*), as well as to His wrath (*ghadâbihi*), the oral tradition of the Prophet enumerates and dissects one by one each of the characteristics of His Majesty, among them "Nearness" (*al-qurb*), which remains one of the most poignant measurements of Islam's intrinsic humanity.

Very little has been explicitly stated about the distance between the believers and God in paradise. There are, however, some testimonies that touch upon an answer to this question, including on told by Jarîr ben 'Abdallah, a Muslim living in the seventh century, who said that the Prophet is reported to have told some people who had gathered around him one night of the full moon: "You will see the Lord even as you see that moon, without having to jostle each other in order to see," and again, from the same witness, "You will see the Lord with your own eyes."[2]

The formula by which God is invoked to bestow His benediction is called the *basmala*: "In the name of God, (the) Merciful, (the) Compassionate" (*Bismillah al-Rahman al-Rahim*). All the suras of the Koran, except the ninth, begin with the *basmala*. Unlike the "good intention" (*niyya*), which is a private thought, the *basmala* is a formula that is either spoken or written. Its importance is such that the Prophet said: "All that is in the Revealed Books is contained in the Koran, all that is in the Koran is contained in the opening sura (*fatiha*), all that is in the *fatiha* is contained in the *basmala*."[3]

During the *basmala*, the following phrase, "Praise be to Allah" (*al-Hamduli'llah*) is used to pay homage to God. It is a phrase that children learn from their earliest days. After each meal they say it in unison, as an expression of their contentment, just as they say the *basmala*. Expressions such as *Subhan'allah* ("Glory to God") or *Istaghfiru'llah* ("I ask forgiveness of God") punctuate a large number of the actions of daily life.

The present list of the ninety-nine names has gradually been superimposed over concurrent lists containing thirty-six, seventy-two, and five hundred names. It is estimated that a secret name, the hundredth, reserved for the Prophet and for men of religious insight, completes this prestigious collection.

Apart from these divine names and that of the Prophet Muhammad, the names of the first four Caliphs, called the "Properly Guided Caliphs" (*al-Khulafa' al-Rashidun*), because they, too, are models of virtue, are held in very high esteem: Abu Bakr (d. 634), 'Umar (d. 644), Uthman (d. 656), and 'Ali (d. 661). The same is true of Khadija and 'A'isha, the wives of the Prophet, as well as of His daughter Fatima, the wife of 'Ali. These "beauteous names" inspire Muslims when naming their children. They add the prefix *'abd* (servant) for boys, to give, for example, *'Abd al-Wahab* (literally, "The Servant of the Giver").

Female first names are constructed on the same roots, although without prefixes: Rahima, Malika, Karima, etc.

1. *Hadith* of the Prophet.
2. El-Bokhari, *Les Traditions islamiques*, vol. 4, p. 598. Paris: Maisonneuve et Larose, 1984).
3. *Hadith* of the Prophet.

MUHAMMAD

*ABOU AL-QASIM MUHAMMAD IBN 'ABD
ALLAH IBN 'ABD AL-MUTTALIB*, THE FULL
TITLE OF MUHAMMAD, THE PROPHET OF ISLAM

The name Muhammad derives from the verb *hamada*, meaning "to praise, glorify." Muslim hagiography gives him another name, *Ahmad.*[1] It draws upon a verse of the Koran in which Muhammad is heralded by Jesus as a future Prophet. In European languages, other variations are often given: thus, Mahomet is a form of Muhammad, and one also sees Mahommed, Mahound, Mehmet, Mahowne, and Machomet.

The Koran lists His other attributes. He is the "Warner" of the religion.[2] He is not the Father of any man, but the Messenger of God.[3] It is said of him that he is the "Perfect Model" or the "Perfect Exemplar," as he is called in this verse from sura 33, *al-Ahzab*, which gives us the fullest portrait of the Prophet Muhammad: "Ye have indeed in the Messenger of Allah a beautiful pattern of conduct for anyone whose hope is in Allah and the Final Day, and who engages much in the praise of Allah" (*The Confederates*, XXXIII, 21). The Arab oral tradition often calls him the Qurayshi ethnotype, since the Prophet was a member of the powerful pagan tribe of the Quraysh, who ruled Mecca. In this respect, he was the one who put an end to the "Pagan Era" ('*Ahd al-jahilia*), re-established the transcendent "Truth" of God, and, moreover, organized the community of Muslims (*Al-Umma al-islamiyya*, sometimes known as the Muhammadan community); he was their guide, their legislator, and their greatest strategist. Muhammad belonged to the clan of Banu Hashîm, which would later be the basis for the family tree of the Hashemites, from which several Arab sovereigns claim to be descended.

Muhammad's date of birth is not certain. It was in the "Year of the Elephant," probably between 569 and 571 A.D. This was a black year, marked by an attack on Mecca led by the Yemeni-Ethiopian general Abraha, a Christian vice-regent, whose army was mounted on elephants.[4] Muhammad was born to 'Abd Allah and Amina bint Wahb. His father died before his birth, and his mother Amina passed away shortly thereafter, entrusting him to a wet-nurse from the nomadic tribe of *Banu Saad*, named *Halima*.[5]

An orphan by the age of six, Muhammad was left poor and destitute, having received no inheritance from his parents. This detail links him, symbolically, with the line of great prophets, all of whom had been poor. He was then taken in by his grandfather, 'Abd al-Muttalib, who was the head of the clan of Banu Hashim at the time, and who looked after him until his death. Thereafter, the privilege of raising him fell to his paternal uncle, Abu Talib. This was in fact his duty, since the very strict customs of mutual aid within families were absolutely binding. Muhammad's disrupted childhood is reported thus in the Koran: "Did He not find thee an orphan and give thee shelter and care? And He found thee wandering, and gave thee guidance. And He found thee in need, and made thee independent…" (*The Glorious Morning Light*, XCIII, 6-8). Soon, however, the Meccans recognized in Muhammad the most pious and accomplished man of his generation and they called him *al-Amin*, "the righteous one" or "the honest one." At the age of twenty, with an unsullied reputation for integrity, Muhammad entered the service of a rich Qurayshi merchant—a woman named Khadija, the daughter of Khawalayd and a distant relative—driving her carts to Syria.

By dint of tenacity and probity, he became her right-hand man, managed her affairs, and married her in 596. At the time, Muhammad was twenty-five years old, while Khadija was nearly forty. Six children were born from this first marriage, two of them sons who died in infancy. Of the daughters, tradition gives pride of place to Fatima, the favorite, who was the future wife of Ali, the fourth Caliph, and the mother of Hassan and Hussein. Muhammad died in Medina on June 8, 632. Throughout his mission, Muhammad was attacked by the pagan leaders of Mecca, who were members of his own tribe. He was mercilessly persecuted until the September of 622, when he fled to

Medina, known as the year 1 A.H. (After the *Hijra*, [*Hegirah*] meaning "exile" or "emigration"). In this place of refuge, Yathrib, known
thereafter as *Madinat an-Nabi* or Medina ("The City of the
Prophet"), he created the first city-state of Islam and its first constitution. It was here, in this city, that the main rituals of Islam evolved.

Two years after the Hijra, the canonical direction of the Kaaba,
known as the *qibla*, was fixed. The Prophet's house therefore became
the first mosque, while Bilal, a freed black slave, was given the task of
calling the Muslims to prayer.

From the eighth century onwards, Muslim hagiographers reported disturbing events, which tended to show that a great *baraka*
(blessing) illuminated the deeds and actions of Muhammad, long
before he perceived the *wahyi*, the supernatural inspiration, divine
in nature, which was the basis of the Revelation.

Muslims have a huge body of texts detailing the life and work of
the Prophet. They were written exclusively by his close Companions,
and later, the best biographers. Called *Sira*, short for the Arabic
expression *Sirat al-rasul*, meaning "The Conduct/Life of the
Prophet," these apologetics are also the logical basis of the *sunna*
(Tradition), which is otherwise known as the consensual "median
way" of orthodoxy. What does this mean exactly? This is an important
question, since, after the Koran, for most Muslims the *sunna* is the
principal repository of the law. The *hadith* consist of all the reported
speech, thoughts, attitudes, or observations made by the Prophet and
authenticated as such by a number of first-hand witnesses. Six collections of *hadith*, thought to be "authenticated," were recorded at the
end of the eighth century and throughout the ninth century. Two of
them, the *Sahih* of Bokhari (810-870) and the *Sahih* of Muslim ibn
Hajjaj, are held in higher regard than all the others. Muslims greatly
revere scholarly theologians including Abu Hanifa, the *imam* Ash-
Shafi'i, Ibn Hanbal, At-Tirmidhi, Abu Dawud, Ibn Maja, An-Nasa'î,
An-Nawani, and Malik ibn Anas, who all lived between the seventh
and thirteenth centuries and left invaluable writings, such as the
famous work by Malik ibn Anas entitled *al-Muwatta*.

As a "Messenger of God" (*Rasul Allah*), Muhammad is, in the eyes of Muslims, the "Seal of the Prophets." He fulfills the monotheistic tradition started by his illustrious predecessors Adam, Abraham, Moses, and Jesus: "Muhammad is not the father of any of your men, but he is the Messenger of Allah, and the Seal of the Prophets" (*The Confederates*, XXXIII, 40).

Muhammad, the founder of Islam, is a universal Prophet and law-giver. His signature is the Koran, the revelation with which he was entrusted. His message is fidelity to an unalterable Divine Word; his mission is the establishment of peace on earth.

Yet Muhammad was a warlord and fine strategist, who ended his mission only a few weeks before his death, having fought for more than twenty years against polytheism and his foes. He suffered numerous betrayals and setbacks, converted a large number of pagans and set free dozens of slaves. In Muslim minds the Battle of Badr, which is named after a place in southern Medina and took place on March 17, 624, tolled the death knell of pagan Arabia because, for the first time, a handful of Muslims defeated the well-trained army of the Quraysh, several hundred strong. On December 4, 656, another memorable battle, the "Battle of the Camel," was fought between 'Ali, the future fourth Caliph, and two enemy high chiefs, supported by 'A'isha. The battle was won by 'Ali.

Muhammad spoke his last words in public on Mount 'Arafat during a farewell pilgrimage, in the very place where, every year, Muslims throng to fulfill one of the five duties of their faith, the *hajj*.

1. "And remember, Jesus, the Son of Mary, said: 'O Children of Israel! I am the Messenger of Allah (sent) to you, confirming the Law (which came) before me, and giving Glad Tidings of a Messenger to come after me, Whose name shall be Ahmad' " (*Al-Saff*, XLI, 6).
2. "And if any stray, say: 'I am only a Warner' " (*The Ants*, XXVII, 72).
3. "Muhammad is not the father of any of your men, but (he is) the Messenger of Allah" (*The Confederates*, XXXIII, 40).
4. "Seest thou not how thy Lord dealt with the Companions of the Elephant?" (*The Elephant*, CV, 1).

5. This is the traditional genealogy of the Prophet as given by Abu'l-Feda: Abu'l-Qasim Muhammad was the son of Abd al-Muttalib, the son of Hashim, the son of Abd-Menaf, the son of Kossai, the son of Kaleb, the son of Morrah, the son of Ka'b, the son of Luwai, the son of Ghalib, the son of Fakhr or Quraysh, the son of Malik, the son of Nadhr, the son of Kenana, the son of Khuzayma, the son of Mudraka, the son of Ilyâs, the son of Mudhar, the son of Nizar, the son of Ma'd, the son of Adnan, who was the direct descendant of Ishmael, the son of Abraham. Muhammad is also the name of the 47th sura of the Koran (XLVII).

THE KORAN

THE NON-CREATED AND INCARNATE WORLD AND DIVINE INSPIRATION

It was in Ghar Hira, a cave near Mecca, in the year 610 or 611, that Muhammad, during one of his retreats, heard the Angel Gabriel (*Jibrîl*) say to him: "Recite, read, announce (*iqrâ*)." Surprised, the Prophet replied: "But I do not know how to read." The Angel Gabriel then asked him to repeat the Word: "Read! In the name of thy Lord and Cherisher, who created. He created man, out of a mere clot of congealed blood. Proclaim! And Thy Lord is Most Bountiful He Who taught [the use of] the Pen—and taught man that which he knew not" (*The Blood Clot*, XCVI, 1-5).

These then are the first words of this non-created and sublime Word expressed by the Angel Gabriel, announced by the Prophet, and transmitted to man by means of reciters (*huffaz*), whose prodigious memories kept it from oblivion.

Revealed in its entirety in the "perspicuous"[1] Arabic tongue, the language of Hijaz, and not allowing a single alteration, addition, or deletion, the Koran is the Book par excellence, the Book about which no doubt can be permitted (the *rayba fihi*), because to doubt the book is to question one's faith itself. "This is the Book; in it is guidance sure, without doubt, to those who fear Allah... And as to those who reject Faith, it is the same to them whether thou warn them or do not warn them; they will not believe. Allah hath set a seal on their hearts and on their hearing, and on their eyes is a veil; Great is the penalty they (incur)" (*The Cow*, II, 1-6).

Moreover, the *mushaf*, the physical Koran that we can consult and touch is, in the eyes of Muslim esotericists, only the visible copy, the divine archetype, of that *materia prima* which has been safeguarded for all eternity in a Preserved Tablet.[2] The word *Qu'rân* comes from the verb *qaraa* and the noun *qirâ'a*, which means reading or recitation, recalling the dictation of the text by the Archangel to the Prophet that began around 610-611 and ended in 632 A. D.

The Koran was revealed successively, first in Mecca—this revelation is called the "first period" (611-622)—and then at Medina, in what is known as the "second period" (622-632). It consists of one hundred and fourteen chapters, called suras, and six thousand two hundred and nineteen verses, the *ayat*. The basic element of the Koran, the verse, is a powerful sign, which is an assurance of the divine presence. It is derived etymologically from "miracle" and signifies the realization of an infinitely superior will. Within the Koran, the suras are grouped together into sixty distinct sections of varying lengths called *ahzab*. The longest, from the second sura (*The Cow*) to the seventy-first (*Noah*), may contain up to several hundred verses. The longest sura in the Koran is that of *The Cow*, which is two hundred and eighty-six verses long. The medium-sized chapters are those from sura LXXX (*He Frowned*) to sura XCII (*The Night*). Some of the shortest chapters consist of only three verses. They range from sura XCIII (*The Glorious Morning Light*) to sura CXIV (*Mankind*), the last sura of the Holy Book, which has six verses. Each section, except the ninth,[3] begins with an invocation to Allah, the *basmala*, the symbolic key that opens the Koranic mystery. The inauguration of the whole, the *fatiha* (which means "The Opening," or "The Introduction") is one of the most frequently recited suras. Its seven verses bear the prestigious title of

"Mother of the Book," since, according to a tradition of the Prophet, it is a distillation of its richness and complexity.

The Prophet's scribe, Zayd ibn Thabit, is believed to have recorded the basis for what later evolved into the vulgate of the Koran by order of the Caliph 'Uthman, between 644 and 656.

Since then, the Koran has been sung and chanted in the mosques, as well as copied, meditated upon, interpreted, and learned by heart in the Koranic schools (*madâris*). It has also been widely translated.[4] Learning the Koran by heart is a blessed act of greatness for all Muslims. It is often a prerequisite for Koranic exegesis, and for Islamic theology and jurisprudence. This powerful text, which takes the form of a continuous stream of consciousness and an uninterrupted explanation, this "great miracle," has at its heart an irrefutable aesthetic argument: "And if ye are in doubt as to what We have revealed from time to time to Our servant, then produce a surah like thereunto; and call your witnesses or helpers (if there are any) besides Allah, if your (doubts) are true" (*The Cow*, II, 23).

1. "The tongue of him they wickedly point to is notably foreign, while this is Arabic, pure and clear" (*Bees*, XVI, 103).
2. "Nay, this is a Glorious *Qur'an* (inscribed) in a Tablet Preserved!" (*The Constellations*, CXXXV, 22).
3. The sura entitled "The Repentance" or "The Disavowal."
4. Since its translation into Latin in the Middle Ages, the Koran has gradually been translated into all the languages known to man. However, the greatest number of translations, and the most accurate, date from the end of the last century and from the present century. Apart from French, which counts no fewer than twelve important translations, German, and English, the following should also be noted: Finnish (1942), Afrikaans (1950), Basque (1952), Gaelic, Lowland Scottish (1948), and Yiddish, in Hebrew script (1950). There have also been versions in Platt Deutsche (1698), Swiss Romansch (1949), and Volapuk (the universal language invented in 1879 by Johann Martin Schleyer) in 1951. Translations also exist, among others, in Hindi, Uzbek, Chinese, Malinke, Swahili, and Peuhl.

THE PROFESSION OF FAITH

THE CORNERSTONE OF ALL BELIEF IN ISLAM,
THE *SHAHADA* IS ALSO THE STARTING
POINT OF ISLAMIC DOGMA

The *shahada*, a real jewel of faith, is in a spiritual sense Muhammad's most important contribution. It consists of saying the following phrase: "There is no god but God and Muhammad is the Messenger of God."

Shahada means "to affirm," "to attest," but also "to bear witness to the existence and unity of God." It is the Muslim's most intimate act of piety, the manifest sign of his adherence to the faith of the one true God, the means whereby the faith of the individual is grafted onto the branch of communal faith and the believer is released from his selfish instincts and the narcissism that assails him.[1]

A precondition, which Muslims call "the good (or praiseworthy) intention" (*niyya*), is required before reciting the *shahada*. A saying of the Prophet brings this home with full force: "No act is valid without good intention and each being will be judged according to this intention."[2]

The very edifice of faith is built on this *niyya*, the primal intention of which can be defined by an expression imbued with psychology: "sincere frame of mind" or *sidq*. The *niyya*, like the *shahada* that crowns it, obviously excludes all ostentation or blameworthy action. Even today, any adult who is sound of mind and pronounces this formula with conviction becomes a Muslim in the eyes of Divine Law, since "The only Believers are those who have believed in Allah and his Messenger, and have never since doubted" (*The Chambers*, XLIX, 15).

While the *shahada* is the simplest act of the Muslim faith, it is also the most important. It influences the dogma on which the religion is built, since it is understood that faith begins with the recitation of this phrase. It is notably the manifestation of the divine attributes, since everything about the Creator is brought back to life by the love that the believers give Him. It is reported that, according to Abu Sa'îd El-Khodri, a Muslim came to see the Prophet and asked him if it were enough to recite the phrase in the Koran: "Say: he is Allah, the One and Only" (*The Purity of Faith*, CXII, 1). Understanding that the believer was afraid of not fulfilling the conditions of the dogma, the Prophet Muhammad is said to have answered: "By the One who holds my soul in His hands, these few words are equal to one third of the Koran."[3]

Thus the act of testifying both to the unity of God (the first *shahada*) and to the authenticity of the Prophetic message (the second *shahada*) are acts that, on the one hand, imply the deep awareness of the believer, and, on the other, his responsibility. These professions are absolutely meaningless if they are gained by constraint, mental manipulation, or any other subterfuge: "O ye who believe! Believe in Allah and His Messenger, and the scripture which He hath sent to His Messenger and the scripture which He sent to those before (him). Any who denieth Allah, His angels, His Books, His Messengers, and the Day of judgement, hath gone far, far astray" (*The Women*, IV, 136).

In addition to being a blessed phrase, the *shahada* is also one of the ways—and without a doubt the most certain—of becoming more sincere in the exercise of the religion. One passes from the simple formula, which consists in saying with conviction the names of Allah and of the Prophet, to the very content of this pronouncement, to its spiritual significance. For Muslims, each human act can lead the faithful either to good or to evil. Faith alone is essential to keep him in the blessing of Allah.

This faith is manifold. Fulfilling the conditions of faith takes different forms: not being slanderous, a liar, or envious is an act of faith; seeking peace and harmony, preaching justice among men, and showing tolerance for others are acts of faith. Sincerely wishing the presence of one's fellow man, succoring the weak, and giving alms are also acts of faith. One hadith in fact tells us that "faith consists of sixty and some branches."[4]

Fundamentally, the profession of faith is the synthesis of the whole life of the individual. At the same time, as it symbolizes his conviction at a given moment, it makes him an active member of the congregation of believers. This explains why the shahada is both the first condition of Islam and the formula that the believer must say when he feels that his time has come, on his deathbed. It is the key to earthly life yet it is also the phrase that offers passage to the world to come.

An authorized tradition claims that this phrase is the repetition of the first phrase spoken by the Angel Gabriel and learnt by the Prophet.

1. The points that the Koran has in common with Christianity and Judaism are: the same God, the same intercessory Angel, Gabriel (*Jibrîl*), and the originary figures of Adam and Eve (*Hawa*). Islam has a sincere respect for the prophets who came before Muhammad, some of whom are referred to by name in the Koran: Abraham (*Ibrahîm*), the Ancestor, father of Ishmael (*Isma'il*) and Isaac (*Ishaq*); Jesus (*'Isa*); David (*Dawud*); and Joseph (*Yusuf*) and Mary (*Maryam*). Others are merely evoked: Elijah, John, Job, Jonas, Saul, Zechariah, and others. Islam recognizes the authenticity of the holy books, especially the Bible and the Koran. On the other hand, the trinity Father, Son, and Holy Ghost is denied, since Allah, the One God, cannot be multiplied nor have progeny. For Muslims this would be like anthropomorphism, and a heresy.

2. *Hadith* of the Prophet.

3. *Ibid.*

4. *Ibid.*

PRAYER

TO PRAY IS TO ACCEPT ISLAM AS THE RELIGION
OF THE ONE GOD AND MUHAMMAD HIS PROPHET

Prayer is one of the five pillars of Islam, immediately following the profession of faith. Prayer is performed five times a day, and it represents the most visible form of the believer's attachment to his faith.

In principle, collective prayer is more meritorious than individual prayer, the former, it is said, having twenty-seven times the spiritual value of the latter. From this, therefore, ensues the importance of the Friday prayer, *al-Jumu'a*, the day of the (great) gathering of the community.

The Koran states that this rite can only be performed when physical and spiritual safety are assured: "When ye are free from danger, set up Regular Prayers: For such prayers are enjoined on Believers at stated times" (*The Women*, IV, 103).

The daily cycle begins at sunset and ends at the same time on the following day. The times of daily prayers thus correspond to the rising, zenith, and setting of the sun. There are five ritual prayers:

– *As-Subh*, performed between dawn and sunrise
– *Az-Zuhr*, performed when the sun is at its zenith
– *Al-'Asr*, performed in the afternoon
– *Al-Maghrib*, performed at sundown
– *Al-'Isha'*, performed during the evening, before going to bed.

When praying, the two sexes are kept perfectly chaste. If prayer is being performed at home, the prayer carpet and surroundings must be spotlessly clean. Indeed, Muslim prayer is only valid when the believer is surrounded by the precise conditions of purification, which calls for a series of ablutions: "O ye who believe! When ye prepare for prayer, wash your faces, and your hands (and arms) to the elbows; and (wash) your feet to the ankles" (*The Repast*, V, 6).

The ritual of ablution is carried out in a precise order. The believer must consciously decide to perform the ablutions with a view to prayer. He must then say the *basmala*, "In the name of Allah," the formula of devotion to God. Only then can the actual ablutions begin. These involve the hands, mouth, nose, face, ears, forearms, head, and feet.

Each action is repeated three times, beginning with the right-hand side, which is sacred throughout the eastern and Semitic tradition. This ceremonial washing clearly shows that water enjoys a symbolic status that far outstrips its merely hygienic function. There is also a "dry ablution," purification with earth or sand. When the Muslim finds himself without water, he is permitted to use a pebble or a fistful of sand: "If ye are in a state of ceremonial impurity... and ye find no water, then take for yourselves clean sand or earth, and rub therewith your faces and hands" (*The Repast*, V, 6).

However, there is an inverse to ritual purity: it is breached each time the believer becomes sullied, wittingly or unwittingly. In certain cases—sexual intercourse, childbirth, or menstruation—the believer is called upon to wash completely, according to a practice called *ghusl*, which is as codified as the ritual of ablutions.

But prayer is an act of faith every time it is observed, not only according to the canonical dictates of purification, time, and place, but particularly when it arises from the ardent desire of the believer. Each prayer comprises several cycles (*raq'a, pl. riqa'*), which follow each other in the same order:
– initial upright position, hands raised to the level of the face
– bowing forwards from the waist, with the hands resting on the knees
– double prostration, with the hands on the prayer mat
– return to the upright position.

After two, three, or four *riqa'*, the prayer ends with a *jalsâ* or seated position. Thus, once the believer has placed himself in the protection of God and reaffirmed His power by a formula known as *takbir* ("Allah is Most Great"), he continues his worship with the recital of the *fatiha*, the opening sura of the Koran, and of another sura, long or short, depending upon the occasion. Finally, there are several phrases of blessing and grace. The glorification of God (*tasbih*) is short: "Glory be to our Lord the Most High," as is the formula of thanksgiving: "Allah hears him who thanks Him, our Lord, praise be to You." There then follows the *shahada* and the *taslim*, which is a final salutation.

Other than these five daily prayers, a limited number of additional prayers are recommended.

The call to prayer (*adhan*) is also made five times a day. Inaugurated during the lifetime of the Prophet himself, this call was first made by a freed Abyssinian slave named Bilal. He is thus the first *muezzin* (*mu'adhdhin*) in Muslim history.

Within the context of canonical prayer, which the Prophet is said to have preferred to all the goods of this world, the part played by meditation, whether individual (*du'a*) or collective (*zikr*), is important to note.

ALMSGIVING

THE ISLAMIC THEORY AND PRACTICE OF GIVING

Lawful almsgiving, which is the implementation of sharing goods acquired in this world and considered as divine bounties, is one of the perfections demanded by Islam, and one of its five conditions of validity.

There are two categories of alms. The first, *zakat*, is compulsory.[1] It is mentioned in the Koran: "Of their goods take alms, that so thou mightest purify and sanctify them" (*The Repast*, IX, 103), and is the most succinct expression of the link between almsgiving and purification. It is calculated on the basis of actual possessions, property, capital, and income, which are subject to donation and sharing.

This is an annual almsgiving, legal, codified, and imposed upon every adult Muslim, regardless of sex or origin. This first category of alms is thus equivalent to a tax on all Muslims to be donated to the community and to the public Treasury as an expression of solidarity between the different social classes.

The Koran specifies: "Alms are for the poor and needy, and those employed to administer the funds; for those whose hearts have recently been reconciled (to the Truth); for those in bondage and in debt; in the cause of Allah; and for the wayfarer" (*The Repentance*, IX, 60). Alms have evolved with society and have been adapted to the historic and economic conditions prevailing under Islam. Nowadays, there are no captives to be bought out of bondage or wayfarers to rescue. On the other hand, a new poverty, especially in the cities, has become very apparent. Today, spending goes on the disadvantaged social classes. The best alms are not those that "cost" the most materially, but those given with the greatest fervor and conviction.

In the early days of Islam, a small group of very poor Muslims came to see the Prophet to discuss the case of rich dignitaries who not only scrupulously observed their Islamic duties but also devoted a proportion of their goods to substantial almsgiving. The Prophet answered them in these terms: "Has not Allah given you the means wherewith to give alms? In truth, each *tasbih* is an almsgiving, each *takbir* is an almsgiving, each *tahmid* is an almsgiving, each *tahlil* is an almsgiving. Commanding good is an almsgiving. And in the work of the flesh of each one of you there is an almsgiving." [2] *Tasbih, takbir, tahmid,* and *tahlil* are the current forms of praisegiving, which are part of Muslim prayer and which, in this regard, are regularly recited by the faithful. Some renowned theologians including El-Bokhari (810-870), Razi (1149-1209), and Qortubi (d. 1273), consider that *zakat* has the power to multiply the goods of those who give it with sincerity.

The Holy Book also reminds us that one can "atone for" one's sins by means of the annual donation, for this has the same value as repentance: "But (even so), if they repent, establish regular prayers and practice regular charity—they are your brethren in Faith" (*The Repentance,* IX, 11).

Finally, a Prophetic tradition reported by El-Bokhari shows the importance of *zakat* in the popular representations of the next world: "He to whom God has given goods and who has not paid his tithe, God will, on the Day of Resurrection, make his goods appear in the form of a python with a bald head and two excrescences of flesh. On the Day of Resurrection, this python will coil itself around the neck of that man; it will seize him in its jaws and say: 'I am your goods, I am your treasure.'" [3]

The second category of almsgiving, the *sadaqa*, is a spontaneous donation is as worthy if is made to a beggar who holds out his hand in a souk or to a needy branch of the family. Here, too, in order to be considered a pious act, the *sadaqa* must be made with legitimate funds and honest gain. It must be given without ostentation, so discreetly, indeed, that the left hand must be totally unaware of the donation being made with the right hand. In addition, the Koran specifies that "By no means shall ye attain righteousness unless ye give (freely) of that which ye love; and whatever ye give, of a truth Allah knoweth it well" (*The Family of 'Imran*, III, 92).

Both forms of almsgiving are associated with prayer and, according to the Prophet, are of an equal value in the eyes of God. The fact that they are evoked in eighty verses that appear in thirty-four suras of the Koran testifies to the central place of almsgiving in Muslim dogma.

1. Most probable etymology: "To purify oneself," from the root *z-k-a*, *zakka*, or *tazakka* meaning both "to fulfill one's alms" and "to purify oneself," in conformity with the Koranic text that says: "But those will prosper who purify themselves, and glorify the name of their Guardian-Lord, and lift their hearts in prayer" (*The Most High*, LXXXVII, 14-15).
2. *Hadith* of the Prophet.
3. El-Bokhari, vol. 1, p. 455.

THE FAST

ABSTINENCE FROM FOOD AND DRINK
IN ORDER TO BE IN HARMONY WITH THE SPIRIT
OF ISLAM AND TO SHARE THE DISTRESS OF
THE MOST UNDERPRIVILEGED

The fast of *Ramadan*, the ninth month of the Muslim calendar, is designed as deprivation from food, but it is a desired and accepted deprivation. This is the holy month during which the Koran was revealed: "*Ramadan* is the [month] in which was sent down the Koran, as a guide to mankind, also clear [signs] for guidance and judgement [between right and wrong]" (*The Cow*, II, 185).

According to ancient custom, the word *ramadan* has also come to mean the practice of fasting itself, and often, and incorrectly, replaces the word *sawm*, which means "abstinence": "O ye who believe! Fasting is prescribed to you as it was prescribed to those before you, that ye may [learn] self-restraint" (*The Cow*, II, 183).

The month of *Ramadan*, which is the fourth Pillar of Islam, is obligatory for all believers, male or female, from puberty onwards. The sick, nursing mothers, pregnant women, and travelers are all exempt, and the mentally ill and young children are not bound by the fast. On the other hand, those who only have a temporary reason for being unable to fast, such as menstruating women, or anyone who cannot fast for other reasons, such as medical treatment, must make up the days of fasting they have missed in the course of the year. The start of the lawful fast is established as soon as a worthy believer sees the form of the crescent moon. In fact, it has been decreed that: "Every one of you who is present [at his home] during that month should spend it in fasting" (*The Cow*, II, 185).

The crescent moon, the ancient emblem of the Sassanids, has gradually become the special symbol of Islam. Although it had for long figured in the coats of arms of the Ottoman Empire, it became associated with the emblems of other Muslim countries only in the nineteenth century. The tradition has persisted, but since the science of astronomy has allowed Arabs to calculate the appearance of the moon with a certain reliability (the first observatory was built in Baghdad in 820), the contribution of scientists has been accepted. However, each time that there is recourse to the letter of the Koran, actually observing the new moon serves as a motivation for the faithful, as it augurs a month of beneficial fasting. Nowadays, this practice is naturally more widespread in desert regions and in the countryside than in the cities.

The actual fast begins a little before dawn (*fajr*) and ends after sundown (*imsak*), at the time of the first evening prayer (*maghrib*). The faithful may take a light meal before daybreak. Widely used manuals give the starting and ending times of the fast. Nowadays, they are also broadcast on radio or television, especially in the cities, in Muslim countries, as well as for Muslims living in non-Muslim countries.

During the hours of fasting, before the breaking of the fast (*iftar*) is announced, the Muslim abstains from eating, smoking, and drinking. He is also prohibited from having sexual intercourse, even within a legitimate union. The same is true of a whole series of antisocial behavior condemned by common morality (for example, back-biting, envy, stealing, quarreling, rivalry, or lying). Committing these acts annuls the spiritual value of the fast.

The twenty-seventh night of Ramadan, the Night of Power (*Laylat al-Qadr*), is very important, since it is the night on which Revelation was first made: "We have indeed revealed this [Message] in the Night of Power. And what will explain to thee what the Night of Power is? The Night of Power is better than a thousand months. Therein come down the angels and the Spirit by Allah's permission, on every errand: Peace!... This until the rise of Morn" (*The Night of Power*, XCVII).

Ramadan is also the month of grace, of great religious fervor, and a time for forgiveness. Collective mutual aid is given more overtly and more frequently. The most devout observers of the fast go to the mosque and spend part of the night in a supplementary prayer called *Salat al-Tawarih* or the Prayer of Relaxation or Rest.

Despite the demands the month of ritual fasting makes, Muslims approach it with joy, trust, and serenity. According to Abu-Horayra (seventh century), the Prophet said: "When *Ramadan* begins, the gates of heaven open, the gates of hell are closed, and the demons are chained up."[1]

1. El-Bokhari, vol. 1, p. 607.

THE PILGRIMAGE

MEETING THE COMMUNITY OF BELIEVERS
IN THE HOUSE OF GOD

After the profession of faith, prayer, almsgiving, and the fast, the pilgrimage to Mecca is the fifth and last pillar of Islam. It is enjoined upon all adult Muslims of either sex, who have the material means to undertake it, even if only once in their lives.[1]

The great pilgrimage (*al-Hajj*) consists of several stages spread out over a number of days, usually from the eighth to the twelfth day of *Dhu'l-Hijja*, the twelfth month of the Muslim calendar. The period mentioned in the Koran is a sacral period, that is, subject to minutely codified purification rituals, the most apparent being those that concern dress and costume. The following saying of the Prophet is reported by 'Abdallah ben 'Omar (seventh century): "The man in the state of *ihram* must put on neither *qamis*, nor turban, nor trousers, nor burnous, nor any clothing that has been touched by saffron or by the *ouers* [a plant dye], nor boots, unless he cannot find any shoes; in which case, he must cut his boots down to below his ankles."[2]

The Muslim pilgrimage consists of four stages. The strict observance of this route is the only guarantee of the validity of the pilgrimage:

I. DEPARTURE FOR 'ARAFAT (*Dhu'l-Hijja* 8), the holy mountain of Islam situated 13 miles from Mecca. Upon arrival in Mecca, the believer must cleanse himself (*ihram*) by removing his usual clothing and dressing in white robes made of unsewn material and by observing the major prohibitions of spilt blood, sexual intercourse and the practice of hunting. In addition: "Let there be no obscenity, nor wickedness, nor wrangling in the *Hajj*..." (*The Cow*, II, 197).

The pilgrim circumambulates the Kaaba seven times on foot (*tawaf*). These circumambulations may be undertaken in the company of a professional guide (*mutawîf*). He then prays to God using prayers and invocations, of which the best known and most important is the *talbiyya*.[3] This cycle is completed with a prayer at the

Station of Abraham, which is on the esplanade of the Kaaba.

Finally, the pilgrim must undertake a seven-fold "running" (*sa'y*) between Safa and Marwa, two small hillocks that are part of the rite. This passage to and fro recalls that of Hagar when, in a panic, she had to find water for her son Ishmael. To keep him from certain death, Allah made a spring of fresh water gush up in front of her near the *mataf*, the path around the Kaaba, where a large portico, recalling the "race" run by Hagar, marks the entrance today. Full of *baraka*, this briny water is called *Zamzam*. The pilgrims take some home with them in little jars known as *zamzamiyat*.

II. STANDING ON 'ARAFAT (*Dhu'l-Hijja* 9). The pilgrims gather in 'Arafat around the hill of al-Rahma and pray to God throughout the day, particularly reciting the *talbiyya*. This standing on the ninth day of *Dhu'l-Hijja* is important. It recalls the last public act of the Prophet when, during his "Pilgrimage of Farewell," he went up Mount 'Arafat to make his final speech and deliver this Revelation: "This day have I perfected your Religion for you, completed my favor upon you, and have chosen for you Islam as your religion" (*The Repast*, V, 3). After the afternoon prayers, the pilgrims stand and invoke divine compassion, because, according to tradition, standing on 'Arafat is the culmination of the pilgrimage. It must not be missed on any pretext. After sunset, the pilgrims leave 'Arafat and head for Mina, three and a half miles from Mecca. At the halfway point of their journey, the pilgrims stop at Muzdalifa, where they spend the night. This is an impressive journey for the pilgrims, especially for the more elderly who often require help from a third party. Indeed, the *nafr* is more than a mere walk, it is an actual stampede, the significance of which goes back to the rhythm adopted by the Prophet himself, who accelerated or slowed his pace according to the stages of the ritual.

III. THE DAY OF THE SACRIFICE (*Yawm al-nahr*), MUZDALIFA (*Dhu'l-Hijja* 10). This is the ritual of the immolation of the animal sacrifice, which is observed on the same day throughout the Muslim world. This sacrifice is in homage to the act of Abraham who, tested by God, almost sacrificed his eldest son Ishmael. Indeed,

Muslims believe, contrary to the story told in Genesis,[4] that it was Ishmael and not Isaac who was the subject of the Archangel's barter during Abraham's sacrifice.[5] God, in His great leniency, having dispatched the Angel Gabriel, substituted a sheep for the beloved child, which has been used ever since in this ritual. This, at least, is what most traditional commentators of the Koran maintain. Ishmael is considered to be the ancestor of the Bedouin Arabs and the father of their nation. Moreover, an ancestral tradition holds that Ishmael helped his father when he saw that the Holy Temple of the Kaaba was crumbling and falling into ruin and so rebuilt it.

IV. JOURNEY TO MINA (*Dhu'l-Hijja* 11). This is where the day of meditation (*tarwiya*) takes place, and sometimes continues through the following two days (the twelfth and thirteenth days of *Dhu'l-Hijja*). Accompanying this stage is the stoning of Satan (*rajm al-shaytân*) with stones gathered the previous day in Muzdalifa, which is an obligatory ancestral rite. The devil is symbolized by three upright slabs, the largest of which is permanently covered with a heap of small pebbles. After painstakingly observing this whole journey, the pilgrim deconsecrates himself, sacrificing all or part of his hair (many shave their heads completely), and thus rids himself of all the taboos that still bind him. These routes and rituals, which are so heavily annotated, have a particular meaning. The circumambulation of the Holy House represents the circumambulation of the angels around the heavenly throne, since, according to Ghazali, "the House of God is a visible symbol in the world of the Kingdom of God, which is hidden from sight."[6] Koranic exegesis examines all the stages of the pilgrimage in this way, seeing in each a multi-layered significance: manifest, secret, deep, very deep, and so on. Only some of the initiated can understand, or, even more, interpret the later shades of meaning.

Apart from the great pilgrimage, Muslims also undertake the 'umra, the so-called "small" or "minor pilgrimage," because it is performed only in the Haram, in Mecca and its immediate surroundings. Both these pilgrimages are mentioned in the Koran, which distinguishes them from a mere visit to the holy places (*ziyara*): "Complete the *Hajj* or *Umrah* in the service of Allah. But if ye are prevented therefrom, send an offering for sacrifice, such as ye may find, and do not shave your heads until the offering reaches the place of sacrifice. And if any of you is ill, or has an ailment in his scalp [necessitating shaving], he should compensate therefor either by fasting, or by feeding the poor, or by offering a sacrifice" (*The Cow*, II, 196).

While it is important for pious Muslims, the *'umra* is left to the discretion of every individual. It can be undertaken at any time during the liturgical year, except during the period of the *Hajj*, although preference is given to the seventh month (*Rajab*), which is one of the four "holy months."[7] Although this is an act of great blessedness, accruing great advantage to whoever undertakes it, the *'umra* is not a substitute for the *hajj*, which can alone confer the title and prestige of the perfect Muslim.

The spiritual strength of the pilgrimage stems from its total immersion of the pilgrim in the sacred sanctuary. It is also the opportunity for pilgrims to encounter the huge Muslim community, *al-umma al-islamiyya*, men and women—millions of whom converge from all over the world—who honor the same God.

1. "Pilgrimage... is a duty men owe to Allah—those who can afford the journey" (*The Family of 'Imran*, III, 97).
2. El-Bokhari, vol. 4, P. 99.
3. "Here am I near to you, O my God, here am I" (*labayna alla-huma labbayk*).
4. Genesis 34: 1-14
5. Those ranged in ranks, XXXVII, 100-113.
6. M. Hamidullah, "Le pèlerinage à La Mecque," in *Les Pèlerinages*. (Paris, Seuil: 1950).
7. Mentioned in the Koran (*The Repentance*, IX, 36), these months are: *Muharram*, the first month, *Rajab*, the seventh month, *Dhu'l-Qa'da*, the eleventh month, and *Dhu'l-Hijja*, the twelfth month. Also called the month of "God's Truce," they carried a number of prohibitions in ancient Arabian times, amongst them inter-tribal warfare.

MECCA

For every Muslim, Mecca—formerly known as Bakkah—a city in the heart of the mineral plateau of Hijaz, at 21°26'17" latitude and 37°54'45" longitude, symbolizes the vibrant center of Islam.

In the Koran it is written: "The first house (of worship) appointed for men was that at Bakkah; full of blessing and of guidance for all kinds of beings. In it are signs manifest; (for example), the Station of Abraham; whoever enters it attains security; pilgrimage thereto is a duty men owe to Allah—those who can afford the journey" (*The Family of 'Imran*, III, 96-97).

While the erstwhile name of the town was "Mother of Cities" or "Metropolis of the World" (*Umm al-qurâ'*),—equivalent to the Greek Omphalos—it was also called "The Navel of the World," particularly by Arab geographers of the Middle Ages. Muslims call it by the prestigious name of "Noble Mecca" (*Makka al-mugarrama*), which is a reference to the four great events that took place there: the birth of the Prophet, the Koranic Revelation, the establishment of the *qibla*, and the annual pilgrimage.

The history of Mecca is a very ancient one, particularly in regards to trade and literature, which prepared it for the part it would play at the inception of Islam in the seventh century A.D. It is sometimes known by honorific names including *al-Bayt al-'Atiq* (the Ancient Place), *al-Balad al-Amin* (the Sure Country), *al-Bayt al-Haram* (the Forbidden City/The Sacred House), or simply *al-Haram* (The Forbidden City), and *al-Mugadassa* (the Holiest of Cities).

It was here that the Prophet was born and lived until he was chosen by God at the age of 40. The epitome of the divine, Mecca is considered in theological terms as the cradle of the first Koranic Revelation, the second having been imparted in Medina. This is why the Koran is divided into Meccan and Medinan suras with the place of revelation systematically indicated at the start of each chapter, along with the number of verses it contains. Although Mecca is geographically situated in an extremely arid desert region, it is nonetheless the center of gravity for several holy places including Safa, Marwa, the cave of Hira, Muzdalifa, the Hill of Light, and, further away, Mount 'Arafat. All these places are extremely important for pilgrimage.

Mecca, where the first conversions to the Muhammadan religion were performed, witnessed the religions victories and defeats, its great rallying cries, and its rivalries. It is also the city which persecuted the first Muslims and eventually drove them to flee to Medina. Later, it would be rehabilitated by the Prophet, who definitively consecrated it as the center of the Islamic universe. Mecca was also the epicenter of a whole network of holy cities, which have been concentrically scattered throughout the Muslim Empire since its expansion between the eighth and twelfth centuries.

Among them, in order of importance, are Mecca, Medina[1]—called in ancient times Yathrib, and also known as the "Resplendent" (*al-Munawara*)—and Jerusalem (*al-Quds*): the three chief holy cities of Islam. Medina, which contains the tomb of the Prophet, was the first city state of Islam, since the community of Muhammad was established there in 623. To this first holy trinity a second circle of holy cities, most of them Shi'ite, can be added:

– Qum, in Iran, where the sixteenth-century tomb of Fatima, the sister of the eighth Shi'i imam, is situated;

– Karbala', Iraq, about 60 miles south-west of Baghdad, this is the place of the martyrdom of Hussein, the son of 'Ali, killed in 680, in an infamous battle;

– Najaf, Iraq, near Kufa on the outskirts of Karbala', the site of the tomb of 'Ali (600-661), the fourth Caliph of Islam and son-in-law of the Prophet.

Finally, over a wider geographic range, there are cities or capitals that have played an important part in the propagation of Islam.

The most important are Damascus, Baghdad, and Cairo, which were successively the seats of the four most important Muslim dynasties, the Omayyads, the Abassids, the Fatimids, and the Mamelukes. Then there are Kairouan, Tlemcen, Fez, Meknes, Marrakesh, Cordova, and Granada, each of which are associated with one of the glorious periods of Islam and which developed certain aspects of its civilization to a point that it never matched thereafter.

Above and beyond its theological importance, Mecca is today the urban face of Islam, because these cities are the natural setting for the flowering of the religion, its creative genius, and personality.

1. Second holy city of Islam, situated some hundred miles from the Red Sea and two hundred miles north of Mecca.

THE KAABA

THE CANONICAL DIRECTION OF EVERY PIOUS ACT, PARTICULARLY PRAYER

The Kaaba is a cube-shaped temple (Muqa'ab) situated in the middle of the courtyard of the great mosque of Mecca. It is the point at which all believers converge, and the focus of all spiritual currents.

By virtue of its central position, the Kaaba, called *Bayt Allah al-Haram* (the House of God) or *Bayt al-Haram* (The Sacred House) is the main temple of the Muslim religion. It embodies the divine presence and inspiration.

The Kaaba, which is said to have been built by the patriarch Abraham and his son Ishmael, is draped in an embroidered cloth (*kiswa*). At one corner is the "Black Stone," which the pilgrims must touch during their pilgrimage.

From this point of view, the Kaaba is truly the earthly *qibla*, the physical lodestone of the Islamic faith and the focus for all the prayers Muslims address to their God daily. In the sura called *The*

Cow, it is written: "Turn then thy face in the direction of the Sacred Mosque: wherever ye are, turn your faces in that direction" (*The Cow*, II, 144).

The temple is a little over 50 feet high, 33 feet wide, and with a 40 foot façade. Six and half feet from the ground, set into an oval frame measuring about 8 inches, is the "Black Stone," the most intimate heart of the shrine.

Legend has it that the stone originally was a white hyacinth that, due to the sins of men, gradually grew blacker and blacker. The Kaaba owes its power of attraction to this black stone, which passes for the *mithaq*, the "primordial covenant" between the Creator and His creature. Touching it has a profound impact on pilgrims. In fact, this act is believed to count in their favor on the Day of Judgement. When the pilgrim arrives before the Temple, he enters it via the Gateway of Peace before beginning his circumambulation in a counter-clockwise direction. The area situated between the black stone and the door of the temple is called *al-Multazam* and acts as a support to the pilgrims when they are praying.

The great Muslim traveler from Valencia, Ibn Jubayr (1145-1217), describes the emotion he felt on touching the Kaaba: "The stone, when one kisses it, has a softness and freshness, which delights the mouth; so much so that he who places his lips upon it wishes never to remove them... It suffices, moreover, that the Prophet said that it is the 'Right Hand'[1] of God on Earth."[2]

The Kaaba is covered in a hanging of black silk brocade, embroidered in gold and silver thread with inscriptions from the Koran, which are invocations to God, the *fatiha*, the first sura of the Koran, and other verses.

Once a year, this covering is changed in a symbolic ritual that takes place during the pilgrimage. In ancient times, the highly colorful caravan procession that brought the new covering from Cairo to Mecca was known as the *mahmal*. Egypt was responsible for the temple hanging from the time of the Mamelukes (thirteenth century) until 1924 when this duty returned to the Wahhabite dynasty of the

Beni Saud. The Wahhabis became the Guardians of the Holy Places by reason of national sovereignty.

The temple itself is made of grayish or gray-blue stone from the outskirts of Mecca, and from mortar that came from Yemen. The interior of the Kaaba has also been of great interest for pilgrims and travelers.

Ibn Battuta (1304-1377) gives a lengthy description of it in his account of his voyage (*rihla*): "The interior of the illustrious Kaaba is paved with marbled shaded with white, blue, and red: the marble covering its walls is of the same sort. It has three exceedingly high columns made of teak wood and placed four paces apart; they occupy the middle of the space that constitutes the interior of the illustrious Kaaba. The middle one faces the halfway part of the side which is between the two corners of Iraq [Yemen] and Syria."[3]

In 1956, with the growing influx of pilgrims, the immediate surroundings of the Kaaba were removed and a larger, more austere, concourse replaced it. Paving stones were laid, while the pathway between Safa and Marwa, the two holy hillocks, was widened.

Ultimately, the Kaaba, the place towards which all canonical directions converge, is the epitome of Muslim monotheism. As the embodiment of the unity of the faith, it is also the sign of the unity of Allah and the indissociable link of the Muslim community.

1. *Yamîn*, a word that is difficult to translate, since it has the same etymology as the word "right," as opposed to *shimâl*, which means "left," and thus leads to a possible laterality and hence anthropomorphism of God.

2. Ibn Jubayr, *Voyages*, vol. 1, p. 291. (Paris: Paul Geuthner, 1982).

3. Ibn Battuta, *Voyages*, vol. 1, p. 105. (Paris: La Découverte, 1953-1956).

THE QIBLA

THE SPIRITUAL KEY TO ISLAMIC GEOGRAPHY AND ORIENTATION TOWARD THE KAABA

The *Qibla*, which was established by the Koran as the result of a prolonged controversy, which set the unbelievers against the Muslims, symbolizes the direction of Mecca, of which the *qibla* is the abstract representation and intense "focalization."

The initial direction of the *qibla*, established during the Medinan period of the Prophet's life, was towards Jerusalem (622 A.D.) until the revelation of a verse, two years later, which signaled the definitive change of direction: "And we appointed the *Qibla* to which thou wast used, only to test those who followed the Messenger from those who would turn on their heels [from the Faith]" (*The Cow*, II, 143).

Since then, Mecca, the Great Mosque and the Kaaba, which provide the "key" to Islam's spiritual geography, have formed the living center of Islam. That is why the believers first check the direction in which they are turning before prostrating themselves before God. Once the direction of the *qibla* has been established, earth joins heaven in a sanctified place, the Kaaba, the Sacred Temple of Islam. Animated discussions can often be witnessed between believers in the absence of a mosque and, therefore, of the *mihrab*, which is the architectural symbol of the *qibla* in a mosque. How should one respond to the dictate of the Koran that believers must turn towards Mecca to pray: "We see thee turning thy face [for guidance] to the heavens: now shall we turn thee to a *Qibla* that shall please thee. Turn then thy face in the direction of the Sacred Mosque: wherever ye are, turn your faces in that direction" (*The Cow*, II, 144). This instruction applies to the whole liturgical cycle and is used to attract divine blessings upon a sacrifice, funeral, or wedding.

Nevertheless, the "people of the *Qibla*" (*Ahl al-Qibla*, as the Muslims are called), do not always refer to this precise point, however sacred it is, since, according to the Koran, "to Allah belong the

East and the West" (*The Cow*, II, 115). This means that the direction taken matters but little, since Allah is at the beginning and end of all things. "Whithersoever ye turn, there is Allah's countenance," as that same sura says.

In fact, as in the Mosque of Two *Qibla* in Medina, the ancient mosque of Qubâ, the very place in which the change of *qibla* took place, such an orientation has meaning because it epitomizes the unity of the centralism of the faith on the one hand and its tolerance on the other: Mecca is not only the center of the world but it is also in the world.

THE MOSQUE

THE PLACE OF ASSEMBLY FOR THE COMMUNITY

Designed in the image of the first mosque of the Prophet, built in Medina in the year 1 A.H. (622 A.D.), the mosque (*al-jami'*, or *masjid al-jumu'a*) is the place in which Muslims worship collectively. As such, it is the physical symbol of Islam and the place in which collective fervor is expressed.

The mosque plays a much vaster and more complex role than that of a place of worship. In particular, it is the institution in which religious instruction is given, thanks to the colleges housed in its outbuildings, the moral academy in which social activities such as marriage are consecrated and especially, after prayer, the meeting place in which community life is discussed. It is at the mosque that disputes between Muslims are settled, and also where innovations are considered, rejected, or approved. Last but not least, religious authority is expressed and manifested at the mosque, notably during the Friday sermon (*khutba*). The Friday sermon is preached in the great mosque. This is the most important act of devotion since it combines many oratorical talents, such as the visionary skills of the preacher, the exemplary serenity of the pedagogue and the teacher, and the theological talent of the inspired religious leader.

There are several types of mosques, usually classed according to their size and the number of devotees who attend them. The small mosque is called the *musalla* or *masjid*. This is the little chapel in which "prostration" (*sujud*) is performed, Muslims being designated in the Koran as "those that bow down and prostrate themselves" (*The Repentance*, IX, 112). Friday prayers are held in the great mosque. Apart from a large prayer hall and sometimes a sort of mezzanine at the back of the hall set aside for women, the mosque contains the following features:

– the minaret: this is the anglicized form of the Arabic word *manara*, but this most prominent feature of the architecture of the mosque changes its name depending upon the effect the orator wishes to give in his description, and varies from region to region. There is *al-manara*, as just mentioned, but there is also *al-sa'uma*, "the protuberance," or *al-mi'dhana*, "the place in which the call to prayer is raised." The prototype of the minaret is that of the "mosque of Bilal" in Jabal Abu Kobays. Certainly the form is basic, but it also shows the characteristic features of a minaret, especially its extra height. The main function of the minaret, apart from that of balancing the edifice in the aesthetic sense, is to allow the *muezzin* to project his call (*adhân*) reminding the faithful of the hours of prayer. The minaret is also a symbol of mediation and verticality, which links the mosque to the higher spheres of Muslim cosmology, giving the ritual of kneeling and prostration the sense of a divine flowering of which it is the outward manifestation;

– the *mihrab*: the focal point of the mosque, the hollow alcove in the wall that indicates the direction of Mecca (qibla);

– the *minbar*: the preacher's pulpit is part of the ritual furnishings of the mosque. In some great mosques, such as the al-Agsa Mosque in Jerusalem, this pulpit is magnificently and ornately carved. Although usually made of precious wood, the minbar is sometimes modestly represented by a mound or other raised object. The Prophet is even said to have celebrated the Friday

sermon perched on the trunk of a palm tree;
– the ablutions hall: before entering the prayer hall, the believer must cleanse himself in thought as well as in deed. It is enjoined upon him to perform his customary ablutions (*wudu'*) in a special room set aside for this purpose and adjoining the mosque, which is an integral part of any mosque. The ablutions hall represents an intermediary space between the profane world of active life and the sacred world of the mosque, a place for meditating, regaining strength and feeling at one with the principles of God, man's Helper. The believer here unloads himself of his major or minor impurities before presenting himself, full of humility, before the Creator.

Aside from the mosques of Mecca and Medina, the most frequented of the Muslim world, several other mosques stand out architecturally:
– The Mosque of Omar or the Al-Aqsa Mosque, and the Dome of the Rock in Jerusalem (late seventh century);
– the university mosque of Al-Azhar (tenth century), in old Cairo, one of the most prestigious in Sunni Islam, since it houses the Academy of Religious Sciences and a High Council of theologians who are highly influential in the fields of Islamic jurisprudence and doctrine;
– the Friday Mosque in Teheran (ninth to eleventh centuries);
– the Quat al-Islam Mosque in Delhi (thirteenth century);
– the Suleymanieh Mosque in Istanbul (fourteenth century);
– the Mezquita of Cordova (eighth to tenth centuries), no longer used for religious purposes;
– the Sidi 'Okba Mosque (twelfth century) in Kairouan, Tunisia, which occupies a place apart since it was the work of 'Okba ibn Nafi', the Muslim general who paved the way for the Islamization of North Africa. In his honor, Kairouan is sometimes considered the fourth holy city of Islam.

The construction of mosques accompanies the demographic evolution of Islam. Wherever it is situated, the mosque aims to become integrated into its sociological and urban landscape. Through spontaneous mimicry the style of the mosque quite easily accommodates the architectural influences of the country in which the mosque is built. Consider, for example, the red earth mosques of sub-Saharan Africa, those of the Indian sub-continent, and of Indonesia, Pakistan, and Afghanistan, all of which are distinctive in style.

THE MIHRAB

THE COMPASS OF THE MUSLIM WORLD
AND THE MATERIAL REPRESENTATION OF
THE *QIBLA*, THE *MIHRAB* IS ALSO AN
ARCHITECTURAL INNOVATION

The word *mihrab* has a complex etymology (balcony, hall, room) but has gradually shed these multiple meanings and come to mean simply "alcove," "prayer niche," or "apsidal." It was instituted in the eighth century, most likely in Damascus, when the direction of Mecca (*qibla*) had to be marked on the building of the mosque.

While in exile in Medina, the Prophet had to turn towards the holy city of Jerusalem to pray, but there is no authoritative documentation to show whether the *mihrab* physically existed at that time. Arab historians attribute the innovation of adding a *mihrab* to the mosque to 'Uthman ibn 'Affan, the third Caliph of Islam. However, the *mihrab* only appeared gradually in the arrangement of the mosque, since primitive Islam, apart from not attributing a prominent position to visual symbols such as those found in churches, for example, also shied away from creating visual symbols because of the terror this aroused in believers who were used to strict religious orthodoxy.

Yet the *mihrab* is a rare example in Islam of a symbol in the fullest sense, since it is the physical representation of the direction of Mecca, which is in itself an abstract concept. Essential to the mosque, the *mihrab* is one symbolic representation that has been used widely.

It can be seen etched in marble in some decorative wall panels and even on the reverse of the most ancient Islamic coins.

With the development of Islam, the layout of the *mihrab*, and that of the mosque itself have become fundamental to the validity of the prayer offered up therein. The complex requirements for the establishment of the *mihrab* are on a par with the philosophical and theological demands of Islam, a religion that preaches the absolute unity of God. After all, what meaning would a mosque have if it did not face towards Mecca? Arab theologians, architects, mathematicians, and astronomers have speculated widely on the possible lines that can and ought to govern the siting and physical representation of the *qibla*. The *mihrab* is the architectural response accepted by the college of Muslim scholars who have studied the matter. Since the eighth and ninth centuries, no deviation from the norm has been tolerated by Muslim doctrine, and the reputations of mosque builders depend upon their following it to the letter.

Several exquisite *mihrabs* are to be found in the Muslim world. They are the acme of a mosque's refinement. Some are embellished with gold leaf, borders of light, and stucco stalactites that give an impression of movement. Others are more austere, without any particular additions. Mention is also sometimes made of *mihrabs* made of wood, such as the one in the Tashun Pasha Mosque in Turkey, the construction of which dates back to the thirteenth century. In the opinion of numerous architects, the most remarkable niches are to be found in the following mosques:
– the al-Aqsa Mosque in Jerusalem (eighth century);
– the Great Mosque in Cordova (the Mezquita, tenth century);
– the great mosques of Isfahan and Yazd. The *mihrab* in the former is set in a decor of stucco vegetation (1310), while the latter, dating from 1375, is of glazed earthenware;
– the mausoleum of Sayida Rukkayya in Cairo (twelfth century);
– the Konya Mosque (Turkey), with its glazed earthenware *mihrab*, in the Sedrettin Konevi (c. 1274).

Two other such prayer niches are worthy of note because they

are among the most original examples of Islamic architecture:
– the Sidi Oqba Mosque in Kairouan (ninth century), the *mihrab* is an excellent example of Arab Islamic art;
– the Ahmad al-Budayni Mosque in Cairo, a *mihrab* which dates from 1628 and has marble inlays in different colors.

Such a list cannot be considered exhaustive, since while experts may agree on the objective history of the building of mosques—and their prayer niches—they disagree on matters of personal taste, so there is no way in which the prayer niches can be ranked in order of artistic merit. On the aesthetic front, the prayer alcove celebrates the art of the craftsmen who devised and designed it, but it is also the expression of a mosque's "personality"; it remains the best reflection of the taste of a particular period and of the Muslim region in which it is situated.

Certainly without the *mihrab*, the mosque would be a building without magnetization or liturgical gravitas, prey to a sort of spiritual blindness.

FRIDAY

THE HOLY DAY OF THE MUSLIM WEEK

Friday is the "day of gathering" or "assembly." It is thus called because of the congregational prayer, which is said in the great mosque as soon as the sun has passed the meridian. It is a holy day for Muslims. The Koran mentions the Friday prayer only once, in the sura entitled Friday: "O ye who believe! When the call is proclaimed to prayer on Friday [The Day of Assembly], hasten earnestly to the remembrance of Allah, and leave off business [and traffic]: that is best for you if ye but knew!" (*Friday*, LXII, 9).

Es-Said ben Yazîd, the source of numerous oral traditions, relates that "in the time of the Prophet, the first call to prayer on a Friday came when the imam took the pulpit. It was also thus under

the Caliphs 'Abu-Bakr and 'Umar. 'Uthman ordained a third call to
prayer during his caliphate as the population had grown. This call
was made at Ez-Zawira [a district of Medina]. This dictate was later
kept up."[1]

It should be recalled at this point that, as in most elements of the
dogma, the Friday prayer was codified at the time of the four first
Caliphs, who have been dubbed al-Khulafa al-Rashidun (the
Properly Guided Caliphs), those same men who had accompanied the
Prophet in his many battles against the hostility and wrongdoings of
the idolaters.

The Friday prayer (salât al-jumu'a), upon which the entire spiritual and esoteric significance of that day is structured, is an act of
great blessedness for all Muslims who can reach the great mosque. A
ceremonial call (adhân) is raised by the muezzin, but a great number
of Muslims are already in their places because they attend the
mosque very early in the morning.

According to Abu-Horayra, a companion of the Prophet,
Muhammad said: "When Friday comes, the angels are standing at the
door of the mosque. They note the first comer, and the second [and so
on]. He who comes early is like a man who gives alms of a fat camel,
and then [successively] a man who gives alms of a bull, then a ram,
then a chicken, then an egg. When the imam comes out, the angels
shut their registers and listen to the mention of God."[2]

Because it is congregational and gathers the whole community in
the mosque (jami'), the Friday prayer is undoubtedly the most
important of the week. It is accompanied by an important instructive
and moral sermon (khutba) given by the imam on behalf of the religious authority of the land, and hence on behalf of Islam as a whole.

This is how Ibn Abî Zayd al-Qayrâwani (tenth century)
described the rite as it was observed in Mâlikism, one of the four
canonical schools of the Sunnis, found mainly in North Africa, black
Africa, and a part of Egypt: "The Friday prayer is obligatory in an
urban center and in a group of believers forming a community. The
sermon is obligatory before the prayer itself. The imam must lean on

a bow or a stick and sit down at the beginning and in the middle (of the *khutba*). The prayer begins when the sermon is ended....Those in the town or within a radius of three miles or less from it must hasten to the Friday prayer. It is not obligatory for travelers, pilgrims at Mina, slaves, women, or children who have not attained puberty. But if a slave or a woman are present at the prayer, they should observe it. Women are placed behind the rows of men. The *imam* who is giving the sermon must be attentively listened to, and the believers should face him." [3]

Having realized the influence of the Friday prayer on the believers, the great dynasties—and later the Muslim states, the best example of which is Saudi Arabia—have done their utmost to control the occasion, by building more and more imposing mosques intended to admit the largest number of believers. Although Friday is a public holiday in many Muslim countries, unlike the Lord's day of rest mentioned in Genesis,[4] it does not correspond to a possible rest from creation. The Koran clearly stipulates in the sura *Qâf* that: "We created the heaven and the earth and all between them in Six Days, nor did any sense of weariness touch Us" (*Qâf*, L, 38).

On a symbolic level, Friday is the pivot of the week and consequently of the liturgical time. It therefore has the same position in time as the mosque occupies in space.

1. El-Bokhari, vol. 2, p. 299.
2. *Ibid.*, p. 303.
3. Al-Qayrawâni, *La Risâla*, p. 95.
4. Genesis I: 31

IMAM AND MUEZZIN

THE *MUEZZIN*, *KHATIB*, AND *IMAM*, THE THREE MAIN FIGURES WHO LEAD THE PRAYER

Perched on top of the minaret (*al-manara*) the *muezzin*, from the Arabic word *al-muadhdhin*, is responsible for calling the faithful to worship in the mosque. It is a canonical duty instituted by the Prophet himself and implemented in the first mosque of Islam, built in Medina the Enlightened (*al-Munawara*).

The Abyssinian Bilal, who had been a slave of Abu-Bakr as-Saddiq (570-634), one of the Prophet's closest companions, was the first to assume this duty. It is one of the most important functions in the ritual. Since the seventh century, the *muezzin*, an officiant specially trained in vocal technique, has been raising a call to prayer, his hand cupping his mouth. The call consists of seven very specific phrases:

– *Allahu Akbar, Allahu Akbar*: "God is Most Great, God is Most Great";

– *Ash-hadu anna la-ilaha ilah-Lah*: "I testify that there's no other divinity as Allah" (twice);

– *Ash-hadu anna Muhammad rasul Allah*: "I testify that Muhammad is the Prophet of God" (twice);

– *Haya 'ala as-salat, haya 'ala as-salat*: "Come to prayer" (twice);

– *Haya 'ala al-falah, haya 'ala al-falah*: "Come to salvation or deliverance" (twice);

– *Allahu Akbar*: "God is Most Great" (twice);

– *La ilaha ilal-Lah*: "There is no god but God."

In the dawn prayer there is a variation and the muezzin twice repeats—for the benefit of those who, tempted into error by Satan, would prefer to carry on sleeping—"Prayer is more meritorious than sleep" (*As-salât khayru mina-nawm*) before pronouncing the final line. The importance of this call (*adhân*) stems from the spiritual value of all congregational prayers, which are twenty-seven times greater than individual prayers.

The *khatib* or preacher is often a theologian of renown, a high-ranking emissary or a scholar from within the Muslim community, with a fund of incontestable knowledge. His primary function is to deliver a sermon, known as the *khutba*, at the Friday prayer. Usually, he will be seated on a raised platform or high chair called a *minbar* and placed on the right (from the believers' viewpoint) of the *mihrab*.

The role of the *khatib* is principally religious and theological, which explains the multitude of Koranic quotations and references to the Islamic era. He does, however, also have to deal with general knowledge or social, political, and juridical issues.

In the past, the caliphate held considerable influence over the ideological orientation of the Friday sermon. There was even a time when this function was the prerogative of the ruling family or its appointed representatives, whether they were a *qadi* (religious judge), an *'alam* (theologian), or even a *talib* (advanced student of religious knowledge). Today, political regimes try to brand the sermon with their own mark of legitimacy and popularity, with varying degrees of success.

After having been summoned by the *muezzin* and having listened to the preacher's sermon, Muslims are invited to stand and perform the great prayer, the leadership of which is entrusted to an *imam*, literally "he who stands in front (of the others)."[1] The *imam*, who stands in the arch of the *mihrab*, is an important figure because he conducts and regulates the mechanics of the congregational prayer, while assuring its validity in the eyes of God. He is chosen from among healthy Muslims (who are free men, particularly in the time of the Prophet), preferably of sound physical constitution and possessing a sufficient level of knowledge and proven skills. In small mosques, the *imam* may also be the *khatib* (preacher); in some cases the same person performs the functions of *muezzin*, *khatib* and *imam*.

On the spiritual front, the *imam* must set a good example. He also sometimes intervenes between the Muslim and the institution, either in matters of theological exegesis connected with the dogma or in personal matters. The imam also intervenes in the various disputes between Muslims outside the context of worship and helps them to concentrate their minds, thus contributing to the permanent process of education characteristic of Islam.

In leading the congregation in prayer, these three figures, the *muezzin*, the *khatib*, and the *imam*, are responsible for religious services that take place five times a day.

Insofar as the Friday prayer is very well attended, it provides the *muezzin* and the *khatib* with the opportunity of expressing the whole range of their talents: in the case of the *muezzin*, he should have a strong, musical voice that is pleasing to the ear; the sermon of the *khatib* should be creative and inspired, while the prayer should be lead in a measured and modulated manner.

1. In the ninth century, the word *imam* was endowed with a new meaning. While for Sunnis it is only one term among others, which is applied to anyone who leads the collective prayer, imam for Shi'ites is a religious title pertaining to several high dignitaries. This theological and religious hierarchy is structured around the advent of the twelfth *Imam*, the hidden *Imam* who will close, at the end of time, the cycle inaugurated and embodied by the eleven other *Imams*.

THE MADRASSA

THE INSTITUTION IN WHICH ISLAMIC
KNOWLEDGE IS TAUGHT AND ACQUIRED,
AND A PLACE OF CONVIVIALITY

One of the main contributions of Islam was to encourage access to learning, especially religious learning. There is no barrier between those who know and those who do not yet know, between scholars (*talib*) and the object of their quest. There are three different degrees of knowledge in Islam:

– Allah is the All-Knowing, He whose knowledge encompasses the manifest and the hidden, the great mystery of the Universe that mystics call by the term *al-ghayb*. The Koran reminds the reader of this immeasurable knowledge and makes it one of the branches of divine truth: "Enough for a witness between me and you is Allah, and such as have knowledge of the Book" (*The Thunder*, XIII, 43). The concept of the "knowledge of God" (*'ilm Allah*) is given numerous interpretations (God knows everything, even the mystery of the hour of the Final judgement; he is perfectly informed of people's actions, their good deeds or their misdeeds, their thoughts, etc.), in over three hundred verses of the Koran and almost all the suras;

– the knowledge of the Prophet Muhammad is an extension of the knowledge of prophecy inaugurated by Adam, the first Prophet recognized in Islam. As the repository of the most recent monotheistic religion, Muhammad possesses the thousand and one facets of belief and faith from all time. He himself had preached for the benefit of his supporters and followers that knowledge should be sought even if this meant travelling as far afield as China. These words of the Prophet are regarded as authentic because they have been reported by several compilers of traditions, the most eminent of whom is El-Bokhari (810-870) and, in the same century, Muslim (817-875);

– a third category of those with knowledge consists of Muslim scholars and sages, whether they are well-versed in the field of the Islamic sciences, know the Koran by heart, interpret it, or seek to resolve social and interpersonal conflicts by specializing in Islamic jurisprudence (*fiqh*). Those engaged in more "intellectual" disciplines such as grammar, historiography, rhetoric, and all the speculative disciplines such as logic and philosophy, which Muslims refer to collectively as *'ilm al-kalam*, also belong in this category.

It is within this context that one can place the rise and dazzling efflorescence of the *madrassa*, "the place of learning," from the verb *darassa*, "to study," and *darrassa*, "to teach." Here the tradition of learning in Islam is perpetuated, especially in regard to the Koran and the *hadith*. These school-universities can legitimately claim their spiritual ancestry from two illustrious institutions: the *Bayt al-Hikma*, the Abbasid "House of Wisdom" built in Baghdad in the ninth century,[1] and the Fatimid university-mosque of Al-Azhar, founded in 972 A.D. in Cairo, a city also built by the Fatimids in 969.

In practice, the *madrassa*, or *médersa* as it is called in North Africa, is not merely a place for lessons and long hours of Koranic recitation (activities performed in the mosque with greater efficiency and comfort), it is above all a focus of life for the many students who attend it, some of whom come from the most far-flung regions of the Muslim world.

Each great mosque has an adjoining *madrassa*, and some are so beautiful and famous that they have acquired a universal reputation.

This is the case with the Nuriya *madrassa* in the Khawasin quarter of Damascus, built in 1167 and described by Ibn Jubayr (twelfth century): "One of those in this world that afford the most beautiful sight to the eyes is that of the late Nur-Ad-Dîn, where his tomb lies. May God illuminate him! It is a most magnificent palace: water flows there, first descending into a channel in the middle of a large waterway, then flowing into an oblong fountain, and finally falling into an ornamental pool in the middle of the building. The eyes are amazed by the beauty of this spectacle. All those who see it reiterate their prayers for Nur-ad-Dîn."[2] The magnificence of the Moroccan *médersas* is also remarkable, especially those of Fez or Marrakesh (the fourteenth-century Al-Attarine *médersa*; the fourteenth-century Bou Inania *médersa*; the seventeenth-century Esh-Sherratin *médersa*).

Along with the masque and the *madrassa*, we should also mention the *zawiya*, the sanctuary that houses the shrine of a saint. A building characteristic of North African Islam, the *zawiya* passes on a popular heritage and memory of Islam. The Koran and the disciplines that derive from it are usually taught there.

Even the modest buildings of country *zawiyas* can also be used as mosques. This accentuates its image as a para-Islamic or even

heretical sanctuary, taking into account of the practices which sometimes take place there.

1. Though it was Nizam al-Mulk (eleventh century), the powerful Vizir of the
   Sultan Malik Shah, who gave it its impetus.
2. Ibn Jubayr, *Voyages*, vol. 3, p. 330.

HOLY DAYS AND RITUALS

THE HIJRA IS THE BASIS OF THE MUSLIM CALENDAR, WHILE THE LUNAR YEAR PROVIDES THE RHYTHM FOR THE LIFE OF BELIEVERS

The rites of birth, protection, and death are a skillful blend of
customs and religious dictates. In daily life, Muslims do not believe in
any power besides Allah, but in moments of confusion they sometimes
have recourse to talismans to guard them from the evil eye and from
the *jettatura*.[1] These amulets contain Koranic verses and recall the
authority of God over Satan.

Rites and prohibitions pertaining to food are especially important. The Muslim dietary laws are rigorously codified. Works on
theology and jurisprudence go into minute details concerning the
thousand and one situations—medical, purifying, sacrificial—in
which meat acquires the status of *halal*, or conversely, is made
unfit for consumption. Food prohibitions extend to permitted types
of meat from an animal not specifically slaughtered in the name of
Allah, or which has not been caught expressly for the purpose of
consumption. "Forbidden to you [for food] are dead meat, blood,
the flesh of swine, and that on which hath been invoked the name
of other than Allah; that which hath been killed by strangling, or
by a violent blow, or by a headlong fall, or by being gored to death;
that which hath been [partly] eaten by a wild animal, unless ye are
able to slaughter it [in due form]; that which is sacrificed on stone

[altars]" (*The Repast*, V, 3). A similar ban is placed on intestines and carrion, since it is written that "It is not their meat nor their blood that reaches Allah" (*The Pilgrimage*, XXII, 37).

As for sacrifice and immolation, part of the ancient Arab heritage, these are reinforced and confirmed in the Koran: "We have placed sacrificial animals among those things that are sacred to Allah: in them there is much good for you: then pronounce the name of Allah over them as they are made ready for slaughter: when they are lying down on their sides [after slaughter], eat ye thereof, and feed such as [beg not but] live in contentment, and such as beg with due humility" (*The Pilgrimage*, XXII, 36). In Islam, the most important of sacrificial rituals is the slaughter of an animal—a sheep, camel, bull, or goat. This is how Muslims commemorate Abraham's act when, following divine injunctions, he would have sacrificed his son Ishmael. The feast commemorating the act, the Feast of Sacrifice (*'Id al-Adha*), is called the *'Id al-Kabir* (Great Feast) to distinguish it from the feast that falls at the end of *Ramadan*. It takes place on the tenth day of the month of pilgrimage (*Dhu'l-Hijja*). Muslim (816-873) reports the following words attributed to the Prophet: "When you slaughter an animal, slaughter it in an excellent fashion: let each one of you sharpen his blade and not mistreat the animal he is about to sacrifice." [2]

In order that the meat should be permitted (*halal*), the person performing the sacrifice—any adult Muslim in a state of canonical purity and practiced in the field of sacrifice—follows very precise ritual instructions: to turn in the direction of Mecca, invoke the name of Allah, and slit the animal's throat deftly, without, however, separating the head from the body. Some animals are unfit for consumption. These include dogs, cats, wolves, foxes, wild boars and pigs. The same applies to the raven, because of the bad omens associated with it, and some birds of prey. Since they feed on human flesh, eating them could create precedents of cannibalism.

Muslim religious judges advise against their consumption. In Europe, meat is supervised by the veterinary services of the great mosque. This festival of sacrifice, the *'Id al-Kabir*, is certainly not the only one. It is part of the wider framework of Arab and Muslim dietary laws that still play a part in some popular beliefs.

The rite of circumcision also occupies an important place. Although the Koran does not contain any references to it, circumcision (*khitan*) is a Bedouin and Semitic practice that is highly recommended for male children to undergo. It has gradually come to occupy a place in the rituals of the Muslim world, especially in the central regions (Iran, Turkey, Egypt, Arabia, Muslim Africa, and North Africa). Circumcision has emerged as a collective tradition symbolizing a form of perfection, but not as a substitute for faith. Circumcision corresponds as much to religious as it does to medical, hygienic, and social requirements. Depending on the region, it is performed when a child is between three and nine years of age. Nowadays, the tendency is to make it as painless as possible by having it done at an early age by a pediatrician or surgeon in properly sterile conditions.

Rituals reinforce the adherence and respect of a Muslim for his religion. They are a source of dogma and law, but also a method of differentiating between beliefs, as expressed in the Koran: "To every people did We appoint rites [of sacrifice] that they might celebrate the name of Allah" (*The Pilgrimage*, XXII, 34). Since they are responsible for relaying identity to millions of people, rituals are the focus for a spiritual revival in religious life.

Other important events in religious life are the feasts that punctuate the Muslim year. The Muslim calendar (or the era of the *Hijra*) is built on the lunar year. It officially began on September 24, 622 A.D., which corresponds to the twelfth day of *Rabi'al-awwal* in the year 1 A.H.[3] The word *hijra* means "exile," "emigration," or "expatriation"; thus, the Muslim year can be seen as the advent of a new cycle and not just the leftovers of the pagan calendar of pre-Islamic Hijaz. This exodus occurred on September 16, 622, when, persecuted by their Meccan enemies, the Prophet and his companions emigrated to Yathrib, as Medina was then called. Medina thus became the refuge of the Islamic community, the place in which the new faith was adopted, and the first city-state. The Muslim year is a lunar year consisting of twelve months, which are twenty-nine or thirty days long. It has 355 or 356 days, a difference of about eleven days from the solar year, hence the annual gap between the Hegirian and the Gregorian calendars. The names of the Muslim months are as follows: *Muharram, Safar, Rabi'al-awwal, Rabi' al-thani, Jumada al-ula, Jumada al-thaniya, Rajab, Sha'ban, Ramadan, Shawwal, Dhu'l-Qa'da*, and *Dhu'l-Hijja*. Four holy months are mentioned in the Koran and are called "months of God":

– *Muharram* (literally forbidden, prohibited, and thus, holy), is the first month of the Muslim year;

– *Rajab* is a month that was venerated even before the advent of Islam;

– *Dhu'l-Qa'da*, which means "the month of rest," is the eleventh month of the year. It is a month of truce, in which rival clans suspend their conflicts and attend to their trading occupations;

– *Dhu'l-Hijja* is the twelfth month of the Muslim year and the month of pilgrimage to Mecca.

There are many other feasts and ceremonies which mark the Muslim year:

I. THE NEW YEAR (*Ras al-'am*), *Muharram* 1. This is the start of the Muslim calendar. Iranians, however, remain attached to *Naw-Ruz* (literally "New Light"), the Sassanid new year, which survived the advent of Islam and is celebrated at the vernal equinox (March 21).

II. 'ASHURA, *Muharram* 10. On this day, many Muslims fast, pray, and perform ritual activities. For Shi'ites, it has a different significance, since this lucky day is a day of national mourning. In fact, 'Ashura recalls the painful memory of the death of Hussein, the second son of the Imam 'Ali, which took place on Muharram 10, 680 in Karbala' (Iraq).

III. THE BIRTH OF THE PROPHET (*Mawlid an-Nabi*), *Rabi' al-awwal* 12. During this birthday feast, which is widely celebrated in the Muslim world, mystic prayers and readings of the Koran are organized. In North Africa, it is called *al-Mouled*.

IV. THE NIGHT OF THE PROPHET'S ASCENSION INTO HEAVEN (*Laylat al-mi'raj*), *Rajab* 27. According to hagiographic accounts, this took place during the second year of the Prophet's dispensation. Although it is not greatly celebrated by believers, the night of the Prophet's ascension is propitious for meetings of meditation and invocation of God, at which ritual libations are also offered.

V. THE NIGHT OF POWER, ALSO CALLED THE NIGHT OF THE DECREE (*Laylat al-Qadr*), *Ramadan* 27. This is the most important night of the month, being the night of the revelation of the Koran: "We have indeed revealed this (Message) in the Night of Power" (*The Night of Power*, XCVII, 1). Spiritually, it is worth a thousand nights together, and the Koran defines it as a night of "Peace… until the rise of Morn" (*The Night of Power*, XCVII, 5).

VI. THE FEAST OF THE BREAKING OF THE FAST (*'Id al-fitr*), also called the "Lesser Feast" (*'Id al-saghir*), *Shawwal* 1. It owes its importance to the fact that it brings to a close the month of the annual fast. It is celebrated on *Shawwal* 1, the following month. An important prayer performed at the mosque marks the beginning of the celebrations, which sometimes last two or three days.

VII. THE FEAST OF THE SACRIFICE (*'Id al-adha*), *Dhu'l-Hijja* 10. This is also known as the "Great Feast" (*Kurban bayram*, in Turkey), commemorating as it does the sacrifice of Abraham. At its center are the practices of donation and sharing. It is within this strictly religious framework that the slaughter of the *'Id* sheep takes place. Once it has been sacrificed and carved into portions, it is meant to be distributed to the family, the poor, and friends. This is also true for those who are in Mecca for the pilgrimage. Their sheep are sacrificed in the prescribed places, and surplus meat is given to the poor.

To this calendar of rituals should be added other social and family occasions such as marriage (*zawaj*) or the completion of a Koranic apprenticeship (*khatma*). Marriage, for instance, demands the active and complete participation of the whole family, and sometimes even the whole clan. The status of marriage in Islamic lands is so high that even the poorest families sometimes hold week-long banquets, although doing so may mean incurring heavy debts. Its religious significance arises from the rejection of celibacy in Islam: Muslims follow the example of the Prophet and his close companions, who constantly praised marriage. Koranic apprenticeship, meanwhile, follows rules of a pedagogical order and of the transmission of memory. It begins in early childhood in the nearest Koranic school, and continues until university. Theoretically, *khatma* involves those who have learnt the whole Koran by heart, but families are delighted if their children have managed to learn only half or three quarters. Often the culmination of this training is celebrated with a meal the whole family is invited to.

1. A note, however, should be added here on a characteristic object of Arab folklore: the hand of Fatima. This is as widespread as horseshoes, which are hung on the pediments of doors to ward off curses, or the drawings of fish in fishing villages. The hand of Fatima is a social symbol going back particularly to popular Arab-Berber culture, but does not correspond to any ritual, Koranic, or traditional dictates.
2. Nawawi, *Les Quarante Hadiths*, p. 46. (Paris: Les Deux Océans, 1980).
3. In fact, the decision to begin the new calendar at the time of the Hijra goes back to Omar, the second Caliph. Historians date this decision to the year 17 A.H., that is, 639 A.D.

POSTURES AND BEHAVIOR

SOBRIETY GOVERNS ALL THE ACTIONS OF A MUSLIM

Muslim theologians believe that in order to be identified and validated, belief must entail a series of significant acts that make it visible to oneself and to others.

This behavior involves social and individual conduct. Manner of dress, prayer, the cut of the hair and the nails, the wearing of the veil by women, and personal hygiene. Abu-Horayra (seventh century) recounts that the Prophet Muhammad had said that five acts were recommended for Muslims apart from those ordained in the Koran, or the *sunna*: circumcision, shaving the pubic and armpit hair for women, cutting one's nails, and trimming one's moustache.

Islam is thus replete with actions that distinguish it, indisputably, from the other great monotheistic religions, Judaism and Christianity, but also from Buddhism, Shintoism, animist religions, Shamanism, and finally, from the Native American religions.

– The body and prayer: the most obvious external aspect of Muslim prayer is the many postures that the body successively takes up: leaning forward, kneeling, prostration, standing upright, gestures of hailing Allah and blessing Him, etc. Stretching out the index finger— the finger of the profession of faith (*shahada*)—is required at the end of every Muslim prayer. All these gestures proceed from the Koranic injunction of humility (*khushu'*), which appears numerous times in the Koran (seventeen times about the first prostration) and the pro- totype of which could be this verse from the sura Al-Fath: "Thou wilt see them bow and prostrate themselves (in prayer), seeking Grace from Allah and (His) Good Pleasure. On their faces are their marks, (being) the traces of their prostration" (*The Victory*, XLVIII, 29).

Bowing down and prostrating oneself characterizes Muslims, since it is said that they are those who "bow down and prostrate themselves" (*The Repentance*, IX, 112). Through this obedience, they oppose Iblis, the archetype of the devil in Islam, who refused to prostrate himself, as recounted in the Holy Book: "And behold, we said to the angels, 'Bow down to Adam': and they bowed down: not so Iblis: he refused and was haughty: he was of those who reject the Faith" (*The Cow*, II, 34).

– Hygiene: Islam's attitude to bodily cleanliness (*tahara, nadhafa*) is linked to faith according to a very famous saying of the Prophet: "Cleanliness is inextricably linked to faith."[1] The entire Islamic philosophy of bathing and ablutions, major or minor, as well as that of the general hygiene of the believer, springs from this precept. This is also true for the *hammam*, the baths, which are the pivot of two complementary worlds, the sacred world of the mosque and the profane world of the exchange, the street, and the souk. Fragrance and cleanliness are recommended in every case, even if—the odor of sanctity being binding!—"the stench of the mouth of he who is fasting is more pleasing to God than the odor of musk." [2]

The length of hair and nails is codified. The Prophet wore a beard, which, it is said, could fit into the palm of the hand without going beyond the base of the neck (*tolia*). He cleaned it, smoothed it, and perfumed it. Since then the length of the beard and, even more, the moustache, have become conditions of hygiene encouraged by Islam. Since excess is frowned upon, in this matter as in all others, a beard that reaches the chest is not considered a sign of greater virtue. Nails must be cut and kept clean. According to the very words of the Prophet, reported by Abu Horayra, and subsequently by El-Bokhari, depilation and shaving of the female pubic hair is encouraged, as is a suitable hairstyle.

– Prohibitions: other than pork and all other meat not sacrificed in the name of Allah, Islam forbids the drinking of all alcoholic beverages, even if the alcohol content is negligible. Thus, for example, aperitifs, wines, cakes containing the merest hint of alcohol, chocolates, syrups, and stews containing a sprinkling, a dash or a drop of any wine or spirit, even a residue, are forbidden. Islam also forbids gambling, condemns illicit gains, games of forfeiture and usury, and disapproves of winnings from gambling at the lottery, the casino, etc. These prohibitions come from a Koranic dictate: "They ask thee concerning wine and gambling. Say: 'In them is great sin, and some profit, for men; but the sin is greater than the profit'" (*The Cow*, II, 219).

The avowed intent of Islam is to allow the individual to have mastery of his own free will, since in freedom of choice there lies the great risk that the Muslim will abandon the most basic religious duties in favor of gaming and its "satanic allures."

1. *Hadith* of the Prophet.
2. *Hadith* reported by El-Bokhari, vol. 4, p. 127.

PRAYER BEADS

MISBAHA: THE ENDLESS RECITATION OF THE NAME OF ALLAH

The recitation of the ninety-nine full names of Allah using the prayer beads (*subha* or *misbaha*) is an old mnemonic practice used in every Muslim country. The symbolism connected with the prayer beads is that of the "chain of worlds." A discreet reference to sacred numerology is also contained therein, as the symbolism of numbers permeates the activity of the mediator.

Custom dictates that litanies called *wird*[1] should be recited with devotion and in a continuous manner, the beads having the purpose of aiding concentration and rhythm as well as punctuating the exercise. More traditional formulas such as the *shahada*, which recalls the unity of God, and *tahmid*, thanksgiving to Allah for His blessings, are also said on the beads. The compound structure of the prayer beads (three sections of thirty-three beads each) contributes to its particular spiritual significance. There are also rosaries with thirty-three beads that are used to complete the prayer cycle. For Islam, the beads number ninety-nine and correspond to the beautiful names of Allah, *al-asma al-husna*, the hundredth attribute being absolute mystery.

In fact, this hundredth figure only appears to be missing, since the two ends of the rosary join up in a sort of long horn that symbolizes the name of Allah. However, theologians remain divided as to this explanation, and some reject the idea that the essence of God the Creator should be reduced to this appendage.

The exact origin of the prayer beads is unknown, but the custom was probably introduced by the Sufi movements of the first two centuries of Islam, inspired by distant Indo-Iranian origins. Long sessions of meditation (*zikr*) indeed involve prayers, which require the use of the rosary.

The prayer beads have become a visible reality in Muslim cities. Some believers are never parted from them. They are often made of wood, but can also be fashioned from more precious materials, such as onyx or ivory. While expressing the believer's attachment to his faith, the use of the prayer beads serves to reinforce the belief of the faithful and their constant self-perfection.

1. "Glorified be God, Praised be God, Allah is Most Great" (*Subhan Allah, Al-Hamduli'llah, Allahu Akbar*).

CLOTHING

SIGN OF DECENCY AND ADHERENCE TO THE SPIRIT OF THE FAITH

When dressing, especially for feasts or to go to the mosque, Muslims favor long white tunics (*qamis*), which cover their shape and at the same time protect them from the intense heat.

The turban and skullcap, the traditional headcoverings of the Islamic world, fulfill the same function. For town wear, extensive use is made of delicate materials such as cotton, linen, and silk; in the country, clothes are rougher and wool is more widely used. The origin of the term *turban* is unclear, since each country has its own name for it. In Algeria, the word *a'mamâ* is preferred, while in Tunisia and Egypt the term *tarbouche* is used. The turban, which is reserved for Muslim dignitaries, has adopted very different shapes according to the various Muslim regions, especially at the time when a united Islam united vast areas of the globe. Indeed, the often successful marriage of the turban and the Ottoman fez, the Sassanid tiara, the Moghul skullcap, the Targhi *litham*, and the North African tarboosh, all used to cover or wrap the head, facilitated the emergence and preservation of distinct local habits of dress. This is equally true of Islam in Asia, Africa, or the Balkans, and even of Almohad

Andalusia, where a mutual tolerance can be observed between so-called Arab dress and some elements of the Iberian costume. From the nineteenth century onwards, under the influence of colonization, the custom of dressing in European style spread. Clothing in Islam functions as an index of the vitality of the religion, since, like religious architecture (mosques, mausoleums, *madrasas*), it has taken root in some newly Islamicized regions.

Ideally, women should veil themselves whenever they leave their homes, whether to go to the mosque or to attend to their errands. This is an important Koranic precept which can tolerate no exception.

Wearing the veil[1] is for women a manifestation of virtue: "Say to the believing women that they should lower their gaze and guard their modesty; that they should not display their beauty and ornaments except what (must ordinarily) appear thereof; that they should draw their veils over their bosoms and not display their beauty except to their husbands, their fathers, their husbands' fathers, their sons, their husbands' sons, their brothers or their brothers' sons, or their sisters' sons, or their women, or their slaves whom their right hands possess, or male servants free of physical needs, or small children" (*The Light*, XXIV, 31) .

In the seventh century, the veil characterized the Prophet's harem; it was a sign of distinction, by which a woman of good birth sought to show that she was virtuous: "O Prophet! Tell thy wives and daughters, and the believing women, that they should cast their outer garments over their persons [when abroad]: that is most convenient that they should be known [as such] and not molested" (*The Confederates*, XXXIII, 59). Later, in the time of the Egyptian Mamelukes, between 1258 and 1512, the veil, which had always symbolized social distinction, was particularly favored by the women of Cairo.

The veil defines the limits of a person's inviolability, especially that of a woman, since it is less a case of segregating women (a new concept) than of symbolizing their modesty and respectability. On the question of the veil, the official attitude of Muslim countries is extremely varied.

Countries such as Iran and the Sudan, enforce the wearing of the veil, while others, such as Egypt or Algeria, accept it with greater difficulty. Still others, such as Tunisia, openly fight it. Women in Arabia, Yemen, and other countries of the Gulf have been wearing veils for a long time, without it ever seeming strange or open to exegesis.

In France, where it is a sign of the way in which Muslim women are different, the veil is still the subject of controversy, while in the United Kingdom, for example, it is tolerated much more. Whether or not the veil is universally worn is often a reflection of the tone set by the leadership of existing parties, especially when Muslims are in individual or collective contact with lay circles, in which women are traditionally unveiled. A similar problem arises concerning co-education. While it is absolutely prohibited in the Muslim world, it is considered a social norm in European countries.

At all times and in all places, the function of clothing is to ensure sobriety, decency, and modesty. Ibn 'Abbas (seventh century), a companion of the Prophet, said: "Eat whatever you please and wear any clothes you wish, as long as you do not commit either of two things: prodigality or parsimony."

1. The veil is called by different names in different countries: *litham* in the Arab world, *chador* in Iran, *chadi* in Afghanistan, *charshaf* in Turkey, *safsari* in Tunisia, *hijab*, *hayq* in Algeria, etc.

WATER

THE SOURCE OF LIFE AND AN
IMPORTANT ELEMENT IN RITUAL

In Islam, more than any other element, water is blessed, because it is the spring that floods man with its divine providence and favor: "And We send down from the sky rain charged with blessing, and We produce therewith gardens and grain for harvests; and tall [and stately] palm trees, with shoots of fruit stalks, piled one over anoth-er—as sustenance for [Allah's] servants" (*Qâf*, L, 9-11).

Water has various origins and functions. There is the water for ablutions, water from the well of Zamzam, water from the caravan water-skins, water from the well and the oasis, water from fountains and taps.

In the sura entitled *The Prophets*, it is written: "Do not the unbe-lievers see that the heavens and the earth were joined together [as one unit of creation] before we clove them asunder? We made from water every living thing. Will they not then believe?" (*The Prophets*, XXI, 30).

With regard to Muslim dogma, and taking into account the explicit dictates on hygiene in Islam, water is present at the beginning of most rituals of sanctification or purification.

Within this symbolic whole, which is as much a matter of regional mythology as allegiance to founding fathers, the sacred water of *Zamzam*, the source of which is situated in the courtyard of the Hijr, at the foot of the Kaaba, is one of the elements which most impresses the pilgrim.

Ibn Battuta (1304-1377), the geographer and traveler from Tangiers, reports a belief of the Meccans of his time, according to which the water of *Zamzam* miraculously augments and swells, every night from Thursday to Friday.[1]

Muslim historiography suggests that the fountain of *Zamzam* surged up at the feet of Ishmael, the oldest son of Abraham, when his mother, Hagar, was desperately searching for water between two hillocks next to the Kaaba, Safa, and Marwa. According to the great Arab historian Tabari (838-923), Ishmael himself unleashed the mira-cle: "Ishmael began to cry, as children do when they are left alone without their mothers, and having stamped his heel on the ground, again as children do, a spring appeared under his heel."[2]

Finally, one should recall the majestic power of the quartet of the rivers Kawthar, Salsabil, Euphrates, and Nile. The two former, called "internal rivers," are in paradise. The Euphrates and the Nile are called "external rivers." The Euphrates flows through Iraq where it forms a vast delta with the Tigris in the Persian Gulf. The Nile is a huge river, the longest in the world (4187 miles). It flows through Kenya, Rwanda, Burundi, the Congo, Ethiopia, the Sudan, and Egypt, into the Mediterranean. From ancient times (as mentioned by Plutarch), until the construction of the Aswan Dam (opened in 1971), its rate of flow was particularly devastating for Egyptian agriculture and sometimes for the inhabitants themselves.

The Muslim paradise, a vast verdant garden, contains the Kawthar and the Salsabil, two rivers mentioned in the Koran, but there also flow rivers of milk, wine, honey, and water: "[Here is] a Parable of the garden that the righteous are promised: In it are rivers of water incorruptible; rivers of milk of which the taste never changes; rivers of wine, a joy to those who drink; and rivers of honey pure and clear. In it there are for them all kinds of fruits; and grace from their Lord..." (Muhammad, XLVII, 15).

There are also gushing fountains for the refreshment of the Chosen Ones who abide in paradise. Finally, however idyllic it already is, this picture would be incomplete without evocations of greenery, oases, receptacles full of water, and silver goblets in which flow rare and sealed wine. The blessing imparted by water is both immediate (water keeps the camel driver alive in the desert) and complex (water is at once cleansing, beneficial, and regenerating). According to medieval Western medical theory, water, when opposed to fire, and sometimes to earth, represents the coldest part of human nature, but it is unlikely that Islam should have been aware of this dimension, who instead favored its surging movement and dynamism.

Does it not also symbolize nature regenerated, the divine omnipotence, the compassion of Allah? This is made all the more clear in the sura entitled *Al-Nûr*, which testifies: "Allah has created every animal from water" (*The Light*, XXIV, 45).

1. Ibn Battuta, Voyages, vol. 1, p. 319.
2. Tabari, *Chronique traditionnelle*, vol. 1, p. 164. (Paris: Sindbad, 1980).

COLORS

ALL COLORS ARE RESPECTED
IN ISLAM. SOME, SUCH AS GREEN, ARE
GIVEN GREATER IMPORTANCE

Green is the color of Islam, since green was the color of the banner of the Prophet, and of the robe of 'Ali (d. 661), the fourth Caliph of Islam. Since then, the Prophet's descendants (*sharif*) have considered green as the mark of their reign, the color serving as a link, however indirect, with the Prophetic period.

In daily life, green plays a part that confirms and reinforces a symbolic significance gained over the course of time. In Syria, it is said of a person who has the *baraka* that they have a "green hand." This person is a good omen.

The symbol of springtime renewal, another sign of life, green is the color of joy, success, and happiness. Arabic has an extensive vocabulary for the different shades of green. It flourishes in the Koran, permeates the language of theology, and is as essential in literature as in classical poetry. Finally, a significant number of professions—dyeing, decoration, illumination, chemistry, botany, horticulture, and agriculture—accord it particular prominence. Even if there is no real link with the Creator, green is so revered that some very pious Muslims hesitate to pray on a green carpet for fear of offending Islam.

On the contrary, in order to express faith and attachment to the teachings, and since green symbolizes hope and peace, mosques, catafalques, house interiors, and royal, tribal, and family emblems are often painted green.

Finally, the domination of green in heraldic symbolism and in the content of national flags is well known. Examples include the Kingdom of Saudi Arabia, Libya, Pakistan, the Comoro Islands, and Mauritania. It also figures prominently in numerous other flags: the Sherif's star on the Moroccan flag, the horizontal or vertical stripes on the flags of Algeria, Kuwait, Jordan, Iraq, Iran, etc.

There are several other colors, which, like green, convey a particular symbolism or sign of belonging.

The color black acquired an importance that has lasted for centuries, when it was adopted by the Abbassid dynasty, which was established in Baghdad at the end of the eighth century. In ancient Persia (now Iran), black represented the devil, while yellow was the color of mourning and sometimes jealousy. Nowadays, the robes of mullahs are either black or white, or both. Since the death of the Imam Hussein, at the infamous battle of Karbala' in 680, black, the mark of mourning, has become the symbol of Shi'ism as a whole and its clergy in particular. The significance of the black veil of the Iranians, the *chador*, is related to this context.

White—the color of the shroud, of angels, and others—is a complex color for Muslims. It is the color of the grand sheikh's *gandura* and of the student's *qamis* (long tunic), but also of the funerary winding-sheet. However, if one goes by a *hadith* of the Prophet: "God loves white clothing, and He has made paradise white," it can be seen that white is a predominantly positive color in Islam.

In North Africa and Egypt, earth colors prevail although green and white still symbolize noble or abstract sentiments. The *kashabia* of the Algerian high plateaus is brown or dark, while around the Algerian city of Constantine the veil is black.

In the time of Andalusian Spain, red, the color of fire and blood, as well as the color of passion, dominated in clothing, as can still be seen in the costume of the flamenco dancer. Today, red is still found in the most wide-ranging domains, especially in folklore and traditional dress. Furthermore, the national flags of several Muslim countries are dominated by red: Tunisia, Indonesia, Morocco, and Turkey. In this last case, red recalls the Ottoman origins (thirteenth to twentieth centuries) of the national flag. Finally, red figures on other flags, in particular those, which, to a greater or lesser degree, are drawn from the four colors of pan-Arabism (red, white, black, and green), such as Palestine, Egypt, Iraq, and Syria, but also the Sudan, Yemen, and so on.

Muslims perceive the hereafter in terms of color. Paradise itself, apart from the white mentioned above, has a wealth of other colors. These are evoked in an abundance of silks, delectable beverages and the murmur of water. On the subject of the Chosen Ones, the Koran writes: "They will be adorned... with bracelets of gold, and they will wear green garments of fine silk and heavy brocade; they will recline therein on raised thrones" (*The Cave*, XVIII, 31). In the sura *Al-Insan*, it is also written: "Upon them will be seen green garments of fine silk and heavy brocade" (*Man*, LXXVI, 21).

The Islamic field of colors, dominated by the peaceful, joyous color green, is intended as a response adapted to the Muslim's aspirations to calm and serenity.

ACKNOWLEDGEMENTS

Marc-Alain Ouaknin

This book is the result of a dialogue and a wonderful friendship among book lovers. I salute and thank Martine and Prosper Assouline.

A book is also those that have helped to make it become a physical object, and to circulate and transmit the passion of the ideas that teach us to always go beyond ourselves. So my very warm thanks go to the teams working in Rue Casanova and Place Vendôme.

To all, again, thank you, and until we meet again...

Dom Robert Le Gall

I should first like to sincerely thank Cardinal Jean-Marie Lustiger, Archbishop of Paris, for the confidence he showed in wanting me to write this book. I am thankful to my community for its support and for the way it took this mission to heart. I accepted the task with the conviction that it could serve as a modern, evangelistic tool, helping the younger generations to discover, or rediscover, their spiritual roots.

The initial idea came from Editions Assouline, known for their high-quality art books: special thanks to the entire team for their inspirational efficiency.

Finally, I should like to give my warm thanks to the scholar Bernard Huchet for his friendly assistance during the revision of this text, destined for a wider public.

Claude B. Levenson

To all those who, through their knowledge and expertise, have contributed to this book in an atmosphere of cordial collaboration. To Marc-Alain Ouaknin, for his helpful hints. To Claudio Tecchio at Carmagnola. To Tenzin Geyche Tethong and the venerable Lhakdor, at Péma-la, Dharamsala. To my first and most faithful and ever-present reader: His Holiness the Dalai Lama, who showed me the Path.

Malek Chebel

I would like to thank my three families: my immediate family, my wife and my son, as well as my Parisian relatives. I owe my mother and my brother, who stayed behind in Skikda, old thanks which were never formulated and which every day have more importance. Finally, my gratitude to my larger and very pious family, who allowed me to discover the unimaginable depths of knowledge, of peoples, and continents.

May these three families find here the marks of my profound attachment to them.